Understanding the Heart

Understanding the Heart

The Art of Living in Happiness

Minh Niem

authorHOUSE®

AuthorHouse™
1663 Liberty Drive
Bloomington, IN 47403
www.authorhouse.com
Phone: 1-800-839-8640

© 2012 by Minh Niem. All rights reserved.

No part of this book may be reproduced, stored in a retrieval system, or transmitted by any means without the written permission of the author.

First published by AuthorHouse   02/22/2012

ISBN: 978-1-4670-0142-7 (sc)
ISBN: 978-1-4670-0143-4 (ebk)

Library of Congress Control Number: 2011917320

Printed in the United States of America

Any people depicted in stock imagery provided by Thinkstock are models, and such images are being used for illustrative purposes only.
Certain stock imagery © Thinkstock.

Because of the dynamic nature of the Internet, any web addresses or links contained in this book may have changed since publication and may no longer be valid. The views expressed in this work are solely those of the author and do not necessarily reflect the views of the publisher, and the publisher hereby disclaims any responsibility for them.

Copyright Holders Chi Bao Co., Ltd.

About the author Minh Niem

* Born in Chau Thanh, Tien Giang Province, Vietnam
* 1992: Entered the monastic order at Hue Nghiem Buddhist Institute in Saigon
* 1999: Began practicing Vipassana Meditation
* 2001: Studied with Zen Master Thich Nhat Hanh in France
* 2005: Studied with Meditation Master Tejaniya in the United States
* 2007: Founded "Understanding Meditation"—combining Mahayana Buddhism and Vipassana Meditation
* 2008-present: Conducting meditation classes and providing counseling for the young in the Washington D.C., metropolitan area

Contents

Preface – xi

Suffering – 1
Happiness – 7
Love – 13
Loving-Kindness – 17
Anger – 21
Endurance – 27
Jealousy – 31
Forgiveness – 35
Exchanges – 41
Support – 45

Loneliness – 49
Offering – 53
Intimacy – 59
Thanksgiving – 63
Boredom – 69
Respect – 75
Doubt – 81
Deep Listening – 87
Judging – 93
Loving Speech – 99

Prejudice – 105
Beginning Anew – 109
Covering Up – 115
Honesty – 121
Principles – 127
Adapting To Conditions – 133
Despair – 139
Faith – 143
Will Power – 149
Hesitation – 155

Failure – 161
Success – 167
Ambition – 171
Knowing When Is Enough – 177
Dependence – 183
Interdependence – 189
Weakness – 195
Repentance – 201
Laziness – 207
Letting Go – 213

Imagination – 219
Concentration – 225
Emotions – 231
Peace – 237
Worry – 243
Relaxation – 249
Authoritarianism – 255
Humbleness – 263
Selfishness – 269
Responsibility – 275

Preface

Eighteen years ago, I was determined to seek true happiness. At that time, the concept of true happiness was pretty vague to me, but I still believed it existed and that anyone could grasp it. However, I couldn't find a way to do this until ten years later, and only now am I confident enough to write it down to share my experiences and discoveries with everyone. I imagine that in the near future I will continue to write about the topic of happiness with even better experiences since I am still on the road to discovery.

I have been extremely fortunate to meet very successful and outstanding teachers on my journey. It was their advice to me in the early stages that helped prevent me from making regrettable mistakes and so greatly shortened the time I needed for my discoveries. In fact, even when I had found the path to enlightenment, I still first sought ideal external circumstances. This was partially because of my old habit of relying on external conditions rather than on myself, and partially because I was not self-confident enough when facing many difficulties. I slipped and fell several times because of those difficulties. More than just tired and bored, I was in a severe crisis of conscience.

When I was at the bottom of the pit of mental suffering, my survival instinct and strong will to live brought me back. I was aware that I had nothing else to lose, so I just needed to live an ordinary life like other wondrous living beings—with no need to struggle to achieve anything, happy to accept myself with what the universe had given me and to live in harmony with all the people around me. To my surprise, at that moment I felt that the universe had opened its arms wide to welcome me, and I realized that I was actually making some headway into the nature of happiness.

Although I knew the secret of mental transformation was not to use will power to influence or change my mind but only to observe and understand it, the instinct to protect my egocentric self still dominated and defeated all the stored energy gained from my initial practice. But after those first failures, I gained more experience about the unreal nature of mental afflictions. I began to become interested in my discovery and gave priority to it because I was fortunate to have chosen that "job" as my lifetime occupation. At times, I didn't believe I could live through days during which I "ignored" the enjoyment of my self, although such enjoyment was just the feeling of being cared for by someone or being recognized by someone. However, I could do without that enjoyment. That is why I believe that it is possible to lift consciousness to higher levels to better understand the conditions and nature of life, especially in this era when there are so many distractions such as material things, power, beauty, etc.

Although I still haven't transformed all my habitual mental afflictions, I have discovered all their operational mechanisms. In observing and experimenting with hundreds of people living around me, I have found the same results. After comparing my discoveries with my successful predecessors' versions of insight, I more strongly believe in the road I'm taking. However, I have never thought that all the understanding in this book belonged only to me. It is a literary work created by blending countless elements, the most prominent of which are Vietnamese culture, Buddhist insight, modern science and even the sufferings and hardships of my network of friends and acquaintances. I am only the person who has selected and organized these discoveries and ideas, adding some of my experiences to find a way to make the ideas easier for everyone to understand and put into practice.

Though this book presents some details of human emotions from simple to complicated, it is not necessarily a book of psychology. It can also heal wounds in your heart as soon as you open your heart to accept it; the better you understand the methods and try to practice them, the more sufferings you can dissolve. However, you shouldn't believe that you can grasp true happiness simply by completely understanding the issues presented in this book. Don't forget that after reading this, you will only have been shown the road. You need other important conditions as well. At least, you will have thought about and gained a proper understanding and strong belief in that road. Then you must be very determined to transform your life by creating good opportunities for it and practicing diligently. The most essential thing is that you must face big problems so that you have opportunities to fully apply what you have absorbed, and clearly see the difference between the understanding of thought and that of verification through experience. Yet you shouldn't worry too much because you will feel the qualities of that happiness as soon as you truly set foot on that road. The farther you move along the road, the greater your happiness will be.

Even if you can't get through this book because some of the ideas are very strange to you or are just the opposite of your current outlook, you shouldn't be quick to think that they are not suitable for you. Whenever you have free time or find it necessary, you can read it again at your leisure. Each time you read it again, you will certainly find something new about it. Since you strongly believe in your own understanding, it is not easy for you to open your heart to those new ideas, or you may prevent yourself from fully accepting this book because of some prejudices. You may throw it into some corner and forget about it, but when you are in trouble or face pain and misery inside yourself, you will realize that your reactions may be different than before. Some power may seem to have come to your aid. Actually, once you have thoroughly understood any of the principles of living a happy life introduced in this book, they will be stored deeply in your mind. They will silently cooperate with the other deep understandings inside you and wait for sufficient conditions to create results.

That is why I hope you will accept this book as a companion and be neither too hopeful nor indifferent. It is certainly impossible to describe all the corners of human emotions in this little book, so I promise I will try to continue to write when the conditions are favorable, especially when I receive valuable input from you. Actually, if you believe in the understandings presented in this book, it will be quite enough for you to take on your road to find true happiness. Especially at the present time when the bad is gradually becoming dominant over the good, this book is an essential catalyst in awakening the spiritual values that have long been asleep inside each of us.

Virginia, cherry blossom season of 2010

Minh Niem

1

Suffering

No matter how talented we are, or how well we have prepared, things contrary to our interest just happen naturally in their own way.

Merely contrary to our interests

We often hear people say "poor and miserable"; much less often do we hear "rich and miserable". In fact, poor people as well as rich people lead their lives miserably in their own way. Poor people don't accept poverty. They hate it and want to become rich. That's why they are miserable, why they suffer. Rich people are afraid their property is not enough to make others respect them. They are also afraid they will go bankrupt. They are even more afraid that other people will take advantage of them or hurt them. That's why they suffer. Compared to that of poor people, rich people's suffering is more complicated and harder to deal with. If everyone in society was equally wealthy and owned the same property, the concept of rich and poor wouldn't exist. However, that can never be true as human beings get more and more materialistic and more convinced that this material wealth is a basic requirement for happiness. We would not have such suffering if we were lucky enough not to be influenced by these societal beliefs. If we were not influenced by the concept of rich and poor, we would see that reveling in material possessions is not the most important reason that we are here in this world.

It is the same for hardship. People often connect the words *hard* and *suffering*. As a matter of fact, hardship itself does not necessarily mean suffering. We resist hardships and don't want to work hard, but we want all the comforts our peers enjoy. That's what makes us suffer. While we are busy making comparisons and demands, we neglect to find the very reason why we have to work hard. We may have seen that some people are willing to risk their jobs or their lives to take care of their seriously ill loved ones. Rescue workers know that it is very dangerous for them to jump into a fire, go underground or run through a line of gunfire, but they don't consider it suffering because of their great compassion for the potential victims. Many people may consider hard mental work to be suffering if a certain task involves a great amount of time and thought. However, it can be seen as very fortunate to have a job that exercises the mind as well as provides an income in the current economic situation. Thus, whether hardship becomes suffering all depends on each person's attitude.

We often complain about our *pain* and *suffering*. Pain is usually accompanied by suffering, like an unchangeable fact. For example, when someone slaps us in the face, it may hurt us, but if we know we have done something wrong to that person and are ready to receive that slap, it doesn't make us suffer. If, however, that person gives us a slap in the face coupled with contempt for us, purely intended to insult us in front of many people, it will certainly cause us to suffer. Any one of us would feel extremely unhappy after a failure in business, facing bankruptcy, because we have been working hard and tightening our belts over the years. There can be, however, a sizeable gap between that pain and suffering if we clearly know the causes of the failure and accept that failure as a good lesson. Perhaps, the worst suffering for human beings is separation from a loved one. That is why separation is usually compared to having a broken heart. But if we are aware that union and separation are results of causes and conditions that we ourselves have helped create, then we may be aware that a separation may be a chance for two sides to reflect upon themselves in order to create new and better bonds in the future. Thus pain and suffering are not identical, for one is physical and the other has various degrees of emotional entanglement.

There are things in life that are pleasing to us while being contrary to other people's ideas and, of course, other things that will satisfy others' needs that are against our interests. That is just natural. We sometimes have conflicting ideas ourselves and may not know why, so how on Earth can external situations always please us? We might have hated some things before but have slowly grown to love them; we might have strongly loved some things in the past but now wince at the sight of them; and we might have disregarded some things as unimportant only to consider them significant later on. Let's suppose we could achieve all our goals. What would we become and what would our world really be like? Instead of looking deeply into this, we just expect things should be as we want them to be and rarely think carefully whether our desires are really reasonable. That is, we rarely think whether they are necessary and suitable to our ability or our current situations, and whether they have any influence or effect on other people. So, most of our complaints, if looked into closely, are merely about what is contrary to our interests. Obviously, our suffering is not necessarily others' sufferings.

So, instead of saying "we're suffering," we should say something is "really contrary to our interests." This way of defining it will help us review our reactions and aid us in deciding whether reactions were right or not. This is certainly preferable to the continual pursuit of external objects. It will also dawn on us that the notion that "life is a sea of suffering" is just an attitude or, rather, a fixed idea.

Suffering can be beneficial

We should never forget that we are not isolated individuals and that we are constantly under the influence of a variety of forces, such as friends, family, society and the vast universe as well. No matter how talented we are or how well we have prepared, things contrary to our interests still happen naturally in their own way. Where there are successes, there will be failures; where there is union, there is separation. Why do we only want successes and unions? Who do we leave failures and separations to then? When we're lucky, why don't we ask ourselves whether we deserve to enjoy our good fortune and should accept it? Yet when we are cursed with bad luck, why do we always complain and demand fairness? We have enjoyed so many of the gifts from the universe, so from time to time if the universe limits such benefits to distribute them among other people, it's only natural and there should be nothing to complain about!

Of course, we may need time to accept bigger losses and regain our balance. Thus, it is quite right for us to have strong emotions and reactions in those situations. However, it is really our fault if we just complain about mediocre, if not trivial, matters. For example, we consider it suffering for us when it rains, when there's a traffic jam, when an appointment is missed, when food doesn't suit our tastes, or because we are not as tall as we want, age faster than we expect, when nobody asks about us, or even when a lot of people love us. The list of trivial annoyances is endless. Take a closer look at those reactions and see that it is our excessive greed that has driven us into "swamps of suffering". We should no longer blame our situations. Nobody can make us suffer if we have correct understanding and a large amount of tolerance. In order to have that large amount of tolerance, we must be able to curtail our desires by eliminating our unnecessary desires. If we see that we can lead our lives steadily and happily without some of the things that we have previously deemed important, we should reject these superfluous things and allow ourselves to be less dependent on our situations, so that we can remain unaffected when these situations change.

We should learn to face difficulties or set up our own way of thinking and living without expecting safety and security at all times so that we can build up endurance. We see children who grow up in protective and comfortable conditions enter society without any social experience to deal with difficult situations, and we see them get disheartened easily and give up immediately if they are criticized just a little bit. It is just like plants growing on soft earth. They look green and fresh but will be blown down easily by a strong wind, while plants growing on a rocky mountain may look tall and thin but are firmly rooted and resilient to wind and storms. Thus, although we don't expect life to push us into severe situations, we can make our mind strong so that we can withstand all life's ups and downs.

To have such a strong mind, we must limit our likes and try to accept our dislikes. Likes and dislikes are just emotions that temporarily serve us. We shouldn't be so quick to complain that life is meaningless without enjoyment. Nobody forbids us to enjoy ourselves, but everything has its price. If we keep serving our foolish selves, we shouldn't ask why our lives are full of suffering. Of course, no fame or wealth can have a negative impact on a person with a strong mind. Such a person is strong-minded and determined enough to remain unaffected by fame and wealth or uses them for the good of others. In reality, however, the number of people wanting to let go of their customary pleasures is very small. The number of those who can let go is even smaller. In our society, many people are ready to lose moral values in an effort to fight for power or to strive for profits without caring about the consequences. That is why more and more suffering is dumped into life. This situation is humanity's eternal saga.

It is true that suffering is an undeniable reality, but its properties are in flux. Suffering is not a defect of life. Actually, there is no suffering in the deepest sense, for suffering is created by our minds. Because our conscious mind doesn't operate in the right way, it creates reactions against situations that it considers contrary to its operation—this is suffering. It is therefore fortunate that our conscious mind is a flexible thing that can be adjusted. We can start by understanding that things related to us are always interconnecting with everything around us. In that way, we won't continue to create selfish reactions. At the same time, we need to skillfully observe and analyze the habits that we have developed over the years. The process of removing those negative psychological emotions is the process of overcoming suffering. The less our self-love gets hurt, the less we suffer. When we stop thinking about our ego, we stop suffering.

Indeed, we should be grateful to suffering because it can help us understand what happiness is as well as build up our stamina so that we develop the survival instincts hidden within us. Similarly, if we never get lost, we will not know that we have fear; if we are never insulted, we will not clearly know how angry we can get; if we are never deceived, we will not know how easily we can be hurt; and if we are never deserted, we will not know our real emotional weakness. It is the expression of our survival instincts that helps us to clearly see all the hidden corners of the mental afflictions that create suffering. By understanding these, we can figure out how to adjust our consciousness and our way of life to be in harmony with the universe. We may then understand ourselves, have compassion grow inside us, and tread a more leisurely path through the trials and tribulations of this world without fear of the unexpected.

So, how we feel suffering all depends on our minds, for it is the mind which has the power to create, as well as cast away, this suffering.

If there were no suffering
We wouldn't know happiness
Thanks to our dreams recently
We've come back to awareness.

2

Happiness

No happiness comes from Heaven, and no paradise consists solely of happiness because the concept of happiness exists only when people can feel suffering.

Satisfying emotions

Happiness has always been mankind's strongest desire. However, happiness has been understood quite differently from society to society and from era to era, and these understandings have been formed by both collective and individual views. There are those who suffer misfortune after misfortune, so they may assert that no happiness exists in the world, while the young may continue to dream, convinced of finding perfect happiness at the end of the road they are following. Generations of people have sought happiness all their lives like a game of hide-and-seek. They sometimes grasp it only to have it melt away immediately. Sometimes when people think they have nothing, happiness unexpectedly comes. Though everyone hopes to find happiness, most people find difficulty defining what it truly is, giving little other than a confused smile when asked.

Haven't we, like many young people, felt the joy of receiving a degree after struggling with books for years? But soon after that, we complain that true happiness will only arrive when we find a well-paid job to gain admiration from friends. Perhaps that feeling of happiness will not stay for long before the desire to marry the one we love becomes the key to being truly happy. Predictably, our anxious expectations to have children, build a happy home and please both families will follow. Those happy days can quickly pass and our aspirations may turn to leaving the extended family to form a nuclear one, to own an expensive apartment and then, of course, to feel "real" happiness. But what is this uneasy feeling when seeing friends drive the latest cars? What about when we see their children going to very prestigious schools or hear of the admiration they receive due to their significant posts? We are worried that if we can't catch up with them, our current version of happiness will be devalued and disappear into mediocrity.

Thus, we keep dropping one piece of happiness to chase another and, believing that the grass really is greener on the other side of the fence, never knowing what happiness actually is. Even though we know that happiness is an emotion we feel when we are comfortable and satisfied upon achieving our expectations, we just can't explain why such good feelings come and go so quickly. We pay no attention. We don't even bother to reflect on it. We keep moving forward, clutching at the next thing that we are sure we cannot be happy without. It's really interesting: if we don't know what can make us happy right now, how can we be sure what will make us happy later on? Is happiness a matter for the present or the future? Does happiness require all the optimum conditions to exist? If so, can people without those conditions ever be happy?

Actually, conditions for happiness always exist, but they no longer attract us. It is not because they lose their significance to us; it is instead due to our limited attention, our uncanny ability to get bored because what we need to feel satisfied constantly changes. It is partially because our "satisfaction instinct" is too strong, and partially because we are affected by the social attitudes around us. Sometimes we struggle for a dozen years to buy a luxury item. Are we afraid that life will be too close to a subsistence level without it? Or will owning it let everyone know who we are? In striving to get it, there is no joy. All our struggles to obtain as many material and psychological comforts (like honor) as possible, serve only to *satisfy our emotions,* and to soothe our never-ending desires for satisfaction.

If happiness can be defined simply as emotions being satisfied, then at this very moment we are holding in our hands countless conditions to achieve happiness. Why then, do we say we are unhappy? We have bright eyes to see the things and the people we love, we have strong legs that can take us wherever we want, we have a stable job that brings a steady income and makes use of our talents, we have a loving family that we can fall back on, we have sufficient knowledge to permit us the discovery of the wide world, we have a good heart which allows us to accept and grow closer to any person on the earth, as well as numerous other benefits we may care to think about. Are they not all sufficient conditions for happiness? If we just look deeply, we will see that we own a lot, much more than we think. There is no need to be so quick in complaining to God or Mother Earth that we are the unhappiest person in the world just because of a few dissatisfactions.

This is why wise people will save the time and energy needed to "create their path" by retaining the happiness values that they have at any time, rather than rushing hastily towards the future to search for things that can only bring fleeting emotional satisfaction. We can find happiness in a peaceful life with few material comforts. We can feel happy even when our lives are unstable simply by recognizing the privilege we have in just being alive. When we look at a dying person in a hospital bed, a person scrambling through the rubble after an earthquake, a person who nearly lost a loved one forever, we can know how happiness feels. Their happiness is very simple—sometimes only requiring a breath of air, a handful of rice or just a final look at each other. When we think of happiness like this, we see no special kind of happiness in the future and so shouldn't waste our time seeking it. To put it bluntly, all the future holds is just different kinds of emotions. These emotions are addictions, and we will never have enough!

Satisfying the mind

We cannot be happy in a warm comfortable bed when we hear that a beloved person is stuck in a blizzard. In such a moment, the feeling of happiness from staying warm in bed loses priority. It would please us to be there in time to help our beloved person get out of trouble, even if we have to suffer the terrible cold of the blizzard. This situation is similar to that of parents who work hard for long hours to make money to pay for their children's food and education. They physically endure a hard life, but they feel truly happy for having fulfilled their wishes for their children. The same can be said for political activists. Although they can be tortured, they still feel proud, happy or even ready to die because they have made contributions towards the liberation of their people. In this, we can see that happiness is only concerned with good feelings. At times, we may have to sacrifice those good feelings for a more significant kind of happiness. That happiness is *satisfying the mind*.

Although satisfying the mind is still a form of satisfying our ego, doing whatever it takes to achieve our goals, it is a more subtle satisfaction that we can only realize by paying it close attention. It goes beyond the mediocre requirements of habit. We make every effort to endure pain and make use of all our understanding and skills to deal with difficulties. Therefore, its qualities are certainly more durable than the kind of happiness that is simply created by waves of emotion. That is because the nature of emotion keeps changing due to consciousness and the influences of our surroundings. Therefore we can see that happiness created by satisfying our emotions requires more conditions than happiness that is made by satisfying the mind.

When we are in a difficult situation and facing hardships, we should take care not to immediately resist it. First, we must understand that we are pursuing an important or lofty goal and in doing so, we cannot expect the usual comforts. Even if the difficulty of a situation becomes painful, we still shouldn't run away immediately. Instead we should realize that it is the pain that allows us to understand what happiness is. It is just like the situation where we value food highly after we have suffered hunger, where we appreciate sunshine because we have suffered the cold of winter, where we cherish every moment of togetherness because we have suffered the loss that is caused by separation and where we have a greater love of life because we have been close to death. It is in this fashion that we should not be afraid of suffering, nor should we separate happiness from suffering because without it, we would be unaware of what happiness truly is. The happiness within suffering is like the gem or jewel that only exists in the rock or the lotus that only grows from the mud. Without toiling through masses of rock, you will never find a gemstone, and without muddying your hands, you will never grow a lotus flower.

Thus, no happiness comes from Heaven, and no paradise consists solely of happiness because the concept of happiness exists only when people can feel suffering. Happiness cannot exist without suffering. What place is more wonderful than this Earth where both happiness and suffering are found!

True happiness

The happiness obtained from living with our loved ones doesn't remain the same after a couple of years. The happiness obtained from being able to buy a dream house usually tends to fade after a couple of months. The happiness obtained from a promotion is usually forgotten after a couple of weeks. And the happiness obtained from being praised usually evaporates after only a couple of hours. Then we crave for something else, readily believing that some new object in the future will bring happiness that will last longer. In this way, we can see our happiness is basically short-lived. Sometimes, it takes us a lot of time and energy to obtain happiness but then it mercilessly leaves us. It is the nature of the things outside of us. We borrow external conditions to invent something that will satisfy us. It is no wonder that we ultimately have no control over it. Despite knowing this, we have no way to remedy this pursuit of happiness because we are unable to escape from under the dark shadow of our own ambitions.

In fact, happiness obtained from emotions being satisfied and happiness obtained from the mind being satisfied both come from inside us rather than from external conditions. But due to a lack of understanding, we just imagine that we can't be happy without a particular object that we have set our sights on. External conditions are necessary, but only minimally. *True happiness* is the psychological state of not wanting anything else to serve ourselves, while not needing to get rid of anything we consider unbeneficial. It is better described as contentment and acceptance. It is true because it is the kind of happiness which is obtained from our peace of mind and is not completely reliant on external situations. That is why *happiness* and *peace* should go together—*peace and happiness*—to be long-lasting. Isn't life worth living for a person who has little money, no power and no admiration from anyone yet lives at ease, can smile at all times and can profoundly feel the miraculous values of the here and now?

To some extent, everyone is greedy and aversive. Many people have undergone some big changes in their lives and their energy for greed and aversion has decreased, but most of those who feel true happiness have made great efforts on a daily basis to transform those old attitudes. Actually, greed and aversion are reactions that have long served our foolish selves. Happiness inside us will extend infinitely if we can realize our essential natures and if we can live while being mindful and understanding of what we are doing, as well as how we are doing it. We will find true happiness if we can learn to let go of unnecessary greed and aversion, and allow our miniscule selves to evaporate into the universe and to work in harmony with everyone and everything.

Thus, we can feel as much happiness as our mind allows, because happiness naturally exists inside us—right here and right now.

Smile while looking at a flower
Let go of all doubt
Happiness is here and now
Though foolishly sought forever.

3

Love

How can we love somebody else while we still love ourselves so much? Even if we do love somebody, we just do it for our own good.

Having fallen in love

People in Vietnam often joke that *"Love hurts, but not to love is to lose/ I'd rather get hurt than lose."* There is truth in this joke. Despite the warning that "love hurts," most people would rather get hurt in order to have the feeling of being in love, because, as the poet Xuan Dieu said: *"How can we live without love, without missing or loving someone."* Life would be meaningless without love. It would then be death. But if we are afraid of pain and don't dare to love anyone, can we be sure that we would lead a happier life? There are lots of other things in life, not just love, which can make us suffer. Countless numbers of people around us suffer in the name of love, so why should we be afraid? Is love really as scary as we think?

Love is basically natural human inclination. If we just love a river, a paddy field, our hometown, or disadvantaged people, etc., we won't feel miserable. But we will feel miserable when the objects we love are so attractive that they can have an impact on our desires, causing us to miss them day and night, lose our appetite, lose our sleep and make us try to get them no matter what it takes. The poet Nguyen Du described this state of mind very well in the following verse: *"Having fallen in love, one traps oneself within it/ Therefore in peaceful places, one can't relax or sit still/ As if under a spell cast by ghosts and devils, one seeks the path to disasters."* When the emotion of love bursts, we can no longer keep ourselves under control. Our minds are turned upside down. Ensnared, we just keep moving forward like a sleepwalker oblivious to where we are going, even though we are about to step on the edge of a spike-trap. People in the West call this state *"falling in love,"* that is, being put under a spell of love, or it may be understood more literally as stumbling into love.

As the feelings surrounding romantic love are so strong, they can dominate the mind and even other feelings and emotions. No wonder we become more or less blind when we are in love, seeing the object of our affections as very different from others and seeing everything else as perfectly rosy. That's why we want to remove "the boundary of our selves" and invite that person to step in, and of course, we also want that person to make room for us in his or her heart. Sometimes, we even want to give that person our whole life, so we valiantly declare, "I love you with all my heart." In reality, nobody would love someone with all their heart without expecting to receive something in return, so that declaration is made out of the loss of emotional control in wanting to satisfy our physical desires or just to feel needed because another person's care and attention. We will withdraw in a hurry when that rosy color of love begins to fade.

Such love is just a way of exchanging emotions while true love must contain loving-kindness, an attitude of being ready to give and share everything in order to support each other. We might have mistakenly thought that romantic love is ranked higher than loving-kindness. But actually, romantic love tends to involve having a good time while loving-kindness tends to involve responsibility. As far as a romance is concerned, if love dominates loving-kindness, that love affair is just like a straw fire—"burning fast and dying out quickly"—but if loving-kindness dominates romantic love, that relationship is like a charcoal fire—"smoldering forever". Though our love starts like a bolt of lightning, we will have true love if we can recognize and let go of any unnecessary demands to pay time and attention to the person we love, to understand his or her difficulties or wishes, and to give our support wholeheartedly.

Loving the wrong way

The poet Xuan Dieu discovered common reasons for breakups: *"People suffer because they love the wrong way/ The wrong person and at the wrong time."* We must understand that everything in this world must rely on other things to exist. Love is no exception. Nothing could be described as love if it is separated from other qualities like peacefulness, steadiness, tolerance, openness, etc. If there were no friends, family, society, economy, politics, ethics or even nature, there would be no place for romance to exist. Thus, we actually take care of love while we take care of those other things.

But when in love, we usually pay attention to our desires for each other, staying close to each other all day without daring to take half a step away. When one person is not satisfied and begins to get bored, separation is sure to happen and the other person will surely collapse immediately because there seems to be no more reason to continue living. The poet Han Mac Tu lamented: *"You left, causing half of my mind to die/ The other half suddenly became insane"*. Actually, we never give half of our mind to anyone. Just because half (or all) our life has become dependent on the emotions of the one we love, we have nothing to rely on when that person is gone, and the addiction to that person torments us.

At times, however, we are practical, trying to find a love affair while aiming at its benefits as if it were an investment. We try to make as many demands as possible. We consider that person an effective protection for our life. The phrase "seeking a good port" now means trying to find a person who can ensure a comfortable life for us so that we are not inferior to our friends. This point of view is greatly affected by social consciousness. Taking a closer look, we can see those requirements only bring about temporary feelings through praise from those who care about looking good, but they are "crazy dreams" that have a harmful effect on love. We believe that married life would be happier with material possessions that impress our friends and others. Our desires continue to grow and the other person is squeezed by us until their energy runs out. As a result, the two hearts grow farther and farther apart over time. If that person loves us so much and tries to pamper us, he or she is actually living in a dream. Neither person's actions have roots in the foundation of true love. It is obvious how both can easily desert each other due to different viewpoints, conflicts, and the failure to satisfy each other.

The poet Xuan Dieu once confessed: *"I was so foolish, so stupid/ I know only love and nothing else"*. Love is just like a plant. If we don't know how to take care of it, too much as well as too little care will make it wither and die. Everyone loves to have their emotions satisfied, but we can only enjoy that forever if satisfaction goes alongside responsibility. If the "boundary of our selves" is removed to really let the other person step into our heart, the responsibility to guide each other toward a life of peace and true happiness won't be a burden or reluctance any more. The matter is whether we can open up our heart or not. If we still highly value material possessions, and are too interested in fame and an attractive appearance, a desire for long-lasting love would only be an ambition. When we love ourselves so much, how can we have room to love somebody else? Even if we do love somebody else, we just do it for our own good. If the other person considers physical possessions and comforts as a reason for love to exist, we know that he or she is not the half we are seeking. But if we are good and tough enough, we will still be able to guide the other person in the direction that we think is right without fearing that we *"Love the wrong person and at the wrong time"*.

So, love is always true, and the secret to true love is that we must, at all times, be conscientious enough to find ourselves and understand the person we love.

Love like the first time
Please support each other
With an understanding heart
Then we won't suffer

4

Loving-Kindness

Only mutual understanding can nurture true loving-kindness.

Loving-kindness means giving

Do we ever ask ourselves why we love someone? Is it because he or she is a nice and kind person? Well, in that way, we just want to enjoy those good personal qualities rather than love the person. Anyone can do it because anyone can love someone with attractive character traits. Such an agreeable person is sweet, gentle, and, more importantly, always behaves nicely and humbly toward us. If she behaves nicely toward another person instead of us, we may not find her so agreeable or love her anymore. The relationships between family members are similar. Do we love them because we have a "responsibility" to do so since they are closely related to us? Or is it because we know how pitiful they are and how much they need our loving-kindness? We can see quite a few people who feel they have suffered too many losses because of their relatives, so they "close their heart" and can't love them any more. They feel that *closeness* only becomes *loving-kindness* when that closeness can more or less bring them benefits, even if they only get respect or a reputation for being a good person.

If somebody loves us, we might love them back; it is not worth our while to love someone who doesn't love us. It sounds like a business exchange, but it is always true. It is certainly very hard for us to love someone who doesn't love us, or even hates us or makes us miserable. It would be acceptable if they would just love us a little. Only parents, religious followers and some others who have developed compassion can love people unconditionally. They love us no matter what we are. However, we may have even seen some parents who mercilessly deserted their children just because they are disabled or naughty, or some people who are famous for their donations to charity programs in public, but turn their back on a homeless child begging for food when nobody is watching. So, although love is a human's natural character, we must train ourselves a lot to transform the selfishness inside us before loving-kindness can truly come out.

True loving-kindness must first be an attitude of giving. We shouldn't mistake it for busily trying our best to please a person while actually wanting to "get more credit". True giving must arise from the feeling of wanting to make the other person more peaceful and happier. Therefore, each gift we give must be absolutely for his or her interests without involving any of our own, even if we just want our feelings to be recognized. To expect someone to recognize our feelings is simply trying to cause him or her to love or appreciate us more. Though our heart is not big enough to love someone without expecting to be loved in return, we shouldn't impose conditions alongside each gift we give; otherwise it is no longer loving-kindness.

After all, loving someone is an enjoyment in itself. Is it not true that lots of people want to have someone to love but can't find that person? There are lots of people, but that "somebody to love" must have something to do with us. We can't just love anybody we want. To be more specific, we can only love someone who has feelings or appreciation for us, who welcomes us and feels happy with our love. Thus, we should feel fortunate enough to have someone to love, and we shouldn't really ask them to do anything else for us. We would feel really miserable if one day everyone ran away from us and we had no one to love. It would truly be a disaster if we could not have the chance to love. Thus, we should love in a way that the person we love will really enjoy. Only then, do we not devalue the great meaning of love.

Loving-kindness is sharing

If giving is to bring happiness, sharing is to take away suffering. Everyone experiences troubles or sufferings at some time, but they won't necessarily feel sad, instead they will feel strong enough to overcome difficulties if they can share them with their beloved by their side.

Though we may be unable to pull them out of the swamp of miseries, at least our timely presence can reduce the miseries by some degree, simply because they recognize our sincerity. They know we really love them, want to share responsibilities with them and want to be their partner for life. A pain shared by two hearts is most certainly not a pain anymore. That is the reason why we need each other in this world.

Love can't bring happiness if we live with a person who always says he loves us but when we are in trouble, pays no attention. Even when we directly inform him about our problem and only need him to sit down and understand our situation, he can find all kinds of reasons to decline. Because he always thinks he has worked very hard to bring home money and honor to us, he has no more energy to accept additional trouble, and we are told to deal with the problem ourselves. That difficulty could have been just a difficulty, but it was his indifference and uncaring attitude that turned it into suffering. Yes, we know he is very busy and doesn't have much energy to help us solve the problem, but we just need his attention. Perhaps just a word of sympathy would be enough to comfort us because it shows that he is willing to share our suffering.

To understand is to love. Without understanding, love will not be strong and may be delusive. Mutual understanding requires mutual listening. We must know what the other person wants or doesn't want so that we can act appropriately. Even if some requests are not reasonable, we need to know what kind of trouble they are in so that we can help them out promptly. If we just act in the name of love and do things our way, we may worsen the situation instead of helping. Of course, goodwill is necessary because at times we must be patient enough to listen to, comfort or beg them before they will tell us all their "hidden miseries". Additionally, we must bear the heavyheartedness from their stories, complaints or anger without getting hurt. Thus, goodwill must be the ability to care about another person rather than ourselves (loving-kindness) coupled with the right way of thinking (understanding) before we can help them out of trouble.

Therefore, if we really love each other, we must always *know* and *understand* what is happening to each other without waiting to be informed of the problems. Only mutual understanding can nurture true loving-kindness. We only need to pay close attention to their health, help them with the cleaning in the kitchen, fix the brakes on their vehicles, not ask for help when they are busy and always be there when they are in trouble or distressed. All that is enough to make the person we love feel our true love.

However, to have sufficient energy to do all those things, we must be aware that sharing and giving are two essential ingredients in any kind of loving-kindness. Without them, nothing can be described as loving-kindness. Our beloved's happiness is our own happiness. If we don't help our loved one, who will?

With boundless love and loving-kindness
Mutually sharing our distress
We always bring joy to one another
And guide each other toward peace and happiness

5

Anger

If we curb our anger when we have yet to understand it, it is just a temporary measure.

Where does anger come from?

When we get angry, we usually blame it on the other party as if our anger is directly provoked by them. Therefore, we always find ways to retaliate, either by saying or doing something to really hurt them before we can feel vindicated. We think that in doing so we will seem strong, meaning they won't dare to make us angry again. In reality, the more we retaliate, the stronger our own anger gets, and the weaker we actually get. We suffer the most because when we are angry, the energy inside us burns out. Our body constantly produces stimulants like adrenaline and cortisone, causing biological disorder in our body, especially with our heartbeat and rate of breathing. Worse still, we will temporarily "lose consciousness", taking everything wrong, thinking unclearly and being unable to keep our behaviors under control.

If getting angry easily is in the nature of the previous generation, especially our own parents, then we can hardly avoid bearing their mark, or being affected by their daily behaviors and actions. Our living and working environments can play a considerable role in developing our trait of getting angry easily. Indulgence and family pampering can easily cause us to develop the habit of demanding whatever we want or wanting to prove our power in front of other people, so just a little something against our will can make us instantly angry. Moreover, we are strongly influenced by social mores, so we always think that getting angry is natural human instinct for self-defense. When we see that other people don't dare to bully us, we start to believe that this "useful" anger is a way to release our emotions and allow us to regain our composure after facing trouble. But actually we have failed because we haven't been able to tame the old-fashioned win-lose attitude, we don't know how to express our dissatisfaction more intelligently, and we are making the situation worse and worse.

Transforming anger

After each outburst of anger, we usually feel remorse and a prick of conscience because of our stupid and vulgar reactions. We know that when we get angry, we lose our beautiful image in the eyes of other people and also their trust, so we often tell ourselves that we will not let our anger control us any more. But when facing something against our will, especially when our interest or honor is at stake, we will sometimes "burst out". Even if somebody reminds us to keep calm at the time, we will reject it outright. While we're angry, emotions take over the rational mind. With one failure after another, we gradually hate our anger, and at times we may blame our parents for giving us such a characteristic that ravages us and other people.

Actually, if the seed of anger inside us is not sustained frequently, it won't be strong enough to make us miserable. However, we unexpectedly create it from mundane things against our will such as getting stuck in a traffic jam, waiting in line to check out, getting no answers from phone calls, eating tasteless food, not receiving greetings from our loved ones, etc. It can be created from trouble we make ourselves such as using a wrong key, burning our mouth by drinking hot water, slipping on a staircase, being unable to find a book, recalling bad memories of the past, etc. If we don't take notice of such negative reactions growing over time so that we can find ways to get rid of them, our anger will naturally grow bigger and bigger. When the energy of our built-up anger is powerful enough, just one annoying act is sufficient to trigger it and turn it into a terrible outburst that surprises even us.

As soon as we realize our anger is growing big and about to "burst out" into words or actions, we should quickly find a way to separate ourselves from the object that has just provoked our anger. The best way is to sit in a quiet room or go for a stroll on a shady road. In the event we can't get away from the situation, we should sit still, trying to not to utter a single word, even if we think our explanations would be satisfactory. We will often regret later any action taken while we are angry. We should forget what the other person has said or done to us; instead, we should concentrate all our attention on every single breath we take in order to calm the storm of emotions. If we already have the ability to keep calm by paying attention to our breathing, it will take us no longer than fifteen minutes to calm down. It is similar to the situation in which our house is on fire: we have to try to put out the fire in order to save all the precious things inside rather than rush to find the person we suspect of setting fire to our house. We can "take care of that later".

Our breath is a safe shelter for us whenever torrents of emotions attack us and we do not know what to do. However, if we always only use this method, we will never know the nature of our anger. If we don't understand the nature of our anger clearly, we will never be able to transform it and it will bother us forever. Therefore, after we have developed the habit of examining ourselves whenever we get angry, instead of trying to retaliate like before, we should spend a lot of time observing the process from the time the anger arises, urges us to act and then when it vanishes. When experienced in this, we will find our anger does not actually exist. It is only a source of energy produced by some things functioning abnormally in the operation of the mind, including wrong perception, an overactive imagination, oversensitive emotions and uncontrolled senses. We just need to keep observing that process patiently for a long time and without prejudice. Gradually we will see the real nature of our anger and be able to transform it easily.

However, we often make the mistake of wanting anger to vanish as soon as we learn to keep calm. In such a short time, it is impossible to kick a habit that has been developing for a very long while. The process of observing anger may cause some unexpected irritation in the first stage, but gradually we will get used to it and may even find it as interesting as watching an action film. We just sit back and watch our anger as if we were reclining on a sofa and watching a movie. In this case it's harmless, just to let it rise naturally but observe it, unlike the other times. Of course, the anger will continue its own course, but we don't want to catch it to put it out. We just observe to understand what its operational mechanism really is. Each observation will help us see something new about the impermanent nature of anger. Our wrong perception will eventually go away. We need to practice patiently to adjust our mind's operational mechanism, rather than suppress or control our anger. When we have yet to deeply understand our anger, controlling it is just a temporary measure.

Love without anger

We shouldn't be satisfied too quickly with this first achievement of our practice, although now we may not get angry as easily as before. Perhaps we can even smile sweetly when receiving a scolding from the boss or seeing a colleague doing something carelessly. However, when coming home, if we are unexpectedly suspected of something or wrongly judged by our beloved, our "old" anger may return immediately. But then we often make an excuse for it, saying that we "get angry because of love". We think that we can ignore and pay no attention to total strangers because they have nothing to do with us. On the other hand, this is someone with whom we have lived for years, have always loved and have been willing to give anything, so it's a terrible insult for us to get that kind of treatment from him or her. In reality, we are angry at this "surprise attack" because we believe that when we love somebody with all our heart, that person doesn't have the right to hurt us. We don't think that it is our immense pride that really hurts us.

It is an illusion to expect that our beloved should never do us wrong solely because we have supported or given them so much. We should put ourselves in his or her shoes to see if we can behave that way. Life puts us under more and more pressure. Having financial problems alone is enough to cause people to "lose their minds," forget who they are and make mistakes easily. If we are understanding and calm, we should help them refresh themselves so that they can see themselves and the miracles of life in the present moment. Otherwise, our efforts to help would be like adding fuel to the fire that's burning them down. We should also never pretend to be angry in an attempt to make the other person see their mistakes and change because nobody welcomes uncomfortable and negative feelings. Though they may know they are at fault and can't express themselves well, they will still get worn-out and mad at us. If we are not careful, they might misinterpret our effort as a merciless punishment and hold a grudge against us, making the situation worse.

Remember that affliction is very subtle. If we don't have good observation skills, we won't discover all the hidden negative emotions, and one day our rage will suddenly surface in torrents. Because we often subjectively think we are no longer angry, or just pretend to be angry to show our authority, or act to please someone else, we fail to see the waves of anger seething inside us. Day after day, little by little, the energy of anger festers and forms a huge mass often called an *internal fetter*. This internal fetter affects almost all our behaviors. It always makes us get mad or quarrel with people even though they may have done nothing wrong to us. It turns out that we have not deeply understood our hearts, which are still stubborn and intolerant, and we don't think we have a problem with anger. So we can see that understanding the hidden corners of our minds is more important than smothering our anger.

To sum up, as long as we continue to pamper our ego, anger still exists inside us because it is the "opponent" of selfless loving-kindness.

Anger is also impermanent
The sun ruptures the veil of fog
Give rise to the mind of awareness
The deeper we look, the more loving we feel

6

Endurance

Enduring without complaint is not an act of cowardice. It is a way to learn to expand the capacity of the heart to accommodate life's difficulties.

Accepting to move forward

When the doctor says that we have cancer, we may get terrified and cry: "Oh no, it can't be! I have done nothing so wrong to deserve this. Why me and not somebody else?" We might even think that we can't stay alive after receiving that bad news. But after a few weeks or months, we learn to accept the truth that we have cancer. Though we need appropriate medications for treatment on a long-term basis, the spreading of the cancer slows down because we have calmly focused all of our energy on treatment instead of wasting it on fear, worry, anxiety, despair, etc., which would hinder our efforts. Medically, the process of treatment has begun. Accepting the truth that we are sick means we are brave enough to face the problems in our bodies to receive care promptly. It is not an act of surrender. Sometimes, we are too busy pursuing our ambitious goals to take care of ourselves. When our health deteriorates and our body can no longer serve us, we get angry, blame it and hate it. This attitude shows a lack of understanding of and loving-kindness for our own selves.

Some people show self-confidence when saying: "I never accept failures". This is a very naive statement because nobody escapes failures, even when they may be enjoying their successes. Since conditions that bring success are sometimes beyond our control, we can't make them come to us when we haven't found the proper connections. Feelings resulting from failures are certainly hard to endure, for example trying to put on a calm front after having lost everything we've worked hard for and our self-confidence. When we make a mistake, we just can't forgive ourselves even if our loved ones forgive us. We simply can't believe that a knowledgeable and experienced person like ourselves could make such a careless mistake, so we hate and punish ourselves. This is because in the past, we tried to force ourselves to be consistently perfect at a time when we still had a lot of vulnerabilities and weaknesses that needed to be taken care of. Accepting our own weaknesses is a way of being honest to ourselves and overcoming our old habits or unnecessary resistance.

Once we have developed the habit of accepting our own weaknesses and accepting things that have happened beyond our control, based on principles of cause-and-effect and causal conditions, we will easily accept other people's weaknesses and mistakes. In retrospect, we mostly don't accept others because we see that they have nothing else to offer us or that their bad reputation might hurt us. However, if we truly want to help them and accept them, our acceptance is not an act of tolerating their bad habits; rather, our acceptance will help them gain more confidence and strength to overcome their weaknesses because they can still see their worth in our eyes and still believe in true love that always goes beyond fairness. Thus, if we choose to accept the facts rather than avoid or resist them, we have begun the process of trying to understand and solve problems. The problems are still there, but we no longer feel uneasy or annoyed. We will be patient enough to find appropriate ways to help transform them.

The ability to endure

We all have very different levels of acceptance depending on our understanding, habits and training. There are things that other people accept easily but we strongly object to, and vice versa. We constantly change our own levels of acceptance, too. We may learn to accept something that we never thought we would, or we may eventually complain that we can't stand something which we readily accepted before. When we can accept some people, we say they are nice; and when we can't stand them later, we say they have gotten worse. It never occurs to us that it is our mind which is in a state of flux. Our understanding may be better or worse, our imagination may temporarily stop being active or suddenly exaggerate more, our emotions may get weaker or stronger, and the annoyance inside us may grow or vanish completely. Therefore, we shouldn't strongly believe in our acceptance, or lack thereof, on any particular day. Though we might be very sure when we make a certain decision, over time we might change our mind unexpectedly.

We should know that our heart always has storage capacity. Suppose someone puts a handful of salt into a bowl of water, the water in the bowl will be very salty, too salty to drink. But if they put that handful or even dozens of kilos of salt into a river, the water in the river is still drinkable. The water in the river is still drinkable not because it doesn't contain salt, but because the water volume is too great for the small amount of salt to take effect. Everybody has troubles and difficulties, but what matters is whether each person's heart is large enough to embrace them all. If our heart is small and the external difficulties are too big, we certainly couldn't bear them. For example, a father decides to abandon one naughty child because he is afraid the child would have a bad influence on his other children. His decision is not necessarily wrong, but he is a failure. If a father's love for his children is basically large like a river, then why couldn't he endure the small handful of salt his child has put in? A really big heart doesn't need to make any requirements from a weak adversary.

We usually mistake the word *enduring* to mean being under pressure or being resigned to something even though its meaning is more positive: *to bear and hold*. To bear means to agree to accept something; to hold implies a capacity to accommodate. Acceptance without the ability to accommodate is worthless. A river is capable of bearing a lot more salt because it is tens of thousands of times larger than a bowl. The poet Nguyen Du said: "Being able to accommodate the inferior shows the generosity of the superior". Mature or superior people are those who can accommodate others no matter how they are, instead of hating or forsaking them. So we see that enduring is not an act of cowardice. It is a way to learn to expand the capacity of the heart to accommodate big difficulties. We can't say that we don't need to bother to be long-suffering. Things in life are not always what we want. If we don't prepare a heart with a large storage capacity, we will fail in difficult situations or lose our beloved because of our inability to accept them.

What is miraculous is that our heart can expand to infinity—a boundless heart—without limits. People in the olden days often said that our heart could embrace both heaven and earth and even the whole universe. We don't need to spread our hearts all over the world to embrace all kinds of species. We just need to be able to accept one person no matter what or how he or she might be. If we can see that this person is a part of our non-self natures, we will realize that we are not actually trying to accept anything. We accept but it seems as though we don't. If we have such calm and peaceful acceptance ability, we will be able to accept anyone. Then we will have found our great true selves, and no impermanent disturbance in this world will be powerful enough to threaten us anymore.

A handful of salt is never salty
In the great capacity of the river
That mistake is really tiny
In the boundless heart of the forgiver.

7

Jealousy

Love that turns a person into the guard of another creates a life no different from being imprisoned in exile.

Duality within oneness

Basically, love must exist on the basis of unity. Our happiness is another person's happiness just as the other person's trouble is our trouble. There's no way that a husband's hopes are not known to his wife or the wife's interests don't attract the husband's attention. Once married, two lives are considered one. What happens to one person affects the other and this person's fate depends on the partner's. *"You and I are two but one"*: two bodies are merged into one heart, one fate. That is truly the love of a couple. In Vietnamese, the word "minh" literally means "body", but it is used to refer to ourselves when speaking to our friends and loved ones as well as to call our beloved in a tender, loving voice. Just that word can show us the unity of the two, and the separation is nowhere to be felt.

Thus when we love someone, we should learn from each other to select the common points that can build a true, long-lasting happiness, and we should try to quickly change our own traits that are not lovable and cause suffering to the other person. Unity doesn't mean that one person must change to become a copy of the other person; that would be over-attachment rather than unity. Unity is harmony, not discord. So, although we and the other person become one couple with shared characteristics and ideas, we should never forget they're still very different from us because they come from different families, have different friends, customs, knowledge, remarks, emotions, hobbies and even ideals of their own. If we want love, we should just ask to take part in their lives, accept and help them, rather than try to push their lives out and put our lives in their place to be in control.

"Though we are one, we are two individuals": this is the other half of the inseparable "heart" of the aforementioned folk song. Based on Vietnam's traditions, the principle for a couple's happiness is for husband and wife to be both one and two. They are "one" because they want to live in harmony, and they are "two" because they want release and freedom. Release means not being kept under each other's control or constraint. It means giving each other space to breathe, relax and live in harmony with everyone and everything else in life. This is a very big challenge because we usually act in the name of love to confine our beloved to our "ivory tower." We want them to love and pamper us, do what we want, always be available for us, stay within our reach when they go somewhere, and always think about us and nothing else. But we are very naive in that way because a person's craving for freedom can be immense. The more they are confined, the more they want to escape. Money, power or lust can't control a person's life, except when he or she becomes obsessed with them. Love that turns a person into a guard of another creates a life no different from being imprisoned in exile.

That way of expressing feelings indicates that we still think the other person is outside of us, not a part of us. Meanwhile, the other person does not consist solely of flesh and bone. All that the other person has given us from the beginning—accepting us, trusting and loving us, missing us, as well as peacefulness, stability and happiness, etc.—are the most valuable qualities that have entered us and helped make us what we are today. When we haven't seen our beloved inside us, we still haven't reached the peak of love where the husband and wife are one. This is not a transcendent philosophy. It is an evident truth of the rule of long-lasting harmony which any couple must understand clearly if they want to live together until the end of their lives. Though it is a long process of learning and practicing, if we take a step toward that end each day, we will be moving closer to each other, and we will no longer conceal our true feelings like masking our anxieties with a smile. We will be honest. We will have strength in love.

Supporting each other through hardships

Jealousy indicates a weakness in our view about the nature of our beloved. It will cause the magic of love to fade away very soon. But we often hear people say *"jealousy arises out of love."* It sounds reasonable because we wouldn't get jealous if we didn't love the other person. However, if we love them very much, why do we make them suffer every time we get jealous? The truth is that we only love ourselves. We feel sorry for ourselves being emotionally hurt because we are deserted or lose value in the other person's eyes. We have seen many people treat their beloved very badly but they still want to keep hold of the other whatever it takes, because they think that the other person is at least a safe spot for them to rely on. Such possessiveness indicates extremely selfish behavior!

There is certainly a seed of selfishness in everyone's heart, and marriage must contain certain firm commitments. But if we let this selfishness become too strong of a source of energy, dominating all sentimental attachments, love is likely to crack and break. This is because love comes voluntarily. If the other person leaves us and breathes a sigh of relief, it indicates that he or she felt love for us reluctantly or as a kind of obligation or a responsibility. So, it is possible that just a little subtle jealousy can surprise someone and make them happy that they are still loved. But if we let jealousy become a chronic fever or an uncontrollable storm, it will make the other person very tired, disappointed and scared. They will see the limited space we created for them in our hearts, not to mention our most despicable acts to "pay them back" and punish them.

Although we are not children, jealously makes us behave immaturely. Jealousy makes us mediocre and ugly because it clearly shows our natural instinct for self-defense. Instead, we should keep calm and reflect on the other person's life and on our own life. If both sides don't have time for themselves because they are busy running around, they will not have time to reflect on each other's life and it will be very hard for both to control their strong feelings. Sometimes the other person loves us very much and highly values a happy home. However, once their energy runs short, and if we are inattentive and keep demanding them to satisfy our needs, while an outsider is willing to offer them what they need, betrayal can happen very easily. They're only the victims of their weak emotions and greed. So, if we really love them, we should try to bring them back to their attractive character of the past. Scolding and punishing would only make them think that we are trying to reinforce the "prison" they see us creating. It will only be easy for them to return if they see that we have made it really safe and warm for them back home.

We are also the poor victim of our own emotions, so we need help too. Don't try to refute the truth because of pride: "Am I jealous? Who do you think you are to make me jealous?" If we have tried all measures without being able to transform the storm of destructive jealousy inside us, and it is going to break out soon, we should ask for a helping hand from our partner. We should write a message to tell them how miserable this jealousy makes us feel and ask them to help remove that harmful energy from us. That person is understanding and will not refuse such a sincere request because of their love for us. Taking the chance of their being willing to return, we should ask them to let us know what we should do and what we shouldn't do to be nicer. Remember not to use a "strategy of suffering" to arouse their compassion or make them feel a prick of conscience. That measure might be a temporary solution, but in the end it would put shame to our values and make our beloved despise us when they recognize our "strategy." After "crying wolf" too many times, they will not be easily moved by our reactions, not even our real ones. Everything will not be hard and complex anymore when we take time to look at them carefully from a broad perspective. Patience, after all, is the evidence of love.

We can take hold of the other person's heart in hundreds of ways without using jealousy to try to bind each other together. Jealousy damages mutual trust and respect, and the more we try to love through it, the more tired we will get. Sometimes, we don't keep hold of anything but we have it all, and other times we want to grab hold of everything, but find our hands empty. That is the secret of life. Anyone who has this key will become the powerful owner of the garden of love.

You are still in me
Like I am always in you
A little jealousy from emotional frailty
Will erode love and trust too

8

Forgiveness

Forgiveness is always a wonder drug that can heal all the pain and suffering of the forgiven as well as the forgiver.

Ingredients for loving devotion

In the principle of love, one side must have the ability to love and the other side must be really lovable. When the latter loses their lovability, it means they no longer want to be loved and therefore can't expect their partner's love to remain unchanged. However, the fault is not entirely theirs. If the love from one side is true, strong and bright enough, it will certainly be able to guide and support the other side so both can soar together. Therefore, when both sides do their best with one side trying to lift themselves up and the other giving wholehearted support, their love will never break.

We know that the biggest drawback of modern civilization is that it makes human beings too busy, giving them little time to rest and enjoy the miraculous things around them, let alone not leaving them the energy to look back at themselves and transform all their negative energy. We are always stressed, tired and full of worries about the future. When our energy levels are very low, we can hardly control our thoughts and actions. An unpleasant remark or an inadvertently offensive gesture can easily cause the other person heartbreak. If we run into bad luck and meet such great obstacles that our energy is depleted, the mental afflictions inside us will break out like a kind of instinct that has never been tamed. Desire, anger and ignorance are the kinds of energy inside us that are always ready to come out when we lose our ability to observe, to think rationally, and when we lose contact with life. This is how mistakes usually occur.

Of course, not everyone living in an environment full of bad energy will become a bad person. It all depends on each person's wisdom and toughness. A child can't be expected to be well-behaved or honest if he grows up in poverty, comes from a broken home, never goes to school and often socializes with rude people or relies on them to make a living. Another child can't be aware of responsibility or be polite and respectful to everyone if she grows up in a comfortable wealthy home but her parents are too busy making money and don't have time to be close to her and understand her. The parents may even quarrel often and do dishonest things in front of their child's eyes, then compensate for their lack of responsibility in educating the child by sending her to a prestigious school or by meeting all her material demands.

We can get very angry when reading about a schoolboy taking a knife with him to school to threaten to kill his teachers, or a schoolgirl who has badly beaten her classmate, filmed it and posted it on the Internet. We consider these acts immoral. We want those schoolchildren to be punished severely. But if we blame all these wrongdoings on the children, how could they bear it all? They would collapse and lose all their future hopes, and we would gradually lose the kids who would continue our roles in the future. They are ignorant children who want to grow up quickly but they aren't psychologically well-prepared; that is why they fail. Homes and schools should always be the most ideal environments that help children understand themselves and nurture their plans for the future. However, some parents just expect their children to do well at school to be successful in life, and schools just want the kids to get good grades without cultivating or investing in their ethics. Admittedly, education can't be successful based solely on individual efforts, but the two environments considered to provide the most sustenance for children to make steady steps in life don't take their responsibilities either. Who then would help problem children to reintegrate into the community and be themselves? Do we have hope in reformatories? Punishment is the worst solution in education. In reality, only a very small number of children are strong enough to be rehabilitated and return to normal; the rest lose all their faith in life, are ready to give up and sink back into the mud.

Therefore, before we pour all our anger on those ignorant kids, we should ask ourselves whether we have done anything to help them. Or do we think that it is not our responsibility, so we just stand aside and blame them, condemn them and stay away from them? We adults still make a lot of mistakes and sometimes commit wrongdoing. Even though our mistakes have not been known or exposed by others, it does not mean we are so squeaky-clean that we can arbitrarily label people who have just made a mistake as the bad guys. In the Gospel of John, Jesus Christ warned: "Let him who is without sin cast the first stone." Give other people a chance to transform themselves because by doing this, we give ourselves a way out in the future. Life is steeped in mindlessness, so uncontrollable behaviors are inevitable. We need to tolerate and help each other to overcome difficulties rather than sit still, expecting other people to be perfect at all times.

How to forgive?

Suppose our loved one's difficulty is equivalent to a hand span and our heart's capacity is a hand span and a half, we are then able to contain their difficulty. But if their difficulty is a hand span and a half or two hand spans, then we must try to expand our heart's capacity to be bigger than that. If we try our best but our heart's capacity is just as big as or smaller than their difficulty, our support for them will be a failure. Even so, the other person will feel our efforts and deeply appreciate our kindness. This is because our love is so generous that we can give up basic comforts and overcome environmental pressures to help the person we love see the light and move forward. This loving devotion only comes out of goodwill and selfless volunteering. It is not found in contracts or in the other person's expectations. And forgiveness is really the peak of this loving devotion.

If we are calm and observant, we will always see that the people who make mistakes are really the most pitiable victims. Though they may have hurt us accidentally, they are the most miserable because the energy of their anger or other psychological problems torments them every single second. The more stubborn they appear, the more pitiable they are because we don't know when they will come to their senses and return to the right path in order to live a peaceful and happy life. They lose trust in themselves and are afraid their beloved will desert them without knowing how to solve the trouble and damage they cause. They are scared of not knowing what their life will be like in the future. That is why they are often puzzled and really need help. They know that we have loved with all our heart, but they have failed us. Now, they are ashamed to ask for more help and they think that they have no right to ask for anything else. So they can only hope for our loving devotion—a genuinely affectionate gift that is spontaneous and without reason-or expectation of any return, and is from the heart of a kind and generous person.

When we are aware that this person deserves compassion rather than blame, we will no longer want to rid ourselves of the difficulty involved in dealing with them. That is, we have accepted their unlovable characteristics, just as we welcomed their lovable traits before. The problem is how we can embrace all their pain and suffering easily when our heart is still not large enough. We really want to forgive but still can't do it. Our heart aches each time we think of their bad behavior or betrayal. If we think it is easy to forgive because it takes just a little effort, we are wrong. Our heart can hardly expand more when we cling to inflexible principles, when we always expect perfection from others, when we are caught in egotism, always seeing that we make more contributions than others and still are unaccustomed to enduring losses or doing our best for others. We must be able to limit our needs for selfish satisfactions before there is room for other people in our heart. So, the more selfish we are, the less altruistic we become, because selfishness is the opposite of altruism.

In traditional meditation centers, there are two ways to teach children: *power* and *devotion*. Power means respect-inspiring deportment, the energy radiated from dignified behavior and ethical conduct, not from shouting and barking orders at other people. *Devotion* here means loving devotion, the dedicated support for those in need, or the generous heart to tolerate them when they make mistakes. This devotion does not come from us loving them blindly. *Power* is actually *devotion*, because *it* helps them to always be mindful and try to improve, making them feel very grateful. *Devotion* is also *power*, because it happens when we help them wholeheartedly and unconditionally, instilling respect in them. Just like understanding and love, power and devotion are never separate, though at times one may be expressed more than the other.

We must be very careful each time we demonstrate power or devotion. Sometimes we think we must do something to make someone see their mistakes and to intimidate them from ever making them again, yet in our hearts we feel very angry and want to punish them. At other times, we really feel sorry for someone who needs help and encouragement rather than blame, but actually we are afraid that they might stop loving us or even hate us. When this person is in trouble and needs help, if we mix our self-interest with our help, then this forgiveness is not sincere anymore. Sometimes we see someone making a mistake that is just too big, so big that it is impossible to act as if it hadn't happened. We can attempt to swallow our bitterness, try to accept their mistake and give them a chance, or, if we know our heart is in pain, we may need some more time before we can accept and transform it. At times like these we may as well tell them the truth: Our heart can only open so much. That honesty is also loving devotion and genuine forgiveness.

Though we are not saints who are willing to forgive everyone for their mistakes, if our heart could hold more, we would forgive each other without further deliberation. Forgiveness is a wonder drug that can heal all wounds for both the forgiven and the forgiver. It is better to wrongly forgive than to wrongly blame. If we realize that it was our intolerance that pushed the other person into a terrible situation or even death, we would spend the rest of our lives regretting our behavior. But when we find out that our decision to forgive didn't yield a good result, we would still have a chance to correct the mistake because our heart is expanding and getting stronger every day. The most terrible thing in the process of love is when we allow our hearts to shrink, grow weak and lose all the sacred sensitivity to be affected by the heartbreaking cries in life. The late song writer Trinh Cong Son absolutely believed in the magical transformation of human hearts when he wrote in his song, "Let's Love Each Other": "*Our heart provides shelter for us to come back, to forget many of our miserable days*"

Let me be present for you
And all of my heart too
In this moment of wakefulness
With unwavering devotion and kindness

9

Exchanges

Why do we always keep complaining and asking life for more without ever wondering what it needs from us?

Caring reciprocity or even exchange?

Long ago in Vietnam, farmers could ask people in the village for help when harvesting a crop without having to pay them any money. When the other people harvested a crop, fixed a house or had some heavy work, these farmers would go to help them in return. That was called *work exchange*. That process was great. Though the work exchange was calculated based on the number of hours or days it would take to get done, people were not so serious about each person's skills or ability. For example, while helping other people to pay back their favors to us, if we got sick or had a family emergency and had to stop working, they would make concessions for us and consider our payback done. On the other hand, when a crop was a failure and they couldn't help us in return, we would be happy to wait until the next crop, or we might even exempt them from doing something for us in return. Treating each other with a kind heart was most important. Country farmers understood that the barter only had a relative value. It did not end when we helped somebody in return. The feelings of gratitude were still there because the payback could never be completely fulfilled.

In modern civilization, people have a strange idea about exchange. For example, when we are new at a job and somebody really takes time to help us, create favorable conditions for us to do a good job or share difficulties with us when we are in deep trouble, etc., we promptly give them an expensive gift or take them to an expensive restaurant in return. We think that that's enough and that we owe them nothing more. But if they help us unconditionally with all their heart and we think their help is equal to the value of those gifts, then we should not be surprised if they feel hurt. We'd better not accept their help then because they would feel hurt if we thought such heartfelt, unconditional help was equal to the payback of a gift or meal. However, a gift or meal would be accepted with pleasure if they could see it as an expression of our deeply felt gratitude. Some people don't expect their help to be "repaid" since they did not set any "price" for helping us to begin with. They may still accept our gift and, though we don't have a chance to do something more for them later, that may be fine with them because at the start they didn't expect anything back.

The concept of fair or even exchange can easily be mistaken for the deeper concept of caring reciprocity. You have one of something, so I should have one, or you give me two of something, so I should give you two. That is basic or elementary reciprocity. But the concept of reciprocity can vary and deepen according to time and place. Reciprocal arrangements are usually decided by both parties based on how they feel at the time, so sometimes two people can reach an agreement about the worth of things they want to exchange without complying with the rules of exchange set out by their community. For example, a calabash squash can be traded for two bitter melons, a boat ride across a river can be bartered for singing a song, a picture can be traded for ten gourds of alcohol, and a heartfelt promise can be exchanged for three hundred sixty-five days of waiting. Although those exchanges are reciprocal, they are more than mere exchanges: they include warmhearted feelings for and in consideration of the other person. Both sides understand that feelings are also involved in the deal and they will make it up later when there's a chance. A merely fair or even exchange, on the other hand, is a cut-and-dried, straightforward equitable exchange without any human sentiment. It is just business.

Of course, in the wide market, people need to make everything clear like the monetary values of the materials or services to be exchanged, so they set up a monetary system to simplify and expand trade. As a result, merely fair or equal exchange modeled on business has inadvertently become an indispensable rule. But can such transactions be described as caring or considerate when it takes so much hard work to produce a bowl of rice only to exchange it for a few coins? Remember that exchange can never exist in isolation. Therefore, people are wrong when saying that peace, honesty or concession are factors that are harmful to the economy and need to be eliminated, describing them as "non-economic." In the natural operation of the universe, everything constantly relies on each other for survival, so the separation of mere economic exchange from the rest of life can never actually happen, despite appearances, even though some people have deliberately claimed the opposite for their selfish interests.

How can we compensate loving devotion?

Some people feel they have fulfilled their duty of taking care of their parents by providing them enough food and medicine every month, or buying them a nice house. So when their parents need them to visit more often or do some errands, they complain that it's too much work for them. *"Parents' love for their children is like an immense sea. Children count the days they have to care for their parents."* Those two lines of folk poetry have always been a painful truth in every era, especially in the current time. When people are attracted by fame and fortune, they can easily make light of or push aside other things that they consider obstacles. But isn't it a privilege to have a chance to love and take care of our parents? Isn't it true that countless numbers of orphans in this world long to have parents to love and care for, and they would be happy to exchange anything for them? Perhaps not until people have children and have to make countless sacrifices, especially when the children are ill, unruly or naughty will they be able to feel deeply their parents' love for them and know that the idea of "paying off one's debts" to one's parents is short-sighted and foolish.

Marriage relationships are similar. We also want fair and equal exchange to prevent the feeling of being used or of having to make unreasonable sacrifices. I do this so you must do that; I paid the bill last time, so it is your turn now; why must I take care of lots of things while you just lounge around all day long; you only take care of your parents' family, so you shouldn't complain that I neglect house chores; if you make me suffer, I will make you suffer, etc. And when a marriage breaks up, the two persons involved quickly treat each other like strangers and ignore each other's current difficulties. Although they used to be deeply in love, the have suddenly become enemies and don't want to look at each other when they meet by chance. They may even speak ill of each other in newspapers or make up stories to cause trouble for each other. The most heart-breaking thing is that when dividing property, they will always demand a fair and equal split. All their happy years together suddenly evaporate and both sides want to fight for their rights, their interests, and their personal victories.

All the aforementioned reactions indicate selfishness rather than caring reciprocity. Property can be divided equally, but how can loving devotion be counted and divided equally? Though the romance has come to an end, all the things we have given each other will follow us all our lives, whether we want it to or not. And when we still owe this person a lot of loving devotion, we will certainly have to pay it back somehow because everything goes around in the cause-and-effect cycle of the universe that nobody can escape.

A leaf never thinks it can pay all its debts of love to the tree when it tries hard to absorb the sunlight to refine all the raw nutrients into sap for the tree. This is because the leaf has observed and seen that it has never stopped receiving love from the tree. Though the tree gets old, it still tries to grow its roots deep in the ground to get the nutrients to feed the leaf. Suppose the leaf can pay the tree back, it still won't be able to pay all the loving devotion to the sun, wind, water, minerals, insects and the whole cosmos around it. Even though all those elements seem to be outside the leaf, they are feeding it every single minute. The only thing the leaf can do is to live a good life, be nice and fulfill all its duties. We are no different from this leaf. We will never be able to pay all the loving devotion that this life has given us, directly or indirectly. Then, why do we keep complaining and asking life for more without ever wondering what it needs from us?

Like an ever flowing river
Always loaded with alluvial soil
Do you ever wonder
What life needs from you?

10

Support

> *Life might not be all winter, but the warm flame of loving-kindness is always necessary for the lost hearts after a storm.*

The hand of loving-kindness

There are times when we fall into despair and get confused about life's many turns. There is nothing more precious then to have a strong and steady hand for us to hold and to receive some energy. That help is not a miracle. Empowered with the energy of loving-kindness, it comes forth appropriately and in a timely way to revive the potential energy and vitality inside us. We all need that hand of support at least a few times in life. Who can always smile and relax all alone when facing terrible problems or sudden disasters?

When you fall, I pull you up; when I fall, you lift me up. We can do that if we have loving-kindness and the ability to support each other. It could be just an act of deep listening, a word of consolation and encouragement, a sympathetic attitude instead of blame and accusations, and it could greatly help to treat the wounds inside us. That is because the energy of support is amazing. It can help us recover our self-confidence after suffering from a failure. It can also help us believe that loving-kindness *does* exist in this world. We can't claim that we don't need anyone because no one can exist alone. Indeed we have never stopped receiving the energy of trust and love from our loved ones. We also have the mutual support of the living things around us even if we can't always see how they do that. Yet we can foolishly make such a shallow statement of not needing anyone out of pride or self-assertion.

When we feel very comfortable and secure, we should look around to see who might need our helping hand. That's the attitude of an experienced person who used to suffer tremendous pains and afflictions. That's also the attitude of a knowledgeable person who understands clearly the karmic laws of nature in this world: This is, because that is; if that ceases, this will cease too. Accordingly, when we raise our arms to support someone, we are actually supporting ourselves. Similarly, when we create safe and peaceful energy to protect the seeds of life around us, we are actually protecting a peaceful life for our own present and future as well. Therefore, that helping hand must be one of compassion, of loving-kindness, with minimal conditions or without.

Character role-playing ability

Once I saw a young woman lingering by a lake trying to save an egret in distress. Perhaps its head got caught in a plastic bag full of water while it was busy hunting for food the previous night. It must have struggled hard to escape because it looked exhausted and desperate. The young woman was so concerned that—without waiting for me to think of a way to help—she hurriedly ran down to the lake, causing a big splash and scaring the egret away. But it wobbled down after only a short flight. Though I was standing some distance away from it, I could feel its trembling and fear. The young woman wouldn't slow down. She eagerly pulled up her pants to wade toward the egret's direction. This time, it also tried desperately to fly away and disappeared.

The poor woman stood there and wept openly. I didn't think the egret could fly very far with its weakening strength. Indeed, half an hour later, she and I found it standing close to a big tree. This time I asked her to let me try. I made each step along the lake calmly in the same way I usually walked on quiet streets. I wasn't anxious or impatient at all. I believed that when the egret could sense my "signal" of loving-kindness and my peaceful energy, it would let me help. Amazingly, the egret stood still to observe and allow me to remove the heavy plastic bag from its head. I called the woman to come and touch its head to make her happy before I released it. Watching it fly away, she smiled and murmured to herself, "It's not easy trying to save an egret!"

There must be many among us who have helped others in times of trouble, but were not always successful. The main reason was often the lack of insight and mutual understanding. Yet we usually blamed the other person for being stubborn and unyielding even in times of difficulty. We thought they deserved what might happen to them, even with death! But then we could not bear to abandon them, so we reluctantly helped them. The result would sometimes turn out worse. We could not do whatever we wanted in the name of loving-kindness without regards for the other persons' feelings and sensitivities. Just like the egret. It wanted to free itself from the plastic bag but it did not want just any help. It had its own pride and self-esteem. It would not need any sympathy if it had not been met with such a disaster. Therefore it would rather die if the help was not trustworthy or the helper had disdainful or tricky behavior. It needed our respect even though it was in trouble. When we cannot "play the role" of an egret to understand all its problems and feelings, we will always stand on the sidelines.

We surely remember the time when we were little and ran around playing. We would trip over a doorstep, fall down and cry loudly. Our grandmothers would rush over to console us. She would take our side and scold the doorstep for being naughty and hurting us so much. Once we got over it, she would advise us to be more careful next time. She would never blame us, get mad at us, or hit us. She could understand our feelings so well because she used to be a child and had plenty of experiences taking care of children. She easily let go of the role of an authoritative woman to place herself in the mind frame of a hurt and scared grandchild. That is the true talent of a rescue worker. It takes lots of training and practice to accomplish this instead of just talking and thinking about it. Similarly, no matter how gifted and talented some stage performers are, they must go through many training classes before they can play many different roles. With new and complicated roles, they have to do research and learn from previous performers or even from real life characters. Only then can they truly live in the roles and portray well the characters they play.

If we want to role-play a character in order to deeply understand all the sufferings of our loved ones so we can help them effectively, we have to carefully look back at our goodwill and abilities. Our desire to help might be very strong, but if we always show an attitude of "superiority," of an assertive person who can make no mistakes, we haven't succeeded in understanding our character. To develop this role-playing ability, first we must have experienced similar problems. Secondly, we must observe and learn from other people's experiences. Thirdly, we must practice letting go of our big egos to willingly become a good friend who can show respect and listen deeply. We might have enough knowledge or experience to understand their situation, but if our heart is still seething with the energy of anger or an urge to punish, no good result will happen, especially without the willing cooperation of the other party. In general, it takes loving-kindness and understanding to help someone.

It takes a heart

There is no place for egotism in loving-kindness. No matter how the other party might treat us, we still help them if we really cared about them. Why do we want them to do something for us before we would help them? Haven't we seen their troubles clearly and hasn't our heart been touched? They are losing strength and really need us. They can't do anything else for us. We should keep our initial feelings in our heart without the infiltration of selfish notions and irresponsible comments. If we still have enough energy, we should share some with them. It will not only revive them but also cultivate the heart of compassion inside us.

We should not get discouraged and give up when the other person doesn't want to change in spite of our wholehearted support. A transformation always requires many conditions. It can't happen with just our support, which might not be very practical. The conditions for that person's transformation are still taking place. Other conditions are on the way too. We should just wait patiently and continue to give our support. Perhaps the ultimate condition for the transformation is the utmost trust they have in us. So if we care about them and want to help them, we should always care and not give up helping them until the end. Life can sometimes be like a wintry gale, so the warmth of loving-kindness is always important for those who are lost in the storm.

Light a blazing fire
To warm up the winter sky
In this cold and lonely world
We all need a warm heart

11

Loneliness

The best strategy to transform loneliness is to find our embodiment in all our loved ones.

The invisible walls

One of the biggest misfortunes of human life is not to find someone who can share and understand all of our secrets and feelings. That melancholy state of the self feeling forsaken and isolated is called *loneliness*.

We might be living with our loved ones or have good friends around us, but there might be invisible walls separating us, so neither side can understand the other and be completely open. The wall may be personality, interests, knowledge, viewpoints or even social position. Sometimes we ourselves are the creator of the dividing wall because we can't easily trust or accept another person. We have caused trouble for ourselves by putting ourselves in a special position since only a very able and willing person can climb over that secure wall.

Life tends to lean more and more toward self-enjoyment. Everyone tries to make money and get good jobs to glorify their ego or to make them feel important. Competition and opposition are unavoidable. Therefore we are always on the alert because we think that the closer someone is to us, the easier he can take advantage of us or ruin us. As a result, our free space gradually decreases, and our spontaneity and openness become more limited. The feeling of intimacy and the spirit of mutual support wither away. Life becomes dull and lonely. The higher we approach the peak of fame and glory, the more isolated we are from others. The more things they own, the more unfamiliar they are with everything else. It's really a paradox that we always try to have our privacy or discourage others from coming close to us, yet we always complain that no one wants to understand or be close to us.

But who would understand us when we still overprotect our own selves and are still unwilling to get to know others? We have to open our hearts to welcome them. If we try to love someone but do not want to change, share, give support or let our pride get hurt too easily, we have not been able to break down our solid wall of selfishness. While love is still warm and we are devoted to each other, we immediately feel lonely and lost when separated from each other for just a few hours. This kind of love is just an exchange of feelings and dependency without any appreciation for the true worth of each other. It's a way to stroke our self-satisfaction. When the other person's beauty or attractiveness fades, we would quickly turn away without a care. Consequently, the more we love, the more we feel lonely.

It is often said that *"loneliness is home for the gifted."* Geniuses often lead a lonely and quiet life to discover and create, probably because they can't find someone on the same wavelength to share and understand. But that gap is only manifested in certain gifted areas. Geniuses still need to be in touch with other people and learn their good points. They are not perfect. They need loving-kindness too. They are only lonely when they think of themselves as exceptional and everybody else as ordinary.

As for the people who have failed many times, they easily lose faith in life and in themselves. They always feel worthless in other people's eyes. This inferiority complex separates them from everyone and brings them loneliness. Generally speaking, when we are caught in a superiority or inferiority complex, we feel unable to integrate with everyone, but we think it's our *karma* or fate to suffer loneliness.

Knowing how to live alone

Being lonely or not depends on our attitude about life. We should try to open our hearts and get to know someone who might not bring us any consolation but can at least give us some experience for future relationships. To have a good friend, we must first be a good friend. We should not wait for luck or feel too sorry for ourselves. That's a weak and defeatist attitude. We can overcome it by reducing unnecessary defenses to create a pleasant and warm feeling for everyone around us. If we open our heart indiscriminately, we will find someone among a thousand others.

However, we should not hurry too much to find an object for our affection right after a failure. An animal when wounded has to retreat immediately to its cave or burrow to heal. Sometimes it has to refrain from hunting for a month to lie still and lick its own wounds. If it can't control its hunger, it will surely die from another animal's attack or from its own wound. Running away from loneliness can also be a way to refuse treatment for a broken heart. We might not get any wound from our failure, but feeling so lonely, lost and unsteady is a psychological illness, depriving us from a sane and peaceful life. So we should practice facing our loneliness to observe its evolution and development for our own sanity. Loneliness actually gives us a valuable opportunity to find ourselves. When we keep facing ourselves with a peaceful heart and an exploratory mind, we will certainly find the deep truth about ourselves.

The great poet Nguyen Du wrote in "The Tale of Kieu": *"Is it possible to find a close friend in a day?"* We simply can't "pick" a dear friend in a short time. We need to be close, share and do things together, understand and accept each other. We need to be more flexible, less stubborn and prejudiced. We also need to respect and have affection for each other before we can become close friends. So it's not really a matter of "picking" out someone because a close friend is not ready-made for us. Sometimes we might meet a few people who seem to understand us from the very beginning. They are quickly in tune with our thoughts and dreams as if we had been friends for ages. In reality, either they are quite smart and sharp or we are revealing our hearts too much. We might have quite a few things in common. However, inside us there are still many deep layers of complicated psychology that will not surface until sufficient conditions are met. Therefore, no matter how smart we are, we still have to wait for time to help us get to know them well.

When we have become close friends, we should be able to see that our friends are always present in us and that we are always present in them. When we become heart-to-heart friends, it seems we can feel or understand our friends' feelings very well. Their feelings are also ours. This is often called *embodiment*. If we cannot see each other's embodiment, we have not touched the entirety, or the true person of each other.

In the poem *"The Vow Between the Mountain and the River"* by Tan Da, a famous Vietnamese poet (1889-1939), the lonely mountain often reproaches the river for forsaking their vow because the river keeps leaving the mountain to flow away: *"Remember the vow between the mountain and the river/ The river hasn't come back, leaving the mountain standing alone/ The high mountain has been anxiously waiting/ Tears from the streams have dried up from waiting for months."* But the mountain suffers because it has not learned to look deeply, to look with formless eyes to go beyond the old form of the river. It does not know that the river has evaporated and turned into clouds, hovering daily over the mountain. Even when the clouds are dispersed, they transform into rain to water the mulberry field at the foot of the mountain. *"Are you aware, mountain?/ The river flows to the sea then returns to you as rain/ The river might keep flowing away/ But you mountain should be happy with the lush mulberry trees."* The mulberry field itself is a part of the river. It is the mountain's mistake not to see it. The river can't always maintain the same form for the mountain because its nature is impermanent, forever changing.

So the best strategy to transform loneliness is to find our embodiment in all our loved ones. The more we open our hearts to share and support them unconditionally, the better we grow as a person. Loneliness might be home for geniuses, but it might also be a prison for those who have not been able to find their place in life and always wait for support. When we still can't transform our loneliness, we can't find true peace and happiness. Happy people are not lonely. They might live alone, but they see friends in everyone.

In moments of loneliness
Mountains and rivers seem far apart
Dewdrop sparkling on the leaf
Or image of someone from a previous life?

12

Offering

For others' sake is also for our sake, and for our sake is also for others'—because there's no boundary separating ourselves and others.

Giving and receiving

When we give a gift to someone, we think of ourselves as their benefactors because it helps make them feel better and happier whether it bears material or spiritual value. In general, we know they owe us gratitude. But if we sincerely want to give it and they decline because they have had enough, or they don't want to owe us anything, or they are not present to accept it, then the idea of offering cannot be realized. So not only does the receiver need the giver but the giver needs the receiver too. Hence the receiver needs to thank the giver and vice versa because they both are necessary conditions for each other. This sounds very strange, but it's an evident truth that creates a balance among relationships in life.

Another truth is when we offer a gift that we really cherish or have spent a lot of time making and it truly has practical value for the receivers, we not only help them feel better and happier but we also receive compensatory energy from the universe. Even if we just want to help without any expectations, the energy radiated from our heart together with the value of the gift will join the energy on the same wavelength in the universe to reflect a great effect on us. This effect may happen right away or it may happen in one of the following generations (your children or grandchildren) after it has met all the conditions. Even if the gift is not what we treasure or what we made ourselves, and has no practical value for the receiver, we still get "merit" for our goodwill.

Yet another truth is—from the time we think of giving till the end of the giving process and even much later—if we never show the receivers any discrimination, preference or disrespect, and never expect anything in return nor feel too proud of our good deed, we will receive full compensatory energy from the universe. This return may multiply many times since it's a pure offering, entirely for the receivers without any self-interest for us. On the other hand, if we only select a favorite receiver or always expect gratitude, even if it's just a respectful attitude, or if we feel noble for having done a good deed, then the compensatory energy of the universe may still happen, but it will be very weak.

In case we use the receivers to burnish our reputation or to accumulate good karmic results in hope of a safer and better life later, or to prove our worth after some miserable failures, then we will only receive a very little energy from the precious gifts we gave. What we don't expect is that if we gain more power and a better reputation from giving those gifts, we will owe the receivers an emotional debt. Although the receivers might be completely unaware of it, the universe is like a judge and might decide to take back some or all of good outcomes from us to give them back to the receivers. So to give is to receive, and possibly to owe a debt. It all depends on our thoughts. This explains why many people are diligent in charitable work but their lives have not and may even have gotten worse.

Another wonderful truth is that when we whole-heartedly give a present that is truly valuable to us and also useful to the receiver, the universe will compensate us. In addition, the receiver's energy will automatically be drawn to the giver in accordance with "the law of emotional balance." The balance level depends on what the two parties think of the gift value and the meaning of the offering. If the receiver does not have enough reserve energy to compensate the giver, the universe will accept the debt until he accumulates enough new energy for the universe to collect and send to the giver till it is paid off. Amazingly, gratitude, respect, or loving-kindness is the most valuable energy source because it comes from a selfless basis. Once we have it, we won't worry about being in debt anymore. In contrast, ingratitude will multiply the debt and it may take many of our future generations to pay it off. Hence to receive is also to give, and maybe to owe more debts.

So we should be smart enough to decline really unnecessary gifts if we know that we don't have enough energy to compensate.

Mahayana Buddhist traditions always mention the principle of turning giving into absolute generosity, which is symbolized by *"the three wheels of emptiness"*: the giver, the receiver and the gift can only exist in dependence on each other. In other words, none of the three has inherent existence; each of the three is empty of self, so "giving" only occurs when they come together in the act of giving, yet there is no giver in himself, no gift in itself and no receiver in herself. In absolute generosity, the giver must first see the whole cosmos within him giving with him, not just his separate self doing it. Second, the giver must realize that the gift is also being made from the contributions of the whole cosmos, so there should be no calculation of the value of the gift. Third, the giver shows no preference toward and makes no demands on the receiver. When these three conditions come together well, we will reach the perfection of giving—the unconditional or purest giving.

This principle may startle us since it appears that we have never really given a gift so far, that our actions have mostly been emotional exchanges: I give you this so you should give me that. But never mind. What matters is that we correct our ideas and try to practice the habit of observing our heart and mind each time we think of giving. We should do the same thing throughout the giving process to prevent negative attitudes. If we can't immediately let go of our conceited attitudes about giving, we should at least not make demands or take advantage of the receiver for our own interests. Of course if our heart is still full of suffering, greed and conflict, our gift can never reach perfection. However, the more we move toward that principle, the closer we approach higher truth so that both the giver and receiver can benefit.

Blessings and virtues

The Vietnamese cultural tradition has always praised humanity's two precious qualities: benevolence and virtue. Benevolence is the energy produced from actions to help others, while virtue is the energy produced from the process of transforming bad energy and developing good energy for oneself. Actually benevolence is also virtue and vice versa. While helping others, we constantly observe our attitudes of possessiveness and laying claims on others in order to let go of those attitudes; then we have both benevolence and virtue. While examining ourselves to take care of our inner feelings, we let go of bad habits and suffering in order to become a humble and lovable person who always radiates peaceful and fresh energy to people around us; then we have both virtue and benevolence. If we have benevolence but no virtue, our kindness is only an exchange. If we have virtue but no benevolence, our actions are deceptive and selfish. Benevolence and virtue are really two faces of one reality. That reality is non-self. For others' sake is also for our sake, and for our sake is for others' too since there is no separate boundary between ourselves and others. Whether we need to pay more attention to the benevolence part or the virtue part depends on each situation. However, we should never forget their inseparable connection.

When returning to our inner life, we should practice in such a way that both we and everybody else can benefit even though we haven't done anything realistic to help yet. While planning to help others, we should try to make sure that the receiver can really benefit and that we can also feel peaceful, serene and relaxed although we haven't quite begun the task of transforming our character. In reality, it is easier to fail in practicing benevolence than in practicing virtue because we tend to be conceited or self-satisfied about what we consider a noble offering. Hence, self-transformation before sharing with others—self-help before altruism—is the most logical path. However, life isn't always at our convenience; it takes much wisdom and experience to apply both benevolence and virtue deftly and effectively.

For the sake of others or for our sake?

One day a woman came to consult with me about a decision. Her dog, being very old and weak, could no longer eat or drink anything and just lay still in one place. The veterinarian advised her not to prolong his life but to euthanize him with an injection. She knew it was necessary but she could not do it. She felt sorry for the dog that had been loyal and close to her for the last 15 years of her lonely life since her divorce. I asked her, "If you know the dog is suffering so much and you still want to prolong his life, then do you love the dog or do you love yourself?" She was silent for a long time and couldn't answer. I asked her again, "If you forget about your lonely feelings and put yourself in the suffering dog's place, you will understand what he wants at this moment. If you really love him, do as he wishes. You must bravely accept this loss so that the object of your affection can be satisfied and happy." Upon hearing this, she was enlightened and agreed to let the dog go.

When informed that a loved one is dying, we often get scared, cry and earnestly pray for their recovery. But do we really want that person to live because they need to live, or because of our own feelings of loneliness and loss? The two attitudes are completely different: one for the other's sake, one for our own sake. There are times when we do things for others' sake as well as for our own sake. But we often can't see that truth and think we have done our best for the other person only. Consequently it's hard for our prayers to be successful since one of the conditions for prayers to come through is for us to put 100% of our heart and mind on the person we want to help. When our mind is not clean and pure, we can't get a loan from the universe. Similarly, when we decide to punish or not to forgive someone, we often think it is to help her wake up. Actually we are driven by our hurt feelings and want to feel better by retaliating. If we were all for their sake, we would have many more effective ways to help them, rather than those tough actions. But the best way is to use our loving-kindness to transform them.

In the song *"Let the Wind Blow,"* musician Trinh Cong Son was very keen when he wrote: *"Bend down your life/ To look through a love/ Look deeply without saying anything/ Let the heart ache/ Let the heart ache."* When we truly want to help someone, we must have the ability to leave our minds and situations and enter the mind and situation of the other person to fully understand him. We must *"bend"* to their side because we are currently in an upright position of a giver with plenty of energy. Two more conditions are necessary: the ability to observe without blaming or accusing and the readiness of the mind to receive negative energy that may overflow at any moment from the other person's heart, which may make our heart *"ache."* We know we will suffer from losses and damage when helping others, but we accept it wholeheartedly because we have a big heart and true loving-kindness. True loving-kindness is unconditional or requires very few conditions. It is very light, so light that the wind can blow it all over the world. *"Living in this life/ We need a heart/ Do you know why?/ To let the wind blow/ To let the wind blow."*

Loving-kindness is exactly the noblest gift that everybody needs. But no matter what kind of gift we offer, only a sincere heart can really set the true value of the offering.

Everything will fade
But loving-kindness stays
What we give these days
Follows us always

13

Intimacy

*Sexual satisfaction is selfishness if you
only think of your own pleasure.*

Consciousness of responsibility

True love is when two persons come together with sincere mutual feelings and are willing to share problems and joys. But when the other person's image and voice are always on our minds and cause us to daydream and become absent-minded, and we always want to see each other, and we are even hungry to touch each other's bodies, then we are "falling in love." Our emotions now lean toward sex; our imagination also amplifies that desire many times over so that we feel there is nothing more wonderful in the world.

At this time, from deep inside us a very strange energy springs up, making us both happy and bewildered. Everything seems to turn upside down. We can no longer keep our balance and self-control when sitting alone, working, or being in contact with anyone. Then the emotion of love within us suddenly wants to soar high, pushing us to join with the other person's very own feelings of love. This union will reach the highest level when both sides agree to surrender their bodies to each other and desire to tighten their relationship. This is essentially the situation when they wish to bring their relationship to a higher level and intertwine with each other's feelings. This union would be an abuse or an emotional exchange if it were not based on true loving-kindness. And this is a distinctive quality about true love—wanting both emotional enjoyment and responsibility for each other's life.

When we decide to become intimate, however, we often focus only on the desire to taste the highest soaring feelings of love without being aware (or vaguely aware) of our responsibilities. Why must we be responsible when both of us are willing to share our emotions? We just need to remind each other to be careful about birth control. Nothing else matters. But reality is not that simple. The emotion of love that explodes after two bodies are united will stir up the entire realm of mind and consciousness. A series of psychological complications like anger, jealousy, suspicion, fear, uncertainty and more will suddenly emerge because deep inside each person is the secret desire to "monopolize" the possession of the other. Furthermore, once the peak of emotion has been easily reached, our satisfaction may weaken because of familiarity, lack of inspiration or willingness to understand and love more deeply to build a stronger relationship, and we may seek affairs with someone else, so betrayal can take place easily.

In any emotional relationship, guidance is necessary with the stronger side pulling the other. Once we start going in the wrong direction, we might lead our beloved in the direction of mere sensual enjoyment instead of helping each other develop understanding and energy to overcome desire and live harmoniously with everyone. Both might inadvertently become addicted to sensual highs. Sooner or later, this kind of love will run dry of vitality and die out. Worse still, the mind addicted to sex will seek higher and higher thrills. This will torture us more or less during the period that we have to live alone. If we can quickly find someone else before we transform the energy of desire, we will surely repeat the same mistake or will stumble if the new object of our desire starts to become interested in the logic of the mind rather than the emotions of the heart.

Attitude of respect

In the Vietnamese cultural tradition, a wife never changes her clothes in front of her husband. No matter how long they have lived together, they still treat each other respectfully like guests (*mutual respect like new*). Though married, they still follow many customs seriously when they make love. They want their partner to understand that two bodies can unite only when two hearts and minds have truly merged. The late poet Nguyen Du wrote some uncommon lines of warning about this topic in *The Tale of Kieu*: "*While joining wings and entwining branches/ Disrespect has been felt from your side.*" Indeed, without subtlety, deep understanding and complete devotion, contempt for each other's immeasurable lust and easy abandon will emerge behind that layer of ecstasy. This disrespect is the deep cause for the emergence of petty conflicts in a couple's life.

The disrespect is worse when two persons have not officially announced their intention to get married and have not followed all the solemn formalities of their religious, legal and family traditions. These traditional practices help the couple suppress other intentions or plans and ensure their loyalty to each other. Therefore "giving body and future to each other" is a very wise principle to protect a couple's happiness. We only agree to "give our body" after we have officially "given our future" to our beloved. One should not happen without the other. Hence a wedding ceremony becomes important and necessary for families, friends, and neighbors to witness the day we officially give our whole life to each other. The energy of the wedding party and guests will add strength to help us overcome many challenges and difficulties in our married life.

In Western society nowadays, many people live together for many years before getting married. Sometimes that day never comes because they no longer see its sacred meaning, or they get bored with each other. In many economically developed countries today, many young couples live together and when some of these couples break up, one of the partners may commit suicide. They just can't bear the feeling of devastation when there is no longer a place for their emotional habits and when their ego is hurt. That is one of the biggest tragedies today. The more opportunities people have for enjoyment, the weaker they become; the more technologically advanced they are, the more their way of life returns to wild and primitive instincts. When they have lost faith in family happiness and life, young people can easily become victims of loneliness and desolation and be ready to abandon themselves on the road to irresponsible indulgence.

A true love should always manifest in joyous enthusiasm. This cannot be the kind of passion that disturbs our life and ruins our health, wisdom and even ideals. So suppose we have someone who loves us a little but respects us a lot and someone else who loves us a lot but respects us a little, who would we choose? The person who loves us very much will certainly bring us emotional satisfaction but also will easily leave us alone to cope with any painful consequences that may arise. Only someone who respects us wholeheartedly will be conscious of a responsibility for our life, and being mutually responsible for each other means truly loving each other.

Therefore, because of the suffering caused by sexual indulgence that goes against righteous principles, we should promise not to give our body to anyone who is not our husband or wife and not to approve of anyone who betrays marriage vows. In addition, we should practice taking responsibility to protect the virtue and safety of everyone and to prevent sexual misconduct from destroying families and society. If young people everywhere can practice these things, the world can save a tremendous amount of energy to rebuild a truly wholesome culture.

Oh! What a fragrant flower
Smiling charmingly yonder
Behold each other with respect and caution
How sweet to live in loving devotion

14

Thanksgiving

If we always express our gratitude to each other, all wounds will be healed, all difficulties overcome, and all peaks reached.

Cultivating the sources

Traditional Vietnamese ethics often reminds us to *"remember the planter when eating the fruit."* When holding an orange, do we ever wonder where it comes from? OK, so it's from an orange tree. That's our very simple answer. But the truth is that the orange in our hand has to go through a hard life-cycle just like all other living beings. Starting from a seed, it has to absorb countless natural elements to become a plant, grow leaves, flowers, and then bear fruit. Next, it has to depend on the loving devotion of water, wind, sun, minerals, and particularly the planter before the orange can become healthy food for us today. Although that proverb only reminds us to remember the work of the planter, it actually wants to awaken the gratitude in us toward all the conditions that forever nourish us.

Similarly, the proverb *"when drinking water, remember the source"* reminds us to ask ourselves where the water comes from that provides us so many convenient uses every time we turn on the faucet for washing or bathing. We should not think that, since we pay the monthly water bill, we can use the water carelessly or take it for granted. How could we live without water? At present, the clean water sources in the world are running dry because of man's greedy and irresponsible way of life. Do we ever care or do we have any sense of responsibility to protect them?

Seeing water without seeing its source, just like seeing fruits without seeing the planters, shows a shallow view and a lack of understanding. Only those lacking understanding and knowledge can consider themselves independent individuals, and can dare say that they don't need others to exist. But even an electron, which is so small that it can't be seen by the naked eye, still has to be formed by the principle of interdependence. Therefore individualism is man's most serious mistake. According to the experience of wise and virtuous masters, showing gratitude is one way to break that wrong perception to create a balanced and steady stand in the world and the universe.

Gratitude is a sincere attitude of thankful appreciation for an offering registered deeply in our heart, and we want to render thanks by one way or another in the future. When the energy of gratitude arises, it can create harmony in relationships. It also has the force to awaken noble seeds in our heart and mind and burn the harmful energy that we have mistakenly and unintentionally created in the past. Just keeping the thought of gratitude in mind can help us a great deal. When we turn it into an action of thanks or gratitude, that energy will intensify many times, making both the payer and receiver pleased and happy.

Before thanking someone, we need to have a notion of deep gratitude in mind. Don't practice the habit of saying words of thanks so easily in a courteous manner, hoping to get sympathy or esteem from others. At least we should choose an appropriate time and place to be able to express our sincerity by using our language carefully. A handshake, a bow, a bright smile, or a thoughtful comment can help create a responsive energy from the other party. Don't wait until a holiday to rush and buy and give a present, or it will appear that we trying to pay off our debt. We should also not pay too much attention to the value of the gift, nor should we want the receiver to practice the habit of judging our heart by the material value of it.

In the United States nowadays, people celebrate the Thanksgiving Holiday with a different meaning from the old days. In spite of grand celebrations, their main purpose is to build relationships for their jobs or to enjoy themselves to the fullest. They spend a lot of time preparing for parties. Very few of them pay attention to expressing gratitude, even to their loved ones nearby. Vietnamese people have many ways to show their gratitude, but there isn't yet an official day for everyone to practice gratitude as a noble custom. I think the death anniversary of our ancestor King Hung, held on the 10th day of the 3rd lunar month, is one of the most important days for the Vietnamese people, and we can choose that day as the day to give thanks to great men in the past and all our benefactors in the present. Making this death anniversary a Thanksgiving Day will make it much more meaningful.

Vietnamese Thanksgiving Day

We can pick out small and meaningful presents for each other, but it's best to give fresh and lovely flowers to send a message of hope for a long-lasting relationship. We should choose roses since they have long been a symbol of love, but pick yellow roses to express warm and positive feelings. Later, no matter where or when, a gift of yellow roses will let us know that it's the Vietnamese token of gratitude.

For a really meaningful Thanksgiving Day, we should limit parties, shopping and trips. Save that day for its main purpose: to manifest our gratitude toward those who have been influential in our lives. We should organize family gatherings. If living far from home, we can participate with a certain friend's family nearby. We can use all our talents to make a "get-together" really nice and warm. We can arrange a lovely flower vase and light a few candles. We should turn off TVs and telephones. We can practice being silent or we can just whisper when necessary in the first 15 minutes, since a quiet place will help strengthen the collective energy, and then everyone will clearly feel the precious presence of each other. Before that, we can have a few appetizers or some cups of tea. Then we can sit close together in a circle and everyone can take turns to walk gently to the yellow flower vase in the middle, take a flower and sit down in front of the person we want to thank. If we have many loved ones to thank, we can take more flowers. After a few seconds of silence, we can say:

"Dear Dad, I'm very proud to be your son/daughter, for what you've done for other people and for us. You have given me energy and a strong faith in the true value of life."

"Mom, I'm so grateful to you because you've given me the priceless treasure of love. When I'm in my most difficult moments, I think of you, your tolerance and generosity the most."

> "My dear son/daughter, your mom and dad thank you for being their worthy heirs. We are really proud of you."
>
> "My dear wife, I'd like to thank you for all your support and for giving me so much joy and happiness in our married life."
>
> "My dear husband, I'd also like to thank you for everything you've brought to my life. There are times when I suffer, but you've never forsaken me."
>
> "Dear sister, you're a wonderful sister who always listens and understands me. I love you so much and I'm very grateful to you."
>
> "My little sister, I'm also very grateful to you for all your help around the house, especially your genuine cheerfulness and lovely smile."

If there is time, we can tell each other stories about the loving devotion and sacrifices of the benefactors in our lives, whether they are present or far away. Sometimes we can sing songs together to add harmony and warmth to the atmosphere.

We can also express those sincere words to our teachers or students, bosses or colleagues, close friends or opponents. If we can see that we have tried to improve ourselves and become successful today thanks to some people's opposition and challenges, we should show them our gratitude. Who knows, maybe our sincere energy will melt away all distrust, anger and prejudices. Thanksgiving Day will then become a special day for everyone to practice tolerance and move closer together. On that day everyone will certainly feel much happier and more positive about life, and their hearts will be filled with the energy of loving-kindness. If we cannot be there directly, we can still call or write letters, but our loved ones will be happier if they can see our smiles and twinkling eyes in our Thanksgiving conversation.

We should begin right now, right in the intimacy of our family, to really see the true worth of Thanksgiving Day. The good transformations after that practice day will spread quickly everywhere and very soon that day will be accepted as an official holiday of our people. If we Vietnamese always express our gratitude to each other, all wounds will be healed, all difficulties overcome, and all peaks reached. The highest peak of the people of Lac Hong origin is precisely the strong brotherhood and sisterhood that no—ism or power can divide. This spirit will contribute to brighten our human faith that the power of loving-kindness can dispel all the miserable darkness in this world.

Thank you so much for giving
Both happiness and suffering
To wake up in the morning
And still remember names for calling

15

Boredom

Affection not moving deeply into psychological states such as peace, understanding, acceptance, sharing, support, tolerance or responsibility will soon become a kind of boredom.

Normalization of emotion

When we fall in love with a certain person and really want to possess him or her but can't wait or don't care what price we pay, then we are being controlled by emotion. Since his or her good points perfectly meet our needs or taste, our minds can't stop producing wonderful images of our beloved on the surface of our consciousness, and it even enhances them many times over to heighten our level of satisfaction. Therefore, if we let emotion interfere too much while we are in love, our perception of that person will no longer be accurate. Such mental distortion also applies to when we are in the state of anger or hatred. A Vietnamese proverb goes: *"Love each other, and even horn nuts look round; hate each other, and even soap nuts look deformed."* Although we don't purposely embellish the images and are even unaware that our mind is enhancing them, once the ideas of love and possession come to mind, the process of consciousness will automatically find a way to exaggerate our thoughts and memories.

The more we love, the more we fail to see our loved ones' shortcomings. Even if we see some, we don't think of them as important and might even find them charming. In general, since we want that person to belong to us, to be part of our life, everything relating to him is lovable to us. But the nature of emotion is that it is only a temporary energy to express love or hatred, at times it soars high and at times it falls down to a very low level. That means whether good or bad, our emotion eventually gets exhausted and returns to a normal state also called "normalized emotion." Therefore, the more passionate our love, the faster emotion becomes normalized. At that time, we will get startled and won't believe our own eyes because suddenly we don't find that person wonderful any more. The longer we live together, the more we see their unacceptable shortcomings. It is often said that after two years of marriage, a couple's "true faces" will automatically be exposed. Perhaps our spouse runs out of energy to continue the pretense or no longer feels it's necessary since all their needs have been met with satisfaction. Another important reason is that our passion has cooled down, helping us get a better look at our spouse.

Once our spouse's shortcomings have the power to arouse bad emotions within us, they easily become a dividing wall, making us unable to go to them as naturally as before. We feel some hesitation and contempt. If that wall gets so big that our emotions cannot return to the old affectionate level, boredom will arise. Though our spouse still maintains their lovable character, we will still fall into a state of *boredom* because our feelings of love have either been normalized or automatically soared beyond the level that our spouses can meet.

Boredom could easily lead to betrayal if there is not enough awareness of responsibility in the relationship. We see that most broken marriages have very legitimate reasons, but there's one profound matter that few people can mention, and that is because one side cannot respond to the other side's level of emotional satisfaction. It is a kind of "marriage casualty" since no one can tell how soon boredom can replace the love that used to be so passionate. So we should watch out for "falling head over heels in love." Passion is normally a disguise for selfish emotional satisfaction. The more we try to heighten our emotions, the sooner we approach boredom because our desire for emotional satisfaction is unlimited while our capacity to satisfy our desire is always limited.

Love in the most well-balanced way possible

We never stop changing our tastes in such things as food, clothing, vehicles, entertainment and daily stuff. This shows that the emotional energy inside us is very strong and often meddles with our lifestyle.

Be careful because emotions can easily bypass experience and deep understanding. Emotions of the shallow kind are often manifested through seeing, hearing, smelling, tasting, touching, and imagining. When these senses have contact with someone, we have the habit of immediately showing an attitude of like and dislike. Some people react very quickly to pictures and images; others are moved strongly by sounds. That is why advertising companies use these facts to exploit consumers' emotions. When attractive pictures and sounds continuously hit our eyes and ears, they will register in our brains, and there comes a time when they form a sudden reaction of wanting to possess that object at any cost.

It is often said that men "love with their eyes" and that women "love with their ears." That means the male emotional mechanism often concentrates on sight while the female focuses on the sound. Reality shows that men almost always focus on beauty when choosing partners while women enjoy listening to praise, compliments, and even sweet promises. But the listening is often greater than seeing, because the eyes are always limited by the space. Therefore, "loving with the ears" is deeper but also has more attachments than "loving with the eyes." This is easy to understand, because words can express understanding, energy, and even levels of emotion more favorably than visual form. But either way, affection can be built on a foundation of shallow emotions and therefore can change easily once those images and sounds are no longer supplied, or when they receive other images and sounds that are more attractive. Affection not moving deeply into psychological states such as peace, understanding, acceptance, sharing, support, tolerance or responsibility will soon become a kind of boredom.

People whose careers require them to show high levels of emotion, or celebrities with numerous fans, always possess a huge treasure of emotions from resonance with others. Their level of sensitivity toward their good or bad emotions is always higher than ordinary people. Consequently they easily get bored with old emotions and always want to look for fresher and stronger ones. This is the cause leading to the lack of sentimental or marital loyalty among highly emotional people. Sometimes they really do not want any breakup. They also try to find ways to salvage their relationships but fail to cope with their annoying feelings of boredom. In general, highly emotional people tend to lose their own battles—knowing they shouldn't do something but still do it, and knowing they should do it but still can't.

Nowadays the word "love" is used for sexual satisfaction, as if love is only that. In magazines and on TV programs, people are always interested in ways to "love" so both sides can be satisfied. But reality shows that the more people today know how to elevate their emotions to the highest peak, the faster they get bored and leave each other. That is a very wrong path, psychologically as well as morally. In *The Tale of Kieu*, the venerable poet Nguyen Du reminded us: *"Love in the most well-balanced way possible."* The term "well-balanced" covers both affection and duty. "Affection" generates emotional satisfaction, while "duty" includes support and sharing. If we say we love someone, we should ask ourselves whether we have both affection for and duty toward him or her. Duty is definitely the factor for long-term attachment while affection is short-lived but cannot be lacking in love. The venerable poet Nguyen Du was really insightful when advising us that we should have both.

However, human consciousness and emotions change with time. By a certain age, especially after having gone through many ups and downs in life, we will naturally live with each other more for duty's sake. If we can do that when we are young, putting duty before affection and still moving forward peacefully, our feelings will certainly shine brightly and steadfastly.

If we know that we tend to get bored easily, we should try our best to practice transforming ourselves right now—letting go of good emotions gradually and acknowledging bad emotions. When we receive any sensation, we should only identify the target and that sensation without adding our attitude if it's not necessary. A sensation without an attitude of likes or dislikes will not turn into an emotion. When we are pushed by the energy of boredom, try not to believe that it's a true emotion and make frivolous decisions. We need to quickly stop all kinds of exterior struggles with emotions that are based on external conditions and try to create a favorable environment to examine and renew our inner feelings. Under the light of wakefulness, petty demands will disappear, and positive energy like love or responsibility will be aroused.

Therefore emotions, while playing a rather important role in the manifestation of feelings and life style, if not led by awareness and correct understanding, will make us a victim of our own suffering in which boredom and betrayal are causes for great regret.

Don't chase after emotion
Always look back at ourselves
Loving must go with understanding
To fulfill duty and affection

16

Respect

Respect is a basis for the survival of loving relationships.

The basis of all relationships

We all need to be respected. It helps us to see our worth in life better. Even when we suffer terrible failures and lose faith in ourselves, the respect someone shows us helps us realize there are other equally important values that we process. In loving relationships particularly, respect is the basis for their survival. Without respect, that relationship is just an outcome resulting from the exchange of emotions from both sides.

Some respect—for age, influential position or social status—is shown reluctantly. While it might create a certain harmony at a certain level, it lacks a voluntary consciousness and therefore it will not nourish and sustain lasting affection for both sides. The honest nature of a respectful attitude always comes from realizing each other's true worth or deep interdependency.

Indeed, the more people we respect, the more our pride and arrogance are contained and reduced. When our respect can overcome social order to readily reach out to others, including those who are in the lowest class of society, then our inner peace and freedom will be boundless. When we respect someone, we are naturally connected with that person and an exchange of energy will occur even though it is not our intention. Moreover, respecting someone is the act of recognizing his or her presence in this life and in the interbeing of all life forms in the universe.

Life is always so full of demands and expectations that we rarely have an opportunity to look within and maintain our stability and clarity. Therefore, we gradually lose our ability to look deeply at each person to realize that everyone is worthy of respect. To really think about it, everyone has his or her own merits. Sometimes it is clearly displayed in front of our eyes but because of our prejudices we might not recognize it. Other times it is hidden or is covered with an unfavorable attitude that may require us to have the skills of discovery and understanding to realize it. Therefore, when realizing we are being disrespectful to someone, we must ask our self whether it is caused by them or us.

Naturally, in order for someone to respect us we have to respect them first. In addition, to be sure that we receive respect from others we must have two main conditions: *powerful influence* and *loving devotion*. We don't need to have authority to generate a powerful influence. On the other hand, authority may generate disrespect if it is abused to intimidate or threaten those in disadvantageous positions. We just have to always live in awareness, always control and take responsibility for all our words and actions, always maintain a reasonable distance between ourselves and others and never cause trouble or violate their rights. Then we will have a powerful influence over them. Loving devotion is also an important condition for respect. Loving devotion is when we love someone without mercenary motives and calculation, without demanding too much, always giving them priority, ready to open our hearts to accept and forgive their weaknesses or awkwardness. Loving devotion is also helping them overcome difficulties and leading them to a bright future. Certainly with such an attitude, they will have tremendous respect for us. In general, those with virtue and benevolence—able to create good energy and willing to offer it to everyone—will definitely be respected. A person receiving respect from many people will receive energy from many sources. It is like a tree with many roots deep in the ground. It no longer has to worry about getting knocked down by storms or hurricanes.

Love must go with respect

When we begin to respect someone, we begin to have affection for that person. Affection within limits is surely a good beginning in all loving relationships. If we can maintain that respect throughout the duration of our lives together, our relationship can easily overcome obstacles and tough times. Thanks to respect, each side conscientiously maintains their good qualities, not letting bad energy flow out freely to cause trouble or suffering to the other side.

But *"familiarity breeds contempt"*—when living together, it is easy to see hidden shortcomings of each other and gradually lose mutual respect. So how should we practice the art of nourishing and maintaining mutual respect?

First we have to know if the other person respects us. If they love us but does not have much respect for us, we should postpone the decision of living together since their love may be just pity or a temporary satisfaction. They might love us only because of a need to love someone. This kind of love might be passionate but lacks security. Only when they really respect us would they have responsibility for our feelings and our life. They will know what to do and what not to do to make us happy. They will know that our happiness and her happiness always go together.

However, when love is soaring high, we seldom think about the issue of respect. Only after we have lived together does this need come up clearly. It is not that we don't need respect when we love, but the loving emotion is so strong that it overcomes our reason. We might have been quite satisfied with the other party's adoration and infatuation. But when we have decided to stay together, instead of continuously trying to nourish each other's love, we might spend too much energy trying to catch up with other needs such as making money or strengthening our position in society. As a result, the original feeling of love quickly falls while the need for respect rises.

Alas, respect is easily deflated after the whirlwind of love dissipates because while in love, we inadvertently lose ourselves and leave some very bad impressions in the other person's mind. In other words, love with too much infatuation or attachment will destroy respect. Once respect is lost, the more we love, the more we get exhausted and feel that love seems to be slipping out of our hands.

In order to tie respect with love, the most important thing is to know how to control our desire to be loved and how to adjust it consciously and responsibly. Do not let the other person think that our love is only a disguise for an exchange, a selfish demand without any concern for their situation or need. If we always cling to each other and never want to take one step away, sooner or later that love will tremble and die. Because the more we cling together, the more our emotional satisfaction increases, and then we become emotionally addicted and demand more. When the other side cannot meet that need sufficiently, we will protest, get upset, frustrated and fed up. Moreover, if we are always attached to each other, how can we have time and energy to at least maintain our own balance and keep all the good and beautiful things that we have inside us? Besides, love is a journey full of creativity and discovery. If we cannot nourish our own life, how can we share it with someone else?

Therefore, when in love, we should always understand each other's necessary limitations. There are times when we need each other, but there are also times when we need to come back to ourselves. When we come back to ourselves, we can repair our body and mind to always be a source of reserve energy for the other person and to offer it when necessary. In order to do this, we have to lead a peaceful and happy life rather steadily before getting married. While living together, we should always remember to nourish our own qualities. Whenever we feel hurt from disrespect, we should quickly come back to ourselves to treat our wound first, instead of urgently attacking or punishing the other person. Ask ourselves what we have done to cause this disrespect. Maybe our loving behavior with excessive emotions has exposed our weakness and dependence. It is most important that we can always maintain our manners, retain our good points that our partner has cherished, and never stop transforming the weaknesses that have often caused obstacles in our relationship. To have enough ability and goodwill for this, we must have strong reserve energy. This energy comes from a life of practice, of awareness.

Respect is the basis of morality, a necessary condition to build peace for humankind. When we have respect for each other, the thought of violating or infringing upon the rights of each other will not have an opportunity to develop. We will see that our existence is closely related to the other side's presence, so we will treat each other with kindness and sincerity. This behavior is in accordance with the harmony principle of the universe where every individual is equal since we were all made of the same substance.

For this reason, whenever we have a disrespectful attitude toward someone, we should first ask ourselves if we are caught in a wrong perception, a prejudice, or a certain need that the other person has not been able to meet. In case it's the other person's fault, we still should remind ourselves that it is only a very small part of their wonderful entirety. We should never forget that there are only bad actions, never bad people. Going from being bad to deserving disrespect is a huge distance—depending on each individual's understanding and size of heart.

Neither high nor low
Neither rich nor poor
Everything is miraculous
The dust of life makes us forget

17

Doubt

When we start to doubt someone, whether our doubt is right or wrong, we have created a very toxic energy in our heart.

Mysterious reality

It's hard to believe that what we see at the present moment is not exactly what those objects are. This is a warning of science. We have great faith in scientific achievements, but scientists still admit the limitation of science, especially the puzzle about the *ontology* of our world. Science is not exactly sure about the nature of all phenomena and what conditions are required for their manifestations. Immanuel Kant, a German philosopher, once said: "What we know about existing reality is from its appearance exactly as we see it. We can never know its real existence with the quality of scientific knowledge." David Bohm, an outstanding American-born quantum physicist agreed with the above opinion and added: "The electrons that we scientists see appearing and disappearing suddenly and continuously changing their structures are controlled by *quantum potential*." And according to David Bohm, this quantum potential is non-local, not limited by space. It contains both mind and consciousness, which impact each other instantly.

So what we consider correct only has a relative value in human perception. And that correctness is once again limited by each person's level and even by the changes of time. Existing reality is always moving and connecting, but we advocate stability and independence. Similarly, our knowledge about a river is certainly quite different from that of a fish. And the way a person dying of thirst looks at the river is not the same as a person sitting on a cruise ship or someone who wants to invest in hydroelectricity. A poet once wrote: *"Only the river can understand itself."* But that is not for sure yet, because we do not even understand ourselves much. The way we see things is quite different when we love or hate, feel happy or sad. And of course an artist's view is very different from a business person's; a spiritualist's view is quite different from that of a politician. So what is the most correct view? There is none. Living in a relative world, we should accept a relative view. This is also the reason why we can only have relative happiness—meaning happiness is always conditioned. Only when we have the ability to overcome the very afflictions that protect the self, which is misunderstood as separate, in order to accept all things in the universe as part of us, can we reach the super-level of perception that accords with existing reality.

But what is the purpose of correctly looking at the nature of reality? Is this an impractical question or a separate matter for science? No. The purpose of science is also to serve human knowledge, helping us get closer to the operation of the universe. Although we are very busy in life and have no intention of looking into the ontology of this world, actually we ourselves and everything around us all lie within the very mysterious orbit of cause and effect and causal conditions. Therefore, the less we understand about the principle of truth, the more we spend energy fighting for things working against nature. This is the source of all suffering.

Yet we always think we are smart, know everything, and can hold our future and our happiness in our hands. What happens when we get a Doctor of Philosophy degree? Can that knowledge help us know where anger comes from and the source that controls it? Is knowledge about our introspective world an impractical subject? Does it directly influence the quality of our life? Spending many years to hold things that are still subject to chancy situations is quite unfair, is it not? Even more unfair is that we live among unreal things which we deem real or among real things but we suspect them false.

Refusing the truth

An ancient Indian Buddhist story tells a heart-breaking tale. There was a very wealthy merchant whose wife died young, leaving him a son. Since he was often away on business, he had to ask his servants to take care of his son. One day, a gang of robbers burst into his village and burned it down. Many villagers perished in the fire, including his son. After the cremation, he put some of his son's ashes in a brocade sachet which he carried by his side everywhere. At night, he would take it out to talk lamentably on and on to it. Then one night, a boy's voice from outside the door claimed to be his son. Thinking it was a ghost or a prank from the village youths, he refused to open the door. Actually, his son was only taken to the forest by the robbers, and the charred boy that he mourned was a different boy from the village. But forever he would never know the truth when doubt and obstinacy within him completely shut down the door to his heart and pushed his son to walk away in despair.

Life is always full of similar stories. Sometimes the truth comes knocking on the door but we still refuse to open it. We believe our judgment is absolutely right. That is a *stubborn* attitude, holding on to old knowledge and experience to look at a new existing reality. In certain situations, of course, accumulated knowledge and experience are a person's valuable properties. But if we do not use them rationally, they will become great walls separating us from the truth. Then they will turn into fixed views and prejudices. In the meantime, everything in this world continues moving and changing. Looking from the outside, things do not seem to be any different from before, but in reality, they are no longer exactly the same as we knew them.

Therefore when we hold on to our knowledge without opening our mind to discover and learn new things, we are removing ourselves from the natural progress of life. We might be present with existing reality, but we have lost it.

The shadow of doubt

When we do not understand the truth, we tend to have doubt, a kind of reaction to protect our selfish ego. Most of the time we doubt other people, thinking they might be wrong. Seldom do we doubt the reverse. The nature of doubt is just having a question, a guess, or posing a hypothesis of what might happen. It is therefore a good place for us to start research to learn the truth about that subject. However, we usually tend to believe that our doubt is true without trying to understand or research further. That is our "classic attitude." When doubting something, we do not open our mind readily to welcome verifiable information that can help us understand more correctly about that subject. We always think: *"Measuring rivers and seas is easy/ Who can use a ruler to measure a person's heart?"* This saying is a reminder for us to be careful before trusting someone, but we turn it into an immutable incantation to cover up our fear, weakness and irresponsibility. As a result, we submerge ourselves in unpleasant emotions and endless erroneous thoughts, and we fall into wrong perceptions even when the truth is obviously in front of us.

The more we live in comfortable conditions, the slacker we become. Our once keen observational skills will no longer be as sharp in judging whether something is right or wrong, true or false. We have lived too much relying on things outside ourselves, yet such externally based happiness is very uncertain, so we are anxious about adversity and worry about bad luck and obstacles. If we have been cheated, drawn into the field of business or are active in politics, we will easily form the habit of keeping a watchful eye on everyone, even on our loved ones. Although we know that they do not show any suspicious signs and are very nice and kind, we still can't help doubting them. We think it is better to be wrong in doubt than wrong in trust. This is a big mistake. If this mistake is not corrected, it will change into something more serious like judgment or slander. A person with strength of character, on the other hand, will never suspect others of doing bad things to him because he is tough enough to face everything calmly.

What if our doubts are completely justified? It seems we are trying to expose other persons' weak points or mistakes to stay away from them or to stimulate other people to boycott them, not to understand and love them more. Our doubts mostly aim at satisfying our ego even though we might speak up on behalf of a certain group or community. Do we ever act on behalf of morality or altruism and praise their good points while remaining silent about suspicious signs so we can observe and find ways to help? Why don't we keep our respect for them in spite of a few doubts? Why don't we ask ourselves if they deserve our doubt or if we are too suspicious? Why don't we dare ask them for forgiveness when we find out that we were wrong in doubting them? Indeed doubt often makes us weaker and more cowardly.

We may not know that, every time a sense of doubt about someone comes to mind, whether that person is bad or not, we have generated a very toxic energy in our heart. It not only burns away the peaceful energy within us, it also causes us to lose a chance to be in touch with that wonderful life because we are always busy looking for more evidence. Though we have not said or done anything to express our suspicions, we have still sent bad energy when we doubted that person. According to "the law of emotional balance," he will find a way to return an equivalent bad emotion upon receiving our doubt. If not, the universe will get someone else to return that suspicious emotion to us. As for wrongly doubting a bodhisattva (a great benevolent and virtuous being)—where a great amount of peaceful energy in the universe has been accumulated—the consequence is immeasurable. This will be a huge emotional debt that would take us many generations to pay off. Therefore we should not be doubtful easily. Once we discover that we have wrongly doubted someone, we should practice repentance or show our remorse directly to lessen the consequence.

Actually doubt is not always a bad attitude. In traditional meditation practice, meditation students themselves must ask questions about their own suffering or about all phenomena happening in front of them. They cannot absolutely believe in the successful experience of previous masters. *"Great doubt, great enlightenment"*—the greater the doubt, the greater the enlightenment. The more we doubt, the stronger our energy for discovery gets, and the more we leave behind settled views. Only when a meditation student is really stuck will they ask a meditation master for help with carefully selected questions. However a true meditation master would never give a clear or concrete answer. Even the master's opening line often goes "off the subject" to destroy the passive attitude of wanting to rely on others' knowledge or to force the meditation student to stop their useless theoretical questioning immediately. In the end, the student must try to cope with their outdated perceptions and their own suffering to find an answer.

Thus a meditation student always has the responsibility for their own doubts. Once they ask a question, they must by all means try to find a valid answer. We can't just throw it out there, unanswered for five or ten years. The meditation student's questions are always on their mind, but they are quite free, completely different from the sickening doubt to protect the weak, fearful and irresponsible ego of those who enjoy looking for mistakes in others.

Minh Niem

> *Light up a meditation candle*
> *Keep the heart forever miraculous*
> *Look at life with right views*
> *And see through dark minds*

18

Deep Listening

Once true listening ability is lost,
a true understanding opportunity is also lost.

Everyone needs to listen deeply

People in the old days often said, *"Listening 100 times does not equate to seeing one time."* This is to remind us not to listen to public opinions without checking the facts carefully or witnessing with our own eyes. But they also said, "What you see is not what it is," because there are things that we see with our own eyes that are still wrong. For example, when we see that the other person flies into a rage and throws venomous words at us, we normally think they must really hate us and want to attack us. But we might be wrong. Perhaps they are having problems or are such great pain that they have lost all their energy and can no longer control themselves. Or perhaps they have intentionally given a "blow" to test our reaction, or it is simply that they are mad at someone else but picks on us to release their emotions in the style of "hitting the chopping board when getting mad at the fish." If we say, "I don't need to know the reason why. I only know that you said those words and hurt me," then we will shut off the opportunity for them to explain and to come back to their true selves. We will lose them.

Life always has many pressures; therefore we can't always be steady enough to control ourselves, especially when we are troubled, terrified, depressed, or lost. We wish to have a loved one by our side to share our problems. Even if that person can't solve anything or give us any good advice, all it takes for us to feel better is their attitude of deep listening. We all have a strong need for deep listening from others. The irony is that we all want others to listen to us but we don't want to listen to anyone. Especially in the current economic situation, everyone lives in a hurry so they are afraid of any task that requires patience and perseverance without getting any compensation. We just need to ask them to sit down so we can share a few of our problems, especially when it concerns them, but they give us all kinds of excuses to decline or to put it off. Courteous people would agree to listen to us, but they would control the sharing time. They would sit there like a bump on a log, their eyes looking far away and once in a while looking at their watches. Then how can we pour our hearts out to them and dare ask them to help us solve our difficulties?

When even those most close to us are afraid to listen to us, then who will? Maybe our way of sharing is not nice or persuasive yet, but most of the time it's because they would look at us with prejudiced eyes saying, "I know! Please! Not again!" Living with authoritarian personalities who always think they are right, or with those who like to use their authority to pressure others, we would have a hard time telling them our opinion. It would be hopeless trying to share our suffering with them. There are children so upset from being misunderstood that they confine themselves in their rooms for days. There are couples who argue and hurt each other more every time they sit down together, so they go to their friends or psychologists to lament. There are old people who have to confide in their pets because they don't get understanding and concern from their children or grandchildren. There are those who have suffered greatly for so long with no one to share their troubles with that they become depressed, mentally ill, or suicidal. There is really nothing lonelier than when we are surrounded by loved ones who cannot help us overcome our difficulties.

Deep listening from original source

When we really want to help someone alleviate the heavy pain in their heart, we should first know how to listen to them. This is like a doctor who must first observe a patient's looks carefully and then listen to their report or complaint about their problem before examining them and writing prescriptions. When we decide to listen to a person in distress, we have agreed to play the role of a doctor to treat their

Understanding the Heart

mental health problem. Although we are not psychologists, we certainly can help him more or less with our sincerity and correct attitude of deep listening. Therefore every time we get ready to listen, we should ask ourselves carefully if we are really being like a social worker who knows how to listen.

The insurance company Prudential is very smart when it uses the slogan "Always listening, always understanding." Clearly they are aware that the fastest and most accurate way to understanding is by listening. But if we don't have money, the insurance company won't listen to us. We certainly can't open our heart to someone while thinking about what we would get out of this. In reality, some people are eager to listen to others, only because they feel proud of being the trusted and chosen one from among many others. Although they are aware of this, the other person accepts the fact since their purpose is to have friends who would agree that they are right or would share some of their frustrations. Watch out for this trap. Do not listen perfunctorily or we will spoil our hearts. Once we lose the ability to listen honestly, we will lose an opportunity for honest understanding.

In Vietnamese, the term *"lang nghe,"* or quiet listening, has a very interesting meaning. We have to "quiet" our mind in order to "listen." If we "listen" without "quieting" our mind, without stopping all other thoughts, without letting go of prejudices or afflictions in our mind, then our listening will not reach the original source of a problem, or we might misunderstand it. Chinese people use the word *"ting"* to mean "listen wholeheartedly." American people use the term *"listening deeply"* to mean "truly listening," but it is not quite like the Vietnamese term *"lang nghe."* The other terms express the goodwill and determination to listen, but not the purification of the mind while listening. "Quieting the mind" to listen is very important. If we are still half-hearted, frustrated, busy thinking about other things, or carrying past experiences about that person in our mind, we will lose our ability to listen from the very beginning, even though we think we are trying to listen deeply.

"Quieting the mind" therefore, is the gate to "listening." From now on, if anyone asks us to sit down and listen, we should look back at our emotions and our minds right away. If we cannot quiet our mind at that moment, we should stop and ask for another time. Conversely, if someone agrees to listen to us, we should carefully ask her if they are ready to listen with a quiet mind. Make sure their mind is "quiet" then;

otherwise do not tell them anything. "Quieting the mind" is the deep silence of the heart.

The Vietnamese musician Trinh Cong Son also discovered this listening art when he wrote, *"Silent sigh, I'm listening."* Without silence we cannot listen. And the fullest silence must overcome all talking, thinking, and fidgeting. Just like when we listen to a love song, if we close our eyes to enjoy it, we can easily feel all the emotions of the songwriter and even the soul of the song; otherwise, the "looking part" can easily distract the "listening part." While listening to others, we should also avoid or minimize what can disturb the "silence" so we can listen completely, even if it is just a sympathetic look. Practice listening with our own hearts. If the other person says things that are not true, or uses bitter words, we should still practice silent listening to feel all of their pain without interrupting or judging. From there, we will understand the deep cause that made them behave that way.

Listening to ourselves

In the song *"I'm Listening,"* the musician Trinh Cong Son shared with us: *"Silent river, I'm listening/ Silent hill, I'm listening/ Silent sigh, I'm listening/ I'm listening, silent sigh/ After the storm, silent faces/ Listen to all the pain on the palm of your open hand."* When we are silent, ceasing all disturbances, letting go all wants and fights, we can listen to many sounds around us, even if it is a lamentable sigh of someone far away, or the soundless voice of the river and the hill. Life is always rushing and busy so we gradually forget the habit of deep listening with our hearts. Sometimes we can't understand even when the other person says something clearly, not to mention when they only say half a sentence or remains silent for us to think about it ourselves. With pain deeply hidden inside, it is not easy to open one's mouth if the listener cannot express sincere sympathy from their heart. Aware of this, Trinh Cong Son did not choose to listen with his ears but to remain silent and let his heart feel it. The musician had experienced listening to his own desperate sigh, pausing to listen to his own life: *"I'm listening to the silence of my life."*

Only when we listen to and understand ourselves deeply can we listen to and understand others. Therefore we should regularly find a quiet place for ourselves to practice listening carefully to our footsteps and our breaths. These sounds are very close to us and very important, but we have long forgotten them. We should practice listening to each stream of emotional remembrance or aspiration, each notion of anger or jealousy, each moment of wrong decision or self-satisfaction, and even when our minds are completely empty, so we can recognize each of these attitudes. We only need to listen without interfering or judging hastily, so that we can have time to understand all the hidden corners of our mind. The more we can listen to ourselves any time, anywhere, while alone or with others, the more we can gradually separate ourselves from the restrictions and controls of the environment, and the more we have an opportunity to be our own masters. Being our own master means owning our life. When we can own our lives, we can have the ability to invite others to participate without causing suffering to each other. We will have enough energy to guide each other through difficult times.

When we can listen to ourselves and to our loved ones beside us, our ability to listen will go even further. During certain moments of silence, we will be able to hear the miserable cries from the dark corners of life hidden by the clamorous and indifferent multitudes.

From the silent heart
I can hear the anxious mind
Where have you been all these years
Unaware of life's calling?

19

Judging

No matter how accurate, judgment is a sword edge that cuts off close relationships, creating more separation among individuals within this interconnected universe.

Judging habit

There are times when we travel hundreds of miles to view the cherry blossoms, only to be disappointed when we get there because the flowers have not bloomed as beautifully as in previous years. We walk along rows of romantic cherry blossoms but we neither enjoy nor eagerly admire each bloom like many other people. Looking at today's flowers, we miss the flowers of the past, so we feel melancholy and downhearted. If someone asks us about the cherry blossoms this year, we would remark honestly, "Very bad! Not half as good as the previous years!" If the flowers could hear these words, they would be very sad. Though they can't bloom to their peak condition like last year, they still had to go through the bone-chilling coldness of winter weather in order to blossom. They tried to do their best, but they could not change the weather to their satisfaction.

But why would we want the cherry blossoms to be this way or that way? What have we done for them? Or have we ourselves contributed to the destruction of the environment which caused the weather to change unpredictably and the cherry blossoms to bloom that way? Is this our fault or the flowers'? Do all cherry blossom viewers this year feel the same melancholy as we do?

Looking back, we see that we often utter those irresponsible comments. Of course life always needs basic principles or criteria for balance and harmony. But not everything needs to follow the same criteria, which are only relative because they are formed according to the perception of each society in each era. There is no criterion for cherry blossom viewing or the enjoyment of beauty. We certainly have the right to express our opinions. No one can blame us if it is harmless. But that mindless attitude of our opinions will cause us to lose our clear views of reality. In addition to not seeing reality, we also cover it with comparative concepts when we include our love-hate attitude. Opinions are necessary if they can help us progress, improve life, and bring us closer to the universe. But in reality, most of our opinions are from our habit of protecting our selfish interests only.

Going from opinion to judgment is a very short distance. Opinion is based on one's perception and emotions, but opinion is more changeable than judgment. Both can be right or wrong. Like opinions, judgments are often used to condemn or accuse others, seldom to support them. For those having the authority to represent justice or the laws, they have to judge right or wrong to solve serious cases, albeit reluctantly, to keep society in order by preventing wrong acts from infringing upon right ones. No one really has all the essential qualities to represent the purity or the truth to judge others. Everyone makes mistakes even though everyone has an inherently holy character. When we judge someone, we can only see one side of that person and mistakenly declare them to always be that way. They might not have been nice yesterday and so committed an error. However, standing in front of us today is a new person—with a sound mind, a transformed consciousness—so the previous judgment is no longer valid. We might intentionally ignore this change and reject it but that is the truth. The more we cling to our prejudices and fixed views, the more we fall behind life. We will fail to grasp the miraculous value of being alive.

Since we have been living with mindlessness, we do not normally pay attention to our attitudes when looking at an object or a certain issue. Every time we make an observation, we always include our attitude of liking. When a person looks at us with trusting eyes and asks us about another person, we can't control our emotions and want to blurt out both our observations and judgments based on our previously formed attitude. If we like them, we will praise them enthusiastically; if not, we will criticize them so mercilessly that the listener would think what we said is completely true! We should have let the listener form their own impression about that person. If for some special reason we need to give information, we should be objective and reveal what is necessary and true without forgetting to add a wise caution: "That's my observation, which might not be accurate." If we were influential, our observations could cause the other people to lose self-confidence. In extreme cases, our judgment could provoke radical reactions.

The story of the Nam Xuong Woman is very sad but worth mentioning. When her husband Truong went off to war, Thiet stayed home and took care of their baby boy. Every night she would soothe him by pointing at her own shadow on the wall reflected from an oil lamp and say, "There's your daddy!" More than a year later, Truong came home from the war. He was so heartbroken because the little boy refused to call him daddy, saying, "My daddy comes when it's dark. When Mommy sits, he sits. When Mommy walks, he follows her." Young Truong was suspicious by nature, so he quickly believed what the boy told him. In spite of the neighbors' advice, he ignored them all, firmly concluded that his wife had betrayed him. Indignant and not having anyone to share her pain, she jumped into a river and drowned herself. When evening came, young Truong tried to comfort his son by the oil lamp. When the little boy looked at the wall, he cried out, "There's Daddy!" At that moment, Truong shockingly realized his big mistake.

If we do not want to repeat young Truong's blunder, we should not let self-esteem or subjectivity cover up our ability to listen so we can understand the whole story before making our judgment.

Are you sure?

On drugstore's counters in Western countries, we often see the sign: *"Even when you're sure, please check one more time."* A wrong prescription can destroy a life in a few seconds. Therefore we have to be very careful and be responsible before rendering a judgment that might decide someone's future. Even though we have heard, seen, and have proof in our hands, we should not be absolutely certain and pass judgment as firm as "a nail driven into a post." There is the possibility that person had to assume an unfamiliar role to carry out a certain lofty task. Or perhaps he has become expert at disguising feelings when performing particular tasks So we should always remind ourselves, *"Are you sure?"* or *"It looks that way but it's really not that way."* Then we can give ourselves more opportunities to discover, to go beyond our own perceptions and emotions at present and to always live with the truth. Emotion is a reaction of likes and dislikes. It can misdirect all observations, leading to impulsive judgments. Unfortunately, by the time our perception clears up again, it is usually too late because that news and our emotional behavior has already spread everywhere.

Meteorologist Edward Norton Lorenz proposed the theory of the butterfly effect: *"The flap of a butterfly's wings in Brazil can set off a tornado in Texas."* The wing flap of a butterfly is very gentle, but it can create a chain reaction to other more considerable moving forces and therefore can have a very big effect. According to this principle, of course, another wing flap can counteract this effect too. No one doubts that all our actions can cause great effects on other people. What is more terrible is that they will return to us with an effect many times bigger. They do not just go away at the time they happen, but readily wait for other forces of the same frequency to form new effects. There is no need for communication technology. No need for the news to be known by other objects. Once the energy is sent out from within us, it will be spread by energies already around in the universe. The effect might be immediate or it might not happen until the generation of our children or grandchildren. If our bad judgments of another person have caused anger and disdain from many people, then we have accidentally caused that person to feel very badly. In that case, we will naturally receive that "debt" plus "interest" from the universe.

Hence, without an agreement for mutual responsibility, or without the goodwill to help others, we should never make judgments directly or indirectly. It will only harm others as well as destroy the kernel of life within ourselves. If we only have doubt, unconfirmed by the other party, we should hasten to find out the truth with an unprejudiced mind to quickly let go of that doubt. Doubt and judgment are close friends; when one appears, the other follows right behind. However, deep listening and loving speech are two treasures that are right inside us and they can help prevent us from being judgmental as well as dissolve all shadows of doubt.

Once Confucius was reading in a hammock when he happened to glance at the kitchen and saw his student Yan Hui using a pair of chopsticks to scoop up rice onto his other hand, squeeze it into small balls and put them in his mouth. Confucius sighed: "Oh dear! My best student is sneaking around his teacher and classmates to eat on the sly. Could he be that depraved?" When all his students gathered for lunch, Confucius said, "Dear students, we walked tens of thousands of miles to move from the State of Wu to the State of Qi. I'm very happy that even in this disturbing and hungry situation, you still maintain your pure and honest hearts, your loyalty to me and your love, and help for each other. Today we are lucky to have a meal that reminds me of our homeland and my parents. I'd like to offer a bowl of rice to pray for them. Do you think it's a good idea?" All his students put their hands to their hearts and replied, "Yes, Master, it is." Only Yan Hui stood still in silence.

Confucius then said, "But is this pot of rice clean?" His students did not quite understand his meaning and looked at each other quizzically. At that moment Yan Hui pressed his palms together and said, "Dear Master, this pot of rice is not clean. When I opened the lid to see if the rice is cooked, a gust of wind blew in. The soot and the dust from the ceiling fell down and dirty upon the whole rice pot. I quickly put the lid down but not quickly enough. After that I scooped up the dirty layer of rice and was about to throw it away. But then I thought it over. There are many of us and only a little bit of rice. If I threw this dirty rice out, we would lose one share of it and my fellow students will have to eat even less. Therefore I took the liberty of eating that dirty rice, leaving the clean rice for you and for my friends. So I've had my share of rice today. Now with your permission, I'll only eat my vegetable share. And dear Master, we shouldn't use this rice for offering since some of it has been eaten already." After listening to Yan Hui, Confucius raised his face to heaven and sighed, "Alas! There are things in this world that we can see with our own eyes but still cannot understand it truly. My goodness! I, Confucius, almost made a fool of myself!"

Judgment, no matter how accurate, is a sword edge that cuts off close relationships, creating more separation among individuals. So we should try to practice the habit of *mere recognition*—looking at reality as it is to let go of unnecessary discriminating observations. We should replace the habit of judgment with sincere opinions in order to create better opportunities for each other.

Minh Niem

The heart and mind are exhausted
From perpetual likes and dislikes
Cease all discriminating talk
And come back to ourselves

20

Loving Speech

A beautiful and sincere word that can build trust and love is a very sweet-smelling flower in mankind's garden of civilization.

Infusing energy to each other

People of long ago used to remind each other: *"Words don't cost anything/ Choose your words carefully to please each other."* We have at our disposal a very valuable property which can bring peace, joy and happiness to people around us and it doesn't cost us any money or labor. That property is lovely words—*loving speech*. It is true that by nature, words cannot express all the depth of feelings or the endlessness of truth, but they are very essential to give energy to each other in difficult times. Gentle and warm words expressed from a peaceful heart and a respectful attitude can not only create pleasant feelings but can also soothe and encourage listeners a great deal. When we express ourselves in actions or words that accord with what is going on in our mind, their energy will multiply many times over. Therefore, a sincere word that can transmit peaceful energy is really a dose of tonic for speedy health and mental recovery.

We seem to have long forgotten the habit of praising each other due to our absorption in personal interests. Sometimes we are afraid our praise might be misconstrued to mean that we do not ask for more. We might feel that they won't respect us if we seem to be content with them. In reality, everybody wants to be recognized and praised honestly and correctly for what they have tried to achieve, especially when it comes from those they love and trust. They might not be perfect yet, but our encouragement will boost their confidence to strive for perfection. Honestly and unconditionally praising someone's good points proves that we have overcome our self-satisfaction and our prejudices about that person. It shows that we have seen and confirmed their true worth.

Naturally, beauty must go with truth to create goodness. When we try to please someone with polished and flowery words that we don't really mean and don't want to say, we might generate temporary, pleasant emotions, but we will also inadvertently distort our relationship with that person. Many people practice ways to talk beautifully or smoothly; there seems to be a "pot of honey" always ready on their lips, so they can easily persuade people to listen to them. Even when they are not pleased with us or dislike us, we have no way of knowing it. That is also a way to adorn the ego—using one good emotion to exchange for another good emotion. Only those lacking discernment and self-confidence would fall into that trap. The nature of loving speech must have the characteristic of building mutual trust and love.

There are those who prefer to live with the truth and pay no attention to beautiful speech. They think that living untruthfully with such beauty is an act of fraud. Therefore, they talk straightforwardly and express clearly what they mean, even if it hurts others at times. The truth is indeed the most valuable thing in life. If one has to choose between beautiful and true speech, an understanding person would choose true speech, of course. But reality is not always as ideal as we might think. This might not matter if we lived alone. But when our loved ones around us are not experienced enough or are still vulnerable, they will be very upset if they have to suffer unpleasant emotions from such speech. Honest words alone will not be enough to support or guide other people.

The harmony between beautiful and true speech is still the best. In case a person might be shocked upon hearing the truth, we must express it with tactful words. Failure to do so shows a lack of responsibility and is a big mistake. Of course we should not forget to reveal the plain truth once that person is strong enough to receive it. There are many people who lack the ability to use kind words, making their listeners feel bothered whenever they talk. Yet they are very proud, thinking that they are living an honest life. But the kind of honesty that merely serves their selfishness without any consideration and support for others is not skillful honesty.

Loving speech includes careful words in making comments. Even when we know that the other person has not done a good job or has made a mistake, we should be careful of our comments. Cold-blooded comments like "Stop it!" "Drop dead!", a frank observation like "It's worthless!", a judgment like "You're good for nothing!", or an angry word like "No!" to turn down a request, etc., can hurt or push the other person into an abyss. Although we meant no ill will, we could not momentarily control our emotions because of disappointment and self-love. Remember, words always lie in wait on our lips, and only a little prompting from a situation can make them jump out on behalf of our emotions. No matter what we think we stand for, our words express our real understanding and moral development. Hence, words can also lay bare our weak points in the most unexpected way.

Words that hurt others usually come from momentarily furious emotions, like a kind of easy and effective self-defensive reaction. But after we have calmed down, we always feel sorry, especially when we realize we were wrong in our blame. Regretfully, the other person believes that we meant what we said, and holds a tight grudge against us. Even if our sincere apologies touch them and they agree to let go, they really can't forget it easily. While those words do not represent our entire self, it's not correct either to say they do not belong to us. We have to be responsible for everything we do, even if it's just a word.

Deep listening to our own words

If we realize that our way of talking is still too clumsy, causing misunderstanding or hurting others each time we open our mouths, we should practice silence for a period of time to look back at ourselves. We also should inform our loved ones around us so they would not worry and can respect our quiet space during the time we are practicing our silence. If necessary, we should pin the words "practicing silence" on our shirts so we would not be disturbed unintentionally. We should turn off our cell phones, stop chatting on-line and stay away from any means that can easily cause us to talk or think erroneously. In case of an emergency, we should only write on a piece of paper instead of quickly vocalizing. We should make up our mind to practice absolute silence for three days or a week to reflect on our desire to talk, the words we often use and even our attitudes so far. During this practice period, we need to reduce our workload to have more of an opportunity to reflect on and observe our minds more deeply. If we are not careful, we might unintentionally use work to kill some silent time and hence misplace our goal.

While doing things, no matter what, we should also try to slow down a little more than usual to observe our attitude reflected from that task. We should practice smiling every time we can feel emotions going by or mental perceptions emerging in our mind, including the moments when they urge us to talk or act. We need to have a journal to record all these chains of reactions, even the darkest thoughts from the deep corners of our minds, especially when we want to say something to another person. When we have stored up some energy for observation, we should look at our own habits of self-satisfaction or arrogance that are usually the main cause for our inability to use loving speech. Though we have no one to trouble us then, with keen observation we can recognize those afflictions when we are faced with minor dissatisfactions caused by our own doing. We should accept and understand them deeply.

If we practice seriously and correctly, we will understand ourselves a great deal during those silent days. We will be quite shocked to realize that we have been running after external conditions and consequently have never noticed all the terrible perceptions and habits that had formed in our mind. We used to think that we never despised anyone, yet we do not know why we lack respect when talking to those in humbler positions. Similarly, we always think that we bear no hatred against a certain person, yet we do not understand why we cannot use kind words to talk to them the same way we talk to friends or customers. Thanks to our practice of stopping and looking deeply within ourselves, we discover that we have considered ourselves too important, smart and helpful, so we give ourselves the right to speak as we please, mindless of other people's feelings. Because of our selfishness, we have refused to rid ourselves of rough and rude speech habits to bring peaceful and happy energy to the loved ones around us, something they may have entreated us to do many times.

When we begin to speak again, we should keep a slow pace so we can listen to each of our words and observe our attitude. Once in a while we should pause to look deeply at our flow of emotions and perceptions if we realize that we are speeding up. We will feel a little uncomfortable in the beginning stage. Since we used to talk either from inspiration or to achieve a certain goal, most of the time we only paid attention to our listeners' reactions. But after a few weeks of patient practice, we will see noticeable changes in ourselves. We will feel our voice getting clearer, fuller, and more positive. We will feel more self-confident and relaxed when talking to people of power and influence. All our relationships will unexpectedly improve quickly. Especially those living around us will appreciate and have high regards for our sense of responsibility.

Another delightful thing is that we will suddenly realize that each mindfully spoken word can create a strong force. It can subdue violent energies as well as uplift weak hearts. So a beautiful and sincere word that can build trust and love is a very sweet-smelling flower in the human garden of civilization. And only those living permanently in mindfulness can own it.

Loving speech is so wonderful
To infuse energy to one another
Like the nectar of compassion
Soothing those who really suffer

21

Prejudice

Look at things and facts exactly as they are happening, not through our existing feelings or experiences.

The wall of separation

We have the habit of looking at any object or situation happening in the present through the lenses of our past experiences. Maybe a number of past experiences fit somewhat right in with present situations, so we are often confident and proud of our quick intelligence and do not bother to investigate and scrutinize them carefully. If we observe thoroughly and look back honestly, we might see that we have made wrong predictions and regrettable slips in our actions quite a few times. Everything in the universe never stops moving. At times they change their contents but at times they change their forms too. They can get better or worse, but never stay the same.

Engrossed in the intensity of life, we usually do not have the willingness to look at every object with fresh awareness. Using old experiences seems an easy and quick way to solve problems. Partly because our self-defense instinct is not completely tamed, and partly because we are fired up by competition in our society, when we see something that affects our interests, we immediately have a psychologically defensive reaction like anger, judgment, doubt, insistence, intolerance, etc., without observing and checking out the facts with a cool head. Most people do not have the habit of getting detached from old experiences when observing reality. As a result, they often come up with wrong perceptions, lose their target, and create their own suffering.

If we have been cheated or betrayed in the past, that scar is buried deeply in our mind. Now when we are about to have feelings for someone new, we might get uptight and worried and so become confused since our new contact is quite different from the old one. But we are not strong enough to overcome our defensive instincts. Though we have tried to look at the new person as he or she is, and not as the previous person, we still fail in the end. Of course it is hard to forget a heart break. However, instead of giving each other a chance to get to know and trust one another better, we tend to carry inside us a sense of doubt from the previous deception or betrayal during our entire journey together. That wall of separation is *prejudice*, pre-judgment.

Prejudice is simply an attitude of imposing old experiences on existing reality, so there can be good or bad prejudice. In other words, we often wear a pair of rosy or dark glasses to look at people and life. From personal contact or by word of mouth, if we know the other person is likable, we will like them and dote on them with no further question or inquiry. Wearing a rosy pair of glasses, we see only the good and wonderful things about them. Now that mass media and publicity can strongly affect a person's consciousness, once a certain person is written up positively in some articles, they immediately win our affection. Later, should we have a chance to meet them, we easily forget our usual observation and cautious steps. In case we hear negative things about a person, we tend to wear our dark glasses to be on the safe side even if we are not sure that the news is reliable. No matter how hard they try, we might not pay any attention or find excuses not to accept them. Over time, that attitude becomes a habit, and we will not even remember that we are wearing a pair of dark glasses. So everywhere we look is just darkness. We see no one likable and good-hearted any more. This is when we lose the clear vision that nature has bestowed on everyone. Without that clarity, our views become narrow, and we turn into a sullen, unsociable and boring person.

Maintaining clear vision

The more modern human beings are, the more they depend on electronic technology, easily becoming superficial and inflexible. What is stored in memory is not easily retrieved. That is a passive and drifting way of life. The more we are unwilling to open our minds to updated information about the other person, the less we can we can understand each other. Certainly some experiences are very useful because they help us solve appropriate problems quickly without having to spend much time and energy. This is especially in today's society, where too many ingenious products make it difficult to tell what is real or fake, so we have to make good use of successful experiences in the past to heighten our vigilance when observing. However, no matter how effective that vigilance is, it leaves us with the habit of doubting others. Moreover, no matter how good old experiences are, they cannot cover all reality. Therefore people long ago often said, "let it [an object] alone and refrain from interfering with the way we see it"—we should look at things and facts as they are happening, not through our existing feelings or experiences. That is the clear-eyed look, not clouded with the dust of life. Looking at each other with clear vision will help us feel more comfortable and closer to each other as well as give us more of an opportunity to understand and love each other.

We should not forget that the nature of all things is impermanent, hence a human is impermanent too, and so is experience. Another person might have made many mistakes but now they might have changed a great deal. We should give them an opportunity to live as a new person and give ourselves an opportunity to live with a fresh awareness of them. It is most difficult with our loved ones who are near us since we do not usually observe carefully those we think we know very well. This is like a mother who always thinks that her child is still naïve, so her concern and hopes are always based on old experiences. Inadvertently, she has limited her child's opportunity to mature. This is also like a wife who always thinks she knows her husband well and only needs to glance at him to know what he's up to, instead of listening to him carefully and observing him more. She does not realize that, by doing so, she has isolated her husband's creative inspiration and intention to change. How dreary it is to live with those who do not recognize our changes, cannot understand our dreams, or our difficulties so they may be able to support us. Perhaps that is why every time we meet a new person, we want to prolong the minutes we can look at each other with the pure feelings of beginning a relationship.

We should consequently try to practice sitting quietly every day to refine our recently accumulated experience. If that experience does not nourish our understanding and loving ability, we should not let it occupy too much of our consciousness. Observe it carefully and let go of it. Experiences that exist like casual habits in our subconscious should be analyzed and let go gradually. Whenever we have contact with someone, we should look at our attitudes to see if we are wearing a pair of sympathetic rosy glasses or a pair of antipathetic dark glasses. If we are, we should find a way to pause and readjust our psychology. Just like when it rains, if the soil is not covered by a plastic sheet or something else, the rain can then penetrate deeply down the earth to nourish plant roots and seeds. With such an enlightened way of life, we will have an opportunity to elevate our perceptions and open wide our views without becoming rigid or worn-out because of selfish and narrow-minded interests.

An old notion dies for a new one to be born; that is a rebirth—a new life for us. The old is familiar but inadequate; the new is not comfortable right away but can help us have a wider and closer view of life. So we should not hesitate to eliminate the old notions or experiences that only protect the shallow emotions of our ego. In doing so, we create for ourselves an infinitely immense space—the meeting place of the minds full of understanding and love.

Use clear eyes for looking
Unclouded by experience before
Open our mind for deeper understanding
Like the soil welcoming rain water

22

Beginning Anew

Only by keeping our mind clear and peaceful can we enjoy happiness and share it with others.

Beginning the garden of the mind anew

Our mind is like a garden; if we neglect it, weeds will grow wild. They will suck up nutritious minerals and prevent valuable plants and trees from growing well and producing flowers and fruit. Engrossed in running after attractive targets outside us, we have neglected the garden of our mind and let it *deteriorate* seriously without any awareness. We always rush around, talk fast, get upset easily when displeased, and blurt out negative comments readily. We are also stubborn, feel hurt and walk away whenever someone makes a suggestion. Looking back at the past year, what did we gain or lose? Did we gain true happiness? Did what we lose have precious qualities to help make us an understanding and loving person? Have we felt our lives getting more and more insipid and our loved ones getting less and less inspiring for us to do our best? Unable to share with anyone, we have retreated to a shell of loneliness, and then blame life and others. That is the inevitable consequence of a way of life that "drops the prey to chase after shadows."

In *The Tale of Kieu, the revered poet* Nguyen Du often reminded us, "*Hurry home to cultivate your garden.*" We should not hope or rely on someone else to cultivate our minds since we are the owner of this garden. No matter how many material comforts and honors that our many interesting projects promise to bring us, our top priority should be the cultivation of our mind. If our minds are not peaceful, but full of impurities and afflictions, nothing can bring us happiness. Now and then we know that our minds are being caught in difficulty and deadlock, but we do not have enough courage to face it. Making money or earning respect from others is sometimes easier than transforming old habits or harmful energy recently developed in our mind. Only by winning over the dark shadows of afflictions and always keeping our minds clear and peaceful can we feel happy and bring happiness to others. In case we feel we are not strong enough to transform loads of problems that are too big, we should put our pride aside and ask our loved ones for help. If it is a problem for both sides, we should work together to begin cultivating the garden of minds anew.

Method of beginning anew

Beginning anew is an opportunity to look back and unravel the tangles that either we or the other person mistakenly caused in the past. Beginning anew is bringing to life what is good and beautiful in an object, or in a relationship being clouded with bad energy. The prerequisite condition for this method is the sincerity and the will to practice so as to change the situation. Before beginning, we should make arrangements by directly inviting the other in person, by phone, or even by email. If the situation on both sides is rather tense, we can invite another person that we both like, respect and trust. Do not invite those only on our side and ready to defend us or there will be more misunderstanding. Depending on the situation, we might want to begin anew in front of the whole family or a group to get more insight from objective views, even if some members are younger or hold lower positions than us. In so doing, the beginning anew session will be more realistic and effective. The beginning anew session should start in a really comfortable and pleasant atmosphere. Hence it should be announced several days in advance so both sides can prepare really well. If we feel that our energy that day is very weak, or the other person is not yet ready to listen, we should postpone the session to another day. Do not be too eager to solve problems that would reduce us to just going through the formalities without sincerity. This will worsen the situation and both sides will no longer believe in the method of beginning anew.

Additionally, we should design a nice and warm environment for beginning anew. We should have a lovely vase of fresh flowers

Understanding the Heart

symbolizing our wish for an outcome as fresh and full of life as the flowers. We can light a few candles and prepare some tea. We should turn off all TVs, phones, and put aside all the hustle and bustle. One thing we should never forget is that, during the entire session, both sides must know how to apply well the arts of deeply listening and loving speech. In case someone else is invited to the session to witness and help us, we should respect their guidance.

The following is the process for beginning anew:

1. **Flower watering:** First we should mention the positive and lovable points of the person we want to begin anew with to make him feel good and have more self-confidence. This is a very important step. If we neglect it or do it perfunctorily due to our hurry, pride, or uncertainty, the other person might think that we just trying to "stage a fight" to attack him or find their faults. Therefore they may no longer be willing to listen.

    Example:
    "I'm very proud and happy to have a husband like you. You are not only good at your job but also a real man for the family. I still remember vividly our newlywed days. We were both poor but you never let me live in poverty. In spite of your tight budget due to a low salary, you always supported me enthusiastically every time I wanted to study more or needed to buy something. Then since your job became stable and our child was born, you have always been very supportive. Everywhere in this house are signs of your industrious and clever hands. My family and friends also admire your work accomplishments. I don't know how to express all my appreciation to you."

2. **Self-examining:** Admit that our relationship is going downhill because of too much turmoil in recent past. We let tension, anxiety, and affliction consume much of our energy, so there were times when we could not control our words and actions, unknowingly causing upset in others.

    Example:
    "Before talking about the difficulties in my heart, I would like to look back at myself. I've indeed changed a lot in my behavior. I've often

phoned you to check up on you and say some harsh words without reason while you were very busy at work. When you asked me if I needed to share some problems, I brushed you off without any explanation. Out of anger, you often passed up family meals, so now and then I would leave you alone on weekends and find excuses to visit my parents. You would have to cook for yourself and worry about me. Those were my wrongdoings. I'm really ashamed. Please forgive me."

3. **Voicing difficulties:** Let the other person know about the heavy pains in our hearts because of their careless words or gestures. We should also add that since our spiritual cultivation practice is not yet established, anger and resentment can still take over easily, so we hope they would help us by not acting or saying things that way any more. While talking, our wounds might be reopened, arousing the seed of anger; if so, we should stop in time. We need to keep calm to control our speech. We just want him to understand clearly the issues we want to raise without feeling annoyed or recoiling from our strong emotions. By doing so, in addition to not blaming us, they will also feel at ease and admire us for being responsible for what we are saying.

Examples:
"I truly love you and trust you very much, but your recent behaviors have affected my trust and love. For example, early last month, because of our disagreement and fight, you left at midnight to sleep at a friend's house. This caused your family to think that I pressured you and they bad-mouthed me to all your relatives. Two weeks ago, when I phoned to ask your opinion on our child's studies, you yelled and scolded me without letting me explain things clearly. Then you hung up the phone. Last Saturday night, you scolded me in front of your colleagues that I lacked responsibility because our child fell down the stairs while playing. But why didn't you see that I was extremely busy at that moment preparing the many dishes that you wanted for the party while you were heartily chattering away with your friends. I don't know whether you did it on purpose or not, but you made me feel that you didn't love me any more. You never acted that way before. Please help me by telling me the reason for your behavior. I really need your support to compose myself."

4. **Deep listening practice:** If we are in the role of the person being renewed, we must wait till the other person completely finishes their sharing before speaking. If part of their sharing was quite different from the truth, and we were feeling very upset or angry, we should hold our tongues. We should focus right away on our breathing or observe our emotions until we feel really calm and collected. If we still can't quite control our emotions at that time, we should ask for another time before we can explain thoroughly. However, we still acknowledge everything that the other person said and promise to reexamine what happened. And whenever we truly recognize our clumsiness or mistakes toward them, we must phone them right away, or write a letter, or better still, see them in person to ask for forgiveness and promise to behave more carefully and live more thoughtfully in the days ahead.

Example:
"I'm very grateful to you for having voiced all the difficulties that you suffered in the recent past without my knowing anything about it. But I'm very glad to see that your sufferings have been reduced somewhat. I also feel reassured now that I know your thoughts about me. Because our two lives have long become one, your suffering is also my suffering. I promise you that I will look back carefully at what you have just mentioned. I'll have an answer for you within three days. But one thing I'm very sure is that my feelings for you have never waned. I'm so sorry you have suffered much because of me. Please forgive me, darling."

If we can "tend our garden" every week or every two weeks like this, we can root out all kinds of weeds. Indeed, once we agree to sit down together, we can solve any problem no matter how difficult. The sincere attitude of another person helps us realize that our worries and doubts about him were unfounded. When we feel they do not respect us, we immediately think that they do not love us any more, and that the current relationship is just an obligation. That is usually the nub of the problem. But thanks to the method of beginning anew, we can deeply understand their sincerity and discover the deep cause for their unpleasant behavior toward us. Once we recognize the root of the problem, we will see that they deserve compassion rather than blame.

They are just a victim of their own habits and afflictions. Thanks to the method of beginning anew, we both have an opportunity to look back at the quality of our life and our behaviors toward each other so that we can help one another develop new, peaceful energy.

Actually, nothing is completely new. When the clouds of affliction disperse, the moon of love will appear and radiate light. That moon has never waned.

Because of erroneous perception
We've made countless blunders and mistakes
Let us turn to a beginning anew session
The old moon always awaits the garden of our heart.

23

Covering Up

When the mind is not truthful, we can never get hold of true love and happiness.

The cover-up culture

The inclination to please one another tends to distance us from the truth more and more every day. Performances always happen in new relationships or quick meetings, with the hope that the person we meet would have a good impression of us. Of course when we dress decently to receive guests or talk gently and modestly with our seniors, it is an attitude of showing respect to others. We call it good manners. But it will become a kind of "cover-up culture" if our only purpose is to be highly respected or to gain more sympathy from others. Those with selfish interests may perform good deeds yet conceal ulterior motives to gain temporary emotional satisfaction. This kind of relationship cannot last long because only by living truthfully together can we actually respect each other.

Since we live our lives filled with desires for enjoyment, we usually do not have much time to observe and understand each person upon meeting. We usually guess what they are like from looking at the way they dress, behave, or show their knowledge. Nowadays people are more involved with appearances than ever before. When going out, we always dress very elegantly and smile cheerfully so other people will think that we are successful or happy, even though the reality may be completely the opposite. All it takes to make us feel quite happy is to have someone praise and admire us—at least we feel good that our lives have more worth. We are even more thankful when our impressive appearances and performances can win important people to our positions or increase our business relationships. Therefore it is now very difficult to tell what is real or fake, since everyone puts on very sophisticated masks to cope with each other. Sometimes we are even worried and try to defend ourselves when others are too friendly with us.

We do not stop being defensive even with our loved ones. We always want to be worthy in their eyes, so we always try to cover up our weaknesses. Once the musician Trinh Cong Son implored, "*Ocean waves, ocean waves, don't push me/ Don't let me see her heart.*" (From the song "*Where Are the Waves Rushing To?*") Seeing clearly the true character of each other might discourage us from loving one another. But in passionate moments with the tendency to possess, love overcomes loving-kindness, so we only want to come together to enjoy what is lovely and beautiful, and we are ready to avoid what is not. Sometimes it is quite fearsome to see the hidden corners of each other's heart. But with a true love, we have to go beyond a limited look at the temporary display to see each other completely. The more we understand each other, the more we know how to offer and share with each other correctly. Hence, from the beginning of the acquaintance to the time of intimacy, we should live truthfully with each other to eliminate illusions about one another, and to help define clearly the goals of our coming together. Then we will not have the habit of enjoying very good emotions that neither partner can sustain. We have heard stories of many love boats that sank as soon as they set out to sea because the "sailors" became disillusioned with each other.

The fact is we live in a very competitive society that generates expectations from others all the time, and these expectations include our playing different roles appropriate to the various situations in which we find ourselves. People who are able to wear different hats have a better chance of being more successful, valued and liked. If we don't know this fact, others believe we are naive and a failure in life. And there are roles that last for months and years, so we practically live those roles and completely forget our true self. Actually, no one has the right to make us perform if we do not want to base much of our happiness on playing the required roles or if we do not want to get physical comforts, fame or position in return. However, we might not come to our senses and urgently return to our true selves until we run out of energy to fight or until we abruptly become awakened to the fragile happiness that we have tried to capture.

Many people have written very touching poems and songs to express their yearning to return to an innocent age, to be in harmony with their village and nature, to be close to loved ones and friends with no one doubting or hating anyone. They have even wished to be naive and trustful without having to be clever and smart. Although that dream is not impossible, it is sometimes just a dream. Not everyone is capable of recapturing and living with their true self. They may be afraid of direct confrontation with the tormenting pain of having to practice living with a new awareness like a child. That is really grueling. To be successful one must have a high degree of determination and a practical method of transformation. And the first condition is to detach oneself more from the theatrical "stage" of life.

Heart winning

Saying "cover-up culture" is a way to describe a lifestyle that worships forms and lies. However, true culture is a way of life that makes people better and more beautiful. But if that beauty and that goodness do not go together with the truth like the inseparable trio of truth-goodness-beauty, they are just a kind of superficial and fake jewelry. They certainly are not the road to lasting happiness.

People in the old days often advised us to *"show off what is good, cover up what is bad"* to remind us that we have to respect others' feelings. Even if we are upset at someone or having difficulties, we should know how to prevent our bad energy. In addition, we also have the responsibility to show our good energy to the person face-to-face. That is the law of emotional balance: if a person brings us good feelings, we should offer good feelings in return. Even with those who are very close and dear to us, if we see that we still have enough energy to overcome our own difficulties, we should try to handle it alone without bothering them or making them miserable. Of course if they are quite strong and steady, we can ask them for help and get their permission to reveal fully all of our troubles. That is an act of wisdom.

People long ago also said, *"Cover what is good, display what is bad"* to remind us to practice modesty and not to use our outstanding talents to pressure or intimidate others. This is also for cases when we know the other party tends to fall for appearances and often depends on others. So we are determined not to create more opportunities for them to entangle themselves and develop shallow habits. Only people of great ability dare to use this approach, unconcerned about how low other people might assess or underestimate them. Such people do not live their lives depending entirely on external conditions; their spirit is strong and they always believe that what is precious inside them will forever shine throughout their journey.

Actually, the guidance of experienced people is to help us improve our personal character and bring practical benefits to everyone around. Therefore truthful living does not aim at satisfying our egos. However, the young nowadays also think they are living truthfully. They look for freedom by coming back to live with their instinct, regardless of consequences that might happen to their self or the ill will and trouble they cause others. They are overjoyed at showing off what they consider valuable, even if those things only arouse craving, jealousy, and even anger from everyone. They are really pathetic. The more they try to prove themselves, the more they lose their self. They still do not know the true value of themselves and of life.

Once, a young doctor and I took a walk on an icy road. Once in a while I reminded him to watch his step because the road was very slippery and he always replied, "Don't sweat the small stuff!" Not too long later, he slipped and fell, but refused my help when I turned around with hands out. It took him five minutes before he could stand up. When I asked how he was, he calmly said, "No problem!" After a few steps, I turned my head to check and saw that he was limping on one leg. I said half-jokingly, "Even doctors can fall and get hurt!" A few days later I called to ask how he was. He seemed uncomfortable and told me he had forgotten all about his fall the other day. But two weeks later, I heard that he had to be hospitalized for broken-foot surgery. I went to visit him at the hospital. He was somewhat uneasy but then tried to excuse his own conduct, "No problem, it was only a minor accident. Everyone has an accident at least once." I smiled and said, "Everyone has accidents, but the attitude of accepting the accident depends on each person's ability." It wasn't until three months later that he wrote me a letter admitting that he did not have a habit of accepting his weaknesses. He also did not want others to think him weak, even if the habit of covering up had made him fail miserably at times. But the recent accident helped him to wake up and come to his senses, so he wrote, "Yes, it's true that doctors also fall and get hurt."

Telling ourselves to let go of frivolous activities

One day we should try to leave our noisy cities for a time, temporarily putting behind us all the plans, projects and responsibilities we need to carry out, to come back and be deeply in touch with nature, with everything existing around us. In that place, we do not have to wear any mask, perform any role, force ourselves to do thing this way or that way till they are right or perfect. At that time, we will feel our minds really at peace as if we have just unloaded a thousand pounds. The space around us will suddenly become boundless. We will no longer feel any difference between our once proud egos and all the living beings and things around us. Our selves at that time are the most wonderful perfect wholes.

The reason for humanity to be present in this world is to live a relaxing and happy life, to understand our destinies, to discover life's mysteries, to support and be in harmony with one another; it is not to fight, whether winning or losing. However, due to wrong perceptions, human beings have turned external enjoyments into the lofty goals of life. As a result, they have created numerous stages and countless roles to bring everyone into happy theatrical plays full of illusions. Even on their death beds, many people still have not found their true value and still try to tell their relatives to continue their roles.

But the period of time when we can find our peace of mind in a quiet space like nature is usually very short. The more we face ourselves, the more we are puzzled to an alarming degree because we cannot realize which phenomena happening in our minds are real and which are being molded by ourselves. The habits of shaping, over-refining, covering up, and eluding things still cling to us even when we do not have to cope with any adverse conditions. Actually, we ourselves are the most terrifying subject to focus on. It is not easy for us to accept the dark shadows in our minds as part of us, so we always disguise them as good and nice. Without understanding our minds, we will go on being a slave of our own afflictions forever. Indeed, the roles we perform have brought us a great deal of satisfaction, but if we look back carefully, they are the very times when we have pushed ourselves into near comas.

When the mind is not truthful, we can never get hold of true love and happiness. That is the very dear price we have to pay for our fun on our roaming trips, which are at the expense of our meaningful life.

Then at the end we also realize that we alone are responsible for our lives. Only when lying sick in bed or facing bitter failures can we see all the indifference and coldness of the stages of life. But we cannot blame anyone because we ourselves have chosen the main role for the play of our lives. Therefore, letting go of clever cover-ups to bring truthfulness back to our life is the necessary task as well as the responsibility of everyone. Though we cannot fully prevent and transform old habits quickly, at least we can see clearly each of our actions. When we feel exhausted or have no more need to perform, we should try to come back to truthful living. To begin living truthfully is to begin giving up mechanical emotions, to find ourselves in the world and to deliberately re-establish a relationship with all living beings and things around us. Only with that attitude do we truly step on the road of transformation to reach everlasting freedom.

However, we have to be careful because afflictions are very sophisticated and complicated. Sometimes we might think we are living truthfully, but there are still many layers of cover-ups inside. Only when adversity comes knocking at the opportune moment can we see our true natures entirely. Therefore we should trust our minds only when we no longer pursue happiness based on external conditions. Nevertheless, when we are determined to live truthfully, we are already on the right track.

My poor miserable wounds
A dear price to pay for living
Let me come back to care for you
And tell myself to give up frivolous roaming

24

Honesty

Loving one another requires mutual understanding; understanding one another requires mutual trust; and trusting one another requires being honest with each other.

Being honest with each other

Human beings tend to lean toward self-gratification more and more every day, always looking for good emotions from physical comforts and friends' admiration. Not many still maintain their honesty. Although everyone knows that honesty is a good quality and expects others to be honest with them, once they are drawn into the never-ending cycle of life competition, they find that honesty is a basic obstacle to success. Many people even claim that trying to maintain honesty in today's society is a very naive attitude. According to them, one must be clever and adept in each action to be abreast of the times and hopefully to become successful.

Thereupon, people approach each other with interesting performances that range from ornate and flowery words to worldly wise and prepossessing acts. As long as they can convince others, they would not hesitate to fabricate things quite contrary to the truth. It is ironic that our most loyal audience is our most beloved. One day when we run out of energy to perform, that layer of makeup will automatically deteriorate, and so will their trust for us. Even if we try to justify our actions with all sincerity, it will be very difficult to restore their belief in us. Only those with great love and understanding can accept and forgive us. Nevertheless, the wound is still there, they will still be on guard and recheck any important thing we want to say. They will not trust us as easily and completely as before.

Cleverness is sometimes necessary in life, but just a little cleverness. We should only use it in cases when the other person is not yet ready to accept the truth. It should not be a habit to add more layers of artificial makeup to ourselves. Even if we must use some tricky way to solve a problem without a hitch, we must have the responsibility of finding another opportunity to present the truth. Do not wait until the other person discovers it or we will be guilty of lying. One of the reasons for our confidence is that other people usually listen and believe each word we utter. And there is nothing more relaxed than being with those that we do not have to watch out for or deal with by some contrived means. Just from looking at each other we can understand each other. The reason is that loving one another requires mutual understanding; understanding one another requires mutual trust; and trusting one another requires being honest with each other.

In reality, honest people are easily abused or exploited. However, the universe is very fair. Honest people are those who are always lucky in life and never get to a dead end from harm done by others. So just because of some small failures while treating others with honesty, we should not try to form the habit of being cautious and dishonest with others. We have countless ways to recover our interests should we lose them, but it will be difficult to find ways to recover our integrity and sincerity. Without this important integrity, we will look at all objects and situations with an erroneous view, and then blame this life for being full of delusive theatrical plays. Delusions are formed by human beings' crazy mind. They are not the nature of life. Life is naturally beautiful.

Being honest with oneself

There is no standard principle to help us know when to be honest or what level of honesty is needed because we all have different ideas about the value of happiness. If we think that happiness means having lots of money or power, we surely cannot use honesty as a magic wand to cope with tough fights in life. Only those who realize that happiness comes from a peaceful heart and from letting go of some unnecessary desires or conflicts are determined to protect their heart. They would rather let their work fail than corrupt their heart since a corrupted heart is hundreds of thousands of time harder to fix than failed work. Work accomplished with a damaged heart can never bring us happiness.

There are times, however, when we are not sure whether we should choose to maintain honesty or continue performing our role to gain more interests. Our internal strength is not always strong enough to prevail against attractive forces from the outside that arouse our greed. That is really a very tough fight. Only those with strong will for the lofty value of life can hope to protect their clear mind. But reality shows that using only willpower is not always successful. We cannot force ourselves to recognize the truth when our consciousness has fallen to a very low level. Even if we are determined to live in truthfulness, the energy from a life-long habit of cover-ups and lies can still crush our will.

Therefore to be the master of ourselves, we have to understand ourselves. To understand ourselves, we should not use our will to hypnotize ourselves into thinking our emotions are good when that's not true in reality. We are angry but refuse to admit it. We are jealous but try to think that we are competing in a race. We are cowardly but think that we are brave. The reason we cannot see ourselves is the instant interference of our willpower does not give us time to get to know ourselves. Willpower is energy moving toward goals and created from accumulated experience and knowledge; whereas reality is something very different from strong willpower. The nature of willpower can only control the development of afflictions, not transform them. If using willpower we tend to prevent ourselves from expressing our bad feelings and thoughts, then we do not see ourselves as who we are and we could make a wrong assessment of our abilities

Looking at our own consciousness also requires an honest attitude. Until we know how to untangle it correctly, we should observe it as it is, instead of forcing it to be this way or that way. That honest look is usually called *intuition*—to look as if it was the first look. That is a look that has not yet been molded by the mind, a look without an attitude of protecting our egos. If we can eliminate the attitude of like or dislike while observing our minds, we will certainly see its true nature clearly. We can also see clearly the deep causes that have pushed and created our current psychology. We only need to be silent and observe leisurely as if we are watching a movie gradually unfolding; then we will understand deeply and can untangle each psychological thread from coarse to delicate. This requires a process of steadfast practice.

It cannot be done quickly. However, when we begin to be honest with ourselves and accept what we have and then find ways to untangle our minds instead of denying or suppressing it, we will have made a very important step in the process of transforming our minds.

In the past we used to be resolute on achieving major self-improvement, but over the years we did not make any progress. We even regressed. The biggest reason is that we only used willpower and did not accept the level we were at. Worse still, we hated ourselves, always having a complex about bad energies emerging from our minds. But that was the consequence of our lacking awareness in life. We cannot command it to change right away when we have not truly practiced hard long enough for us to form a steady new habit. The most important condition to transform bad habits within ourselves, therefore, is that we must understand them deeply and accept them as part of ourselves. But in order to understand them deeply, the best way is to be gentle and kind to them, even to treat them like friends.

Many people who consider themselves virtuous or living a religious life for years often get caught in this trap. They try their hardest to become saintly, while the gap between saintliness and their existing level is still quite wide. Perhaps it is their eagerness to become saintly that has covered up their true consciousness. From admiring to emulating their predecessors' valuable experiences, they happen to think it is their level. While they cannot forgive someone because their mind is still narrow and prejudiced, they try to force compassion on their consciousness; hence they appear to have forgiven but are still full of resentment within themselves. This attitude of "self-suggestion" is a very big obstacle in the process of discovering the truth. To arrive at the truth, we have to live honestly with the truth instead of using our intelligence to grasp, imagine or shape our minds.

Naturally we don't always have an opportunity to observe our minds honestly. We still have to deal and interact with everyone, and still have to struggle for more enjoyable comforts. So at times we have to use our wills to temporarily overcome or to hide our afflictions. Gaining one thing at the expense of losing another is a necessary law of life. However, we can still save our minds in time after such a performance if we can look back and remind ourselves to try not to repeat it. When we have a strong consciousness about the value of true happiness, about the lofty purpose of life, we certainly will save more opportunities to live with our honest minds. We will be willing to reject what can harm the precious seeds in our minds. We will know very well that whatever is built on a dishonest foundation cannot last long, and it is a big obstacle for our getting close to each other.

Therefore the highest art of living is not based on the skillful ability to shape our minds into a certain wonderful model without a foundation for true transformation. We should practice in such a way that we can always see our minds clearly and understand it deeply. We should patiently observe it many times with a gentle and kind attitude and we will see good results. By practicing like that, the opportunity for attaining happiness will be within our reach. We will no longer complain that life is too complicated or too difficult for us to win our selves. If we can live with our natural and true minds, we can be in harmony with the workings of the universe. That is the life of those who understand how to live, the dream of all those who have not found the value of true happiness from life plays full of drama.

Although we have not found our natural and true selves, we firmly believe that it is available instead of having disappeared. This is because there are many times when our minds are truly empty, without the shadows of ambition, greed, or conflict, and then we can suddenly see it show up as if is it had never been away—*"Many times in the late night from the garden are the very gentle steps of someone returning, like the heart of the years past"* ("Fading Away", a song by Trinh Cong Son).

To heaven and earth my appreciations
For helping me come back to myself
After years of being a traveler
Suffering from life's afflictions

25

Principles

> *Principles for right living are yardsticks to measure mankind's discipline for living.*

Necessary protection

During the evolutionary process, human beings have found the necessary conditions to tame their instincts and attain happiness. We call these "principles for right living."

Human instinct always aims at enjoyment—looking for pleasant feelings and avoiding unpleasant feelings. However, in order to achieve genuine peace and long-lasting true happiness, we sometimes have to practice letting go of unnecessary pleasant feelings and accepting necessary unpleasant feelings. Identifying these feelings and whether to let go or not comes the valuable experiences that our previous generations learned at great expense. If we follow the principles right living, we may not live as we please, but we will save time and energy from trial and error, and especially avoid regrettable mistakes. It is for this reason that those who follow such principles will always feel safe to move forward without fear.

Principles also have an effect on the harmony among many individuals. Everyone has their own perceptions and living habits. In particular, human minds regularly change and transform, so some principles are necessary to regulate the level of "emotional balance." It only takes one person to love and interact with us to make these principles necessary so that one side does not inadvertently encroach on the other. No matter how close or intimate we are with the other side, they are not us. They have definite needs that we must respect. A greater number of people interacting with each other mean a greater number of differences between perceptions and living habits, so the number of principles must increase more and more and become the standard voice of the group.

There are principles that have been written down with proper dates of issue, e.g., rules and laws, and there are also "unwritten" principles, e.g. morals. Both of these depend on the needs of different individuals and the degree of their mutual respect. Therefore, principles must regularly change to be appropriate with human beings' levels of awareness, which never stop progressing. We can say that principles for right living are yardsticks to measure mankind's discipline for living. People living with such discipline are people of great ability and willpower, daring to put themselves in the right environment to reach truth, goodness, and beauty.

But many people hate principles. They are those who live by feeling, do what they like, and don't do what they don't like, regardless of the consequences. They think that principles are restraints spoiling what is natural. Those who succeed easily by their good luck (thanks to favorable external conditions) or those born with talent (without a need to develop skills through training) have the tendency to disregard principles. They are even "allergic" to principles. Many people who are successful, famous, or uniquely talented often have different ways of living, socializing and interacting with people. Sometimes they don't follow common principles on purpose to show their unusual differences. To them, being different from others makes them a special class. So they feel free to be late to appointments, to wear fancy clothing, to talk with a condescending tone, or to do things that shock others but delight them because they think they are stars. This is usually called "the star disease," meaning those who give themselves the right to bypass "the law of emotional balance" of their society. Although they have the ability to contribute to society in certain areas, they forget that they have been famous and successful thanks to the interest, concern and support of the public. If they just rely on their talent, but lack of respect for the fundamental principles of society, then sooner or later they will be ostracized and forgotten. Therefore, when their talent no longer shines, they will not know how to live in harmony with everybody. That is a necessary price to pay for a wild life of immoderation and lack of understanding.

Going beyond principles

It is true that life always needs principles to help individuals tame their instincts and live together in harmony. But people establish principles, so there are principles that are close to the workings of the universe and there are principles that are wrong or only have a relative value in a limited space or time. For example, the Vietnamese proverb *"When close to the ink, one gets inky; when close to the lamp, one gets bright"* is a principle for living that is very necessary and almost compelling for those easily polluted by the exterior environment while unable to control their own self. But with people who are already strong and can "integrate without dissolving," that principle is no longer effective. To be more exact, people who are truly mature must go beyond a limited framework and be ready to meet all objects or situations to realize big goals aiming at helping humanity and the world.

There was once a novice monk who entered monkhood a long time ago but still could not give up his pilfering habit. His brothers reported this to their master many times without getting any reaction from him. One day the novice monk was caught red-handed stealing a valuable item. His brothers immediately escorted him to the master and unanimously asked that he be expelled right away; otherwise they would all leave. After sitting with a meditative look for a while, the master nodded, "If you want to leave, go ahead. You have awareness and are responsible for all your actions, so you can live anywhere. But this novice monk is still too foolish and needs to stay with me for more practice." Everyone was stunned by the master's words. Many thought with resentment that he was being over-protective, saving one person in exchange for the entire group. But once they calmed down and thought it over, they all recognized their master's immense heart.

A monastery is a place for people to come and take refuge, to practice giving up wrong deeds and developing right ones, to transform the bad into the good. It is not a center for those who are already cultivated. The nature of the rules is to prevent people from developing bad characteristics in order to purify their mind. A monastery is not a place for worship and dividing the good from the bad. Becoming a good person is a never-ending struggle, at times successful but other times not, of course. Punishment does not stop people from making mistakes, but education and transformational practice do. It is impossible to consider a person "good" just because they've never made a mistake or "bad" just because he's broken a monastic rule. Truly transforming the bad into the good is the essence of the cultivation practice.

Of course when a person violates the monastic rules, the community has the right to expel them. But is this because we are not strong enough to help them, or is it because we are afraid to execute the monastic regulations incorrectly? While it is fair to enforce the rules properly, isn't it an injustice to use them as a yardstick to measure a human being's level of understanding and love? Laws only reflect the accepted norms of society or monastic communities, while understanding and love can touch the nature of people. We know very well that the dividing line between good and bad or good and evil can be as fine as a silk thread or a strand of hair. That person might have been a bodhisattva yesterday and a demon today. And whether or not they can come back to being a bodhisattva or remain a demon depends on the support of people with understanding and love. This is a very tough math problem—on one side is the rule, and on the other is loving devotion.

In real life, we are not always successful in solving a problem with deep love and sound principles. But at least we should have a policy to try our best to examine both aspects. If we are required to choose reason to protect the majority, we will have to sacrifice our love. Though that decision is not wrong, we have actually failed. If one person who is unable to embrace the mistake of another person is a failure, what about a community of a few dozen people? Why can't the community have the courage to go beyond the law for once to mutually protect and help that person find a way out, and then everyone together will be responsible for this flexibility?

If we say that we only have laws or rules here—that we reward those who deserving and punish those who are guilty—then we can only protect a few rights temporarily, but we have pushed our levels of acceptance and tolerance down to a very low level. After a long time, this level can become hardened and fixed. Despite the fact that we are required to abide by the laws on a battlefield or in the business world, life is not only a battlefield and business world. Applying laws rigidly and without feeling is only an attitude to protect our weakness, stubbornness and indifference. We have witnessed parents who could not forgive their children for fear of suffering disgrace for not educating them properly. There are many spiritual masters who coldly turned away from their student's sincere penance only because they are afraid they might get sneered at for their lack of order and discipline. They tightly hold onto rules and regulations to cover their ungenerous heart while believing they are protecting the truth. Therefore, rules not applied carefully can become a stronghold that confines and destroys boundless benevolence.

Therefore, to live is to enjoy freedom and happiness, not to hold tightly or venerate rules. Only when we feel weak should we agree to and respect a few rules in order to restrain the impetuosity of our instincts and avoid regrettable consequences. When we can control our emotions or basic afflictions, we can live peacefully and serenely and be ready to take responsibility for all our actions. However, we also need to confirm our characters in the light of the public, or at least of the loved ones around us. Be careful about making a mistake between the need to live wildly and the spirit of living beyond rules and regulations. When our practice is really solid, rules or the lack of them will not cause any problem or obstacle any more. We can adapt to all objects and situations. Because we no longer have the need to hold on too much to outside conditions, we have found the strength from our very own hearts.

So we should practice keeping rules as if we do not keep them because we want to set examples or remind others; as for us, we have gone beyond rules. We should also practice not keeping rules as if we do, because we want to let go the relative in order to achieve the absolute. That is the art of living that we must thoroughly grasp if we want to reach the height of happiness and assist everyone. Any rule is just a means; only the attitude of living and interacting with each other is truly the most important value in life.

Don't create principles
Like solid ramparts
Benevolence once confined
What's the use, to be right or wrong?

26

Adapting To Conditions

The bigger is our ability to adapt to conditions,
the greater is our peace of mind.

All things are caused by conditions

All things in this world and even this universe are created by many conditions. Even an extremely tiny unit like an electron is not a separate entity, but is always linked to others. Since every individual thing has to depend on countless conditions to manifest and exist, we call those *causal conditions*. Watching a rain shower, we know one more condition the rice fields just received is water, and one condition the sky gave away is clouds.

The process of causal conditions is extremely mysterious. There are no fixed forms and at times they are formless. Therefore we cannot use our normal eyes, science or technology to know well their working process. Only when we can overcome the erroneous notion about our separate selves and break open that thin shell can we see clearly the working process of all conditions from our own selves to all things around us. Furthermore, all things follow the law of cause and effect, so it is also called *cause and condition*. Cause is what happened before. That means there is never a completely new cause, but there are always a number of small causes that meet and connect with each other to produce today's conditions, which are also the causes of the future.

There is an old saying that three important elements must be met to succeed in doing anything: clement weather, favorable terrain, and human harmony. Clement weather is a favorable condition from the universe. Favorable terrain is a social situation appropriate to the work we are doing. Human harmony is the enthusiastic support from everyone around. People in the old days thought clement weather was not as good as favorable terrain, and favorable terrain was not as good as human harmony. With human harmony on our sides, it is easy to get the remaining two elements. We can take the initiative to create human harmony because this element lies right inside ourselves. We only have to let go our haughtiness and jealousy, and try our best to respect and support everyone around us. In other words, if we live a good and virtuous life, then we can naturally get connected with the other two elements. No matter how talented and capable we are, we can never succeed if one of the three elements is missing, especially when we fail to win people's hearts. Even if we succeed, we will soon fail. Conditions come and go, gather and disperse, so we should not believe that what we have today will last forever. While we cannot take the initiative completely to create all causes and conditions for ourselves, we can influence the better or worse direction that causes and conditions will take.

Our minds also work in a very mysterious process. Each good thought will generate a great amount of good energy and each bad thought will generate a great amount of bad energy. They will join directly with other good or bad energy moving all over the universe. When enough appropriate causes and conditions have been met, they will create unimaginably great effects. Therefore our minds are the source that creates most of our appropriate causes and conditions. But if we do not have enough energy to develop our mind's positive traits to improve our current causes and conditions, we will have to accept their absence. This attitude is called *adapting to conditions*. In addition, not wishing for any other causes and conditions is also an attitude of adapting to conditions.

We adapt to conditions when we gladly accept what is happening in the present, temporarily stop struggling and calmly wait for appropriate causes and conditions to come around. Many times it is this attitude of not struggling and calmly waiting that is the important cause and condition to join with other good causes and conditions. We should not forget that success requires the union of millions of causes and conditions and one missing condition alone can cause failure. If we have deep understanding or experience, in some cases we can guess and know what to do and what not to do for good causes and conditions to gather again or bad ones to disperse soon.

We usually refer to good causes and conditions as *favorable conditions* and bad ones *unfavorable conditions*. There are conditions that are favorable to us but unfavorable to others, and there are conditions favorable to others but unfavorable to us, as far as human beings are concerned. All the while causes and conditions happen with all things everywhere in the universe. Therefore, in another sense, the nature of causes and conditions is not favorable or unfavorable, good or bad. They gather or disperse according to the adaptability among different levels of energy from all individual things.

Most of us, however, habitually feel happy when receiving favorable conditions and want to keep them forever. When we run into unfavorable conditions, we always feel uncomfortable and try to avoid or eliminate them. But favorable conditions do not necessarily bring us happiness or unfavorable conditions real suffering. Sometimes the unfavorable one makes us mature, while the favorable one makes us weak. Many times the favorable one in the beginning becomes the unfavorable one later on, or vice-versa. All depends on our ability and our attitude to life. Therefore we do not need to urgently change unsatisfactory conditions, or try hard to look for favorable conditions. When our minds are strong enough to create peaceful conditions, similar ones will automatically join them. In fact, when we can find the life force within ourselves, we will not pay much importance to exterior conditions any more. Any cause and condition will be fine. We are serene.

Adapting to conditions while remaining unchanged

Adapting to conditions is also an attitude of making the most of new causes and conditions currently present to solve problems or to create better breakthroughs. It is willing to forgo plans, including set rules. This attitude can only come from really able and steady people because they have to make sure that the quality of mind will not only stay unchanged but will also get much better than before. This is quite different from an explosion of emotions—determined to do what we want, then quickly get bored and let go.

There is an interesting story in the meditation world. Two monks were walking from place to place for Dharma teaching when they happened to see a girl trying to find a way to cross a stream with strong current. The elder monk approached her and asked: "Hello miss! Would you like me to carry you to the other side?" The girl happily nodded her head right away. After crossing the stream, the two monks said good-bye to her and continued their journey. But they had not gone very far when the younger monk could no longer contain his indignation and spoke up: "How could you do that, elder brother?" The elder monk was surprised and asked: "Do what?"—"Carrying the girl earlier. Aren't we monks already?" The younger monk was irritated. His elder brother smiled, patting his shoulder: "I left her by the stream already, why are you still carrying her?" There was nothing wrong with the younger monk not helping the girl cross the stream. Since his practice level was still weak, he needed to adhere to the rules so his mental concentration would not be disturbed. But he was wrong in thinking that his elder brother had the same level of attainment and also needed to practice exactly the same way and so felt indignant with him for helping the girl. Despite the fact that purity of mind is a compelling condition for those who leave home to become Buddhist monks, it is not the end of religious practice. Practice does not aim only at obeying religious rules carefully while ignoring other people's suffering. Rules and regulations that merely protect purity are only for those who are still weak or just live for themselves. They have no real value for very capable people who can stay unaffected in tumultuous situations. Therefore we cannot base our understanding on a few external happenings to make our judgment without considering motives and outcomes. The question is whether a person loses himself or herself or improves his or her qualities after an action that seems to break the rules.

"*I left that girl by the stream already, why are you still carrying her?*" This saying confirmed somewhat the unaffected level of the elder monk. Certainly other practical verifications are needed before we can believe in someone's ability to adapt to conditions without his quality of mind changing. There are many people who like to strike out, always want to use all their energy to get hold of causes and conditions in the present to carry out difficult tasks, but few can succeed. Most failures come from their over-confidence in themselves or under-evaluation of the situation. Or they let their ambition take over, have the habit of changing plans of action, or follow their inspiration blindly. Although they also adapt to conditions, they do so from overconfidence, etc.

Changing strategy suddenly, bypassing important rules, ignoring objections from surrounding people, and in the end having to pay a high price without reaching the goal is a very serious psychological wound. That wound will cause us to lose self-confidence and become uncomfortable with changes later on. Because of such unpredictable consequences, many experienced people prefer a normal life that is safely within the limits of the rules. However, life is not always normal. There are times when it requires us to overcome conventions to save ourselves or help others; then what should we do? Therefore, preparing ourselves with a capacity big enough to cope with adversities is the action of experienced and understanding people.

Meditation Master Tran Nhan Tong of Vietnam's Tran Dynasty used to advise us: *"One must adapt to conditions to enjoy the Dharma way in life/ Eat when hungry and sleep when tired."* The art of maintaining a peaceful mind among life's multitude of troubles is an attitude of adapting to conditions. According to Meditation Master Tran Nhan Tong, adapting to conditions means eating when we are hungry and sleeping when we are tired. But we should eat properly and sleep properly, do each task properly without mixing them up or treating one more important than the other. What comes first should be dealt with first without hastiness or hesitation. However, it is easier said than done, since we have to change our dominant habit of living in a hurry, in worry, and in fear. Even those living in a calm environment are still full of anxiety and ambition, let alone us who are living in a turbulent world.

Of course no one forces us to adapt to conditions. But the more we are able to adapt to conditions, the greater is our peace of mind. If we continue to seek happiness only from the outside, we will certainly accept only the conditions that are favorable to us. Only when we can find true happiness within ourselves can we accept all situations. Adapting to situations to help our lives and others' lives without getting lost in the tumult of ordinary worldly is the most ideal model in all ages.

Come and go peacefully
Causes and conditions unnecessary
Winter ends for spring to come forth
No less and no more henceforth

27

Despair

Hope can easily turn into disappointment,
but from disappointment to despair is a very big distance.

Losing one's self

Living in this world, one must have hope. Believing in a better tomorrow is a necessary way to save our hearts from torments or bitter and harsh realities. But if we pour all our energy into hoping for a better future, it is like gambling all of our property on the last game, and should we lose, life will have no more meaning for us. Indeed nothing is more devastating than not knowing where to put our faith. Actually it is our hearts that does not have enough strength to hold tormented feelings bigger than we have ever had before or that we have never prepared for. Our egos no longer have a place to hold onto, so it falls into a lost and lonely place without recognizing ourselves or anything around us.

When desperate, the mind becomes more clouded than ever before. We look at things with a pessimistic and embittered eye with the impression that there is nothing meaningful and believable in this life any more. But the truth is that the universe is still embracing us, our loved ones are still supporting us, and favorable conditions are still surrounding us. It is only our minds that are attached to a certain attractive object and unintentionally assimilate our own lives to that object. That means that while having faith in that object, we have readily gathered all our energy for that object. This kind of faith causes us to limit or end necessary relationships with others around us. We lose our balance as soon as we put all our faith in someone, so if by chance that person changes or disappears, naturally we will collapse. We have nowhere to hold on. Our self seems to have been lost.

We forget that failure in fame, love, or ideals is only a part of life. We still have many reasons to live and to hope. Hope can easily turn into disappointment, but from disappointment to despair is a very big distance. Not everyone who is disappointed becomes desperate. And not everyone who is desperate drowns forever in suffering. Understanding people always consider disappointments as lessons from experience for future successes. They believe that what they have worked hard to build will never disappear, that the energy from that hard work will continue, though perhaps take different forms. Thanks to strong internal energy, they are always ready to accept heavy losses without complaining or giving up. They know they are bigger than what has not yet been accomplished or what has been taken away. The important thing is that they have never gambled away or sold their life.

Not knowing where to go

However, most people want to give up everything when falling into the deep abyss of despair. If we are among them, we should ask ourselves: Who has really caused us to be this way? If we can identify the culprit, we should ask ourselves another question: Why does that person have the right to control our life so easily? They can hurt us, but they have no right to make us suffer. We should remember that this body is not truly our own, so we have no right to disrespect or destroy it. The truth is that our parents, siblings, friends, and even ancestors and countrymen all have their presence in our every cell and breath. They are walking into the future together with us. So if we fall down, they will fall too. The outcome of our future will affect part of theirs.

We know that when we choose death, we have suffered extremely, and our hearts are about to be broken because they cannot stand the pressure of too much. But if we think things over, we will realize that we are making a very selfish decision. We just want to run away from the emotional storm of our selves for which we are partially responsible. We think we are the most miserable person on Earth, so everyone needs to respect us and has no right to blame us. It's true that no one should blame a suffering person. But we have no right to make our loved ones suffer because others make us suffer. And would we have peace in that certain faraway world where our minds are still full of hatred, anger, and our human responsibility is still unfinished?

The future is not separated from the present. The characteristics of the future will be similar to those of the present. Suffering comes from the mind and therapy also comes from the mind. We should not keep on chasing the source of our suffering to question it or punish someone for it, nor should we find an absolutely safe place to escape to. Even if we could do it, our wounds would not heal well. That approach can only temporarily satisfy our emotions because we can never fully recapture what we lost. Stay calm and look back. Many times we do not escape the abyss of suffering not because we lack energy, but maybe because we want to remain in that terrible situation to make the other person feel guilty as punishment. Or perhaps we want to submerge ourselves in that painful emotion to feel sorry for ourselves. This is often called "the pleasure of pain."

Upon falling into painful emotions that are too big, weak and self-centered people often gnaw on the pain for self-pity instead of actively finding a way to get out. They like to huddle themselves like shrimps to listen to heart-rending love songs. Or they like other people to water their miseries by agreeing that they are the most miserable and pitiable persons on Earth. They would not let anyone pull them out of that dark abyss. This is a form of depression—wanting to hold emotions at a low level of the consciousness to satisfy their inferiority complex. Looking deeply, it is actually a way to let everyone know about the pain we are suffering but we would rather have their pity than their help. We only feel assured if they can help us get back to the exact position full of hope we had in the beginning; otherwise, let us be.

Garbage is also flowers

In the song *"Dear Self, Don't Despair"* the musician Trinh Cong Son proposed a very good treatment: *"Be natural and you will be the dawn."* It takes a very experienced person who has risen up from desperate sufferings to express that. Previously, the musician also affirmed: *"You are me and I am also you."* You are the desperate psychology, a temporary manifestation of a big ego, but we cannot say that despair is the whole of us. Though it is dominating our thoughts and actions, its nature is still impermanent like all other psychological phenomena, and thus will disperse sooner or later. The marvelous thing is that drifting to the bottom of the sea of suffering helps us discover that the nature of all afflictions is unreal and nameless. They are just the temporary reactions of our egos that are weak and still lack understanding. However, it is thanks to those strong reactions that we can see clearly all our profound weaknesses to help us and change our way of life. Therefore we can say that if there are no afflictions, there will never be enlightenment; if we were not desperate yesterday, we would not be steady today. The two are not separate.

Garbage can turn into organic fertilizer to nourish flowers and help them bloom. Flowers turn into garbage, and garbage also turns into flowers. So the borderline between a desperate you and a steady you is just a silk thread or strand of hair. When lost, the crybaby of years ago emerges, but when awakened, the steady ego will return. Therefore, to experience a new dawn in our lives, and to overcome bouts of desperate pain, we have to renew our minds instead of chasing others to punish them or to hold on to them. The only solution is to be "natural"—to live with the original true self. It is the self that has never received any social position in life, has never known how to cover up or perform. That self looks at everything with the crystal-clear eyesight of a child, not covered with the colors of prejudices and fixed views. With courage to let go all struggles, temporarily returning to a quiet place close to nature, saving all energy to nurture each flow of our emotions or thoughts, and being deeply in touch with all things existing around us openly and lovingly, the innocent child will appear gradually. That child will see no wound or suffering because this whole process is the most harmonious work of the universe.

Believe in impermanence—everything will change. We will no longer be psychologically desperate and the other person will no longer be foolish and make us suffer. Although there are very worldly desires inside both of us, life also contains great joy and happiness.

> *To this wonderful life with much appreciation*
> *For creating existence, then non-existence*
> *Non-existence, then again existence*
> *For new days to be budding with blossoms*

28

Faith

Self-love and the lack of self-confidence are two culprits regularly robbing the faith we have in others.

Having faith in people

Living together, we have to trust each other. When we have faith in each other, it means we show respect and recognize each other's presence in this world, even if we are not closely related. Trusting others means we can see their true worth, whether their worth is already manifested or still latent. Therefore, we need to look deeply into their nature instead of only relying on actions and events before strongly believing in them. All phenomena constantly change with time, either for better or for worse. This is impermanence—the nature of all things.

When looking at a forest full of red autumn leaves, those with poetic mind tend to feel heavy-hearted, sad, and sometimes doleful like the leaves falling in the wind. They think that autumn is dying and that autumn will be gone. That is a limited or framed view that only sees autumn in its present colors. They do not know that the nature of autumn is also the nature of summer, winter, and spring, too. We call it autumn to differentiate the colors and even the formation process of the leaves according to the weather. We do not think that autumn exists separately from other seasons. The truth is autumn never dies; it only changes from one phase to another. Who denies that the spring leaves this year are completely not the rebirth of the autumn leaves from last year? So believe in autumn; it will return.

Life tends to be competitive. Everyone fights for their own interests even if they have to use clever means, including lies, so it is difficult to have faith in anyone. If someone is dishonest with us once, uses gestures hard to understand, or tells unfounded stories, we immediately shut our door of faith tightly. We think it is better not to trust. That means we would rather not accept, not cooperate, or not have a close relationship with the other person. We might not receive any benefit from them but at least we would not be cheated or be taken advantage of. It seems when we put trust in someone, we want to have more benefits. At least we have one more places for our lost hearts to lean on; it is not to share or support the other person. So when that person cannot shine any more, we withdraw our faith right away. That kind of faith is selfish, and no one needs it.

Sometimes to protect our own interests, we need to check carefully before putting our faith in someone. However, life is interacting with, connecting with, and having the responsibility for supporting one another to keep balance and harmony long lasting. Therefore we have to think about others and trust them to help them have more self-confidence so they can overcome difficulties or obstacles within themselves. Look at ourselves: surely we have not forgotten the times when we lost faith in life to the point of despair, but it was really fortunate that we had someone who had great faith in us. Although we only received a sympathetic look or a few sincere encouraging words, it was enough to make us feel warm and have more strength to go on. So when we think we cannot trust some people, ask ourselves if we are being caught in erroneous perceptions about them. Are we prejudiced against their clumsiness or mistakes in the past? Do we worry that they might take advantage of us instead of bringing us some benefit? Do they lack respect for us or hurt us? Or is it because we lack self-confidence? Indeed, self-love and the lack of self-confidence are two culprits regularly robbing the faith we have for others.

There are cases when we quickly trust other people because their strengths hit our temporary loving emotion right on target! Because of love, emotional attachment, or desire to relate, we easily put all our faith in them. This kind of faith is shallow, blind, and often comes from the psychology of those who tend to lean on others. When we are calm and clear-minded enough to observe and understand other people, we should be brave enough to trust each other. Of course, time is the most efficient way to test the sincerity of each other. But if we need to have strong faith in one another to help overcome the difficult road right now, we should not hesitate too much. In our sincerity is abused, we might lose some property or honor but our faith is still whole inside us. As long as we still have faith in human beings, we can still find a steady footing in this life. Having faith in each other is closely connected to supporting each other; doubting each other is cutting off the support energy that is very necessary to the survival of each other.

Having faith in life

Many people lost their faith in life because they suffered bitter failures or were harmed by bad individuals. They live with a very fixed view, firmly believing no one is honest in this world, and all those nice words or actions are only theatrical performances. From that perception, they stubbornly affirm that this life is no different from tragicomedies on stage. So there is no need to eagerly maintain or build anything more. A number of people with such views live and do what they like recklessly without caring about consequences or the reactions of those around them. A number of other people seclude themselves, live sorrowfully and indifferently, avoiding contact and doubting everyone. The remaining number entrust their heart to a certain high and mighty power, hoping to be saved and led to a world without a shadow of lies and deceptions.

Succeed or fail, win or lose, get together or depart are the ups and downs of life that we all experience. All that happens to us today follows the principle of causes and conditions since the universe gives priority to no one and forsakes nobody. Because we do not have enough wisdom to clearly understand how the process of the causes and conditions works and what causes we create to get certain consequences, we believe our destiny was all arranged by the Almighty. This is a very human interpretation of minds still full of the desire-anger-ignorance energy to protect their small egos. If there were a true Almighty, that Almighty would have to act fairly and reasonably. It should not be due to our fervent belief that the Almighty noticed us and treated us favorably. The reason for our blind and delusive belief is because our minds are too weak with no place to lean on. Once the ego is suddenly nurtured and promised attractive benefits in the future, superstition will turn into fanaticism—we will be ready to do anything for the one promising future benefits, even if the belief is irrational.

We should think of ourselves as a beach of sand, not a grain of sand. When strong winds blow some grains of sand from this place to fill up another place, it also blows sand from somewhere else to fill up this place. This and that place all belong to the beach, so we should not worry or be concerned. If we are able to go beyond the tiny scope of this physical being, we will see that we currently are also present everywhere. If we can recognize the truth that we never stop interacting with all things and living beings in the universe to exist, then we will never suffer or lose faith when experiencing the unavoidable ups and down in this life. Do not be quick to blame impermanence. Without impermanence, flower buds could not blossom, snow could not melt, children could not grow up, dictatorships could not collapse, and miserable beings would drown forever in miseries. Therefore, only when we think less of individual interests and know how to look at life with loving and supportive eyes will our faith never fall. We have faith in human beings because we can see their good nature; we believe in life because we can see the interdependence of ourselves and everything else.

Having faith in ourselves

It is difficult to accept that when we lose faith in human beings or in life it is because we do not have enough faith in our own selves. But that is the truth. Believing that favorable and lucky conditions from outside will bring us safety and lasting happiness, we try our best to chase, catch, indulge, and hold onto them. By letting our minds run after the external world, of course, the mind becomes lost and desolate when the world oscillates or disappears. Though we cannot live apart from the external world, we should try to practice depending less on the chance of the situation by having faith in ourselves. Naturally we must understand our true worth before we can have faith in ourselves. In case we do not, we should ask those with great knowledge to point out our true worth for us. Then we can find ways to develop our good points and arouse our potential energy. By firmly believing in our real strength, we will be able to cope with all situations.

The young nowadays appear very self-confident, but their self-confidence is really simplistic. Just because their knowledge was recognized and they were awarded a degree by a well-known university, their communication skills brought them many good business relations, their tall figure attracted a lot of attention, or because their clothes bear expensive labels, they are full of self-confidence and put on airs in front of everyone. How pitiful! Those who only see their worth through the shallow recognition of others must be resigned to losing their sacred self regularly because people's observations and feelings are also very impermanent, always changing. Besides when we only concentrate on the points that only bring temporary loving emotions from others, we will certainly neglect deep qualities inside. How can we be steady in this tumultuous world without important virtues such as calmness, patience, modesty, tolerance, optimism, flexibility, etc.?

To have faith in ourselves therefore is to believe in our talents as well as our virtues. Talent is not only for making money or getting admiration from others; it should also bring peace and joy to ourselves and our loved ones around us. Talent without virtue, serving only our selfish petty egos, sooner or later will lead us to destruction from subjectivity and haughtiness. Virtue without talent might not bring about great work or help many people financially, but it will truthfully bring long-lasting peace and happiness to our minds. When we have true peace and happiness, those qualities will radiate to everyone around through our attitude toward life. It does not necessarily take a great deal of talent to accomplish it. Be calm and reflect! Don't be engrossed in running after general tendencies; instead, be brave and come back to arouse our true worth to go forward steadily.

Remember that the mind is the source of all happy and suffering emotions, and the situation only plays the role of an agent. So instead of running after crazy or delusive thoughts and trying our hardest to catch one object after another, we should come back and make unnecessary or unreasonable demands in our minds disappear. Even in this moment when our minds is very disturbed or falling to a very low level for having made numerous mistakes, with determination and practice to improve our bodies and minds correctly, we will certainly recover from those wounds. We will also recover the ownership of our lives. Believe in the originally pure and wonderful nature of our self. It never gets damaged or destroyed.

Minh Niem

> *Don't mourn sorrowful sights*
> *Changes are necessary in life*
> *Flowers wither then bloom again*
> *In the old garden sweet scent will remain*

29

Will Power

Will power is only ambition if it is not put into the training framework of our own selves.

The strength of will power

A little boy was assigned the job of getting to the schoolhouse early to light up the fireplace before the arrival of his teacher and friends. One morning, everyone was shocked to see the schoolhouse in flames. The boy was seriously burned when he was pulled out of the fire. He was taken to a hospital nearby. A few days later, the doctor told his mother that he would die because the lower part of his body had been destroyed. Faintly hearing this while he was semi-conscious, he was in tears but was determined to survive. And he overcame death miraculously to the doctor's surprise. The danger was past for the time, but the doctor informed him that his lower body part was injured so badly that he would be a cripple for life with useless legs. Once again the boy suffered, but he still cultivated a will to walk steadily as before.

Though his emaciated legs had no feeling, no control, and no life, he was not discouraged. He confined himself in the wheelchair all day and never stopped finding ways to exercise. One morning he suddenly threw himself out of the wheelchair, dragged his body to a grassy area with his two legs trailing. His mother was surprised to see him reaching the fence surrounding the house and swinging himself to stand up to lean against the fence. Just like that, every day the boy dragged himself from one fence post to another, making a trail around the fence. He always told himself that he would walk again someday. Eventually, thanks to his mother's loving hands and his strong will, he could pull himself up, then limped one step at a time, and then walked by himself. And then he could run. He began to walk to school, run to school, and then run to the university campus he had long dreamed about. In particular, he joined the school's track team. The young man everybody thought could never live, could never walk, could never run was Dr. Glenn Cunningham—the fastest man in the world for the one-mile race.

When we have the intention to do something and firmly believe that is within our ability to complete it, sooner or later this will immediately turn into a strong force to push us through all obstacles. This is will power. That means when we keep repeating in our minds the will to carry out a task, our nervous system will automatically generate an internal command continuously, and find ways to arouse and connect with potential forces to achieve the result. Therefore, self-confidence is the foundation to build will power. There will not be will power without self-confidence. To believe in ourselves is to believe in our real strength already available, and also to believe in the forces that are still potential and will be aroused through the training and nurturing process. There are times when we do not see any sign that it is possible to transform "impossible" things into "possible" things. There are also times when everyone thinks those things are impractical or have never been done before. However, we can still achieve spectacular success if we firmly believe that anything can happen when we find the right conditions to create it.

To believe that anything can happen is to believe in causes and conditions, in the wonderful connections of the energy sources with the same wavelength. Those forces often include the ancestors' blessing and virtues and even the energy that the universe sends to us on loan. Naturally we must have appropriate causes and conditions for these connections. This depends on the accumulated energies that we created in the past and the notable transformations in the present. This means when we first set our minds on something, we gather up all energies to come back to ourselves in order to continuously arouse all good energies not yet produced and nourish those already produced. At the same time, we also try to isolate bad energies not yet produced and find ways to quickly transform those already produced. Before setting our minds on something, we might not understand all our available strength, but during the training process we will discover the wonderful mysteries of our whole selves. Sometimes it only takes one certain point to be cleared for countless other favorable conditions to be pulled along right away. Sometimes those conditions lie right in the middle of a difficult situation and this is when our survival instincts can bring out deep potential forces that we normally cannot see. For this reason, it is often said that those with will power will always see opportunities in all difficulties while those lacking will power will always see difficulties in all opportunities. Successful people, therefore, overcome not only situations but actually overcome their own self and can find their own greatness.

Arousing will power

People with will power must first be optimistic, and always look at the bright side of life. Though they might be facing a big event, optimists believe all difficulties will pass if we can make maximum use of favorable aspects, no matter how few. To be optimistic, we must have the right view of the nature of life; we must have the ability to overcome old knowledge and understanding that have solidified into fixed views and prejudices deep within us. We also must have the ability to observe carefully all things and all facts around us with a true attitude of discovery.

The secret of creating an optimistic spirit, therefore, is to practice ways to enjoy life. When we temporarily take one step back to observe the wonderful values of life, we will see that nature always embraces great lessons that only those bold enough to get detached from an ego eager for self-justification can fully understand. Those lessons can be seen in the vitality of the cherry blossoms in the freezing cold, the flexible gentleness of the bamboo in stormy weather, the bees' harmonious working principle, or even the unity spirit of the ants. Nature not only shows us the road to success but also the art of living, so we can have the joy of living right in the present before reaching success. This spirit is necessary to cultivate success.

The time living with nature and enjoying life is also a valuable opportunity for us to look back at ourselves. This is why those who set their minds on something great often go on retreats to "polish their piece of jade," instead of busily accumulating temporary favorable conditions from outside. When the jade is shiny, there is no need to worry about crises or adversities anymore. We are strong enough to overcome them and moreover to look at them from a different level of perception. We will know clearly what to do and what not to do to make dreams become reality. Actually, when our jade is polished, all those energies of the same wavelength will automatically connect together without us having to look for them. Therefore the process of polishing jade is the most important and most difficult task. We will have to leave behind great enjoyments. We even have to put ourselves in a strict regimen to save our energy for health, to build endurance, and especially to transform harmful habits.

We have seen many people with the will to reach high, but actually they have only tried to collect favorable conditions from the outside and make no changes within their own self. Their level of understanding and ability to endure stay the same. Their dreams of reaching faraway goals in the end are still beautiful dreams only. Therefore, will power will just be an ambition if not placed within the training framework of the self. That attitude is the desire to have more than what we have, but not having enough energy to arouse potential forces in order to overcome our present limitations.

We should not forget that the energy inside us grows strong or weak at times, so our will power is not always steadfast. But we should not worry. That is only the return of our habit of enjoyment, our hope for a sign of improvement or the pressure of a situation that intensifies abruptly. All are temporary phenomena. We just need to adhere to our practice steadily or try a little harder and everything will pass. We will get a new valuable experience after that effort. Those people who never have the habit of acting from emotions, always live deeply in the here and now, look back at their own self, and have experienced difficult situations are people who have netted more than half of the decisive factors to make their dreams come true. Therefore, the jade polishing of the ego should be done at a young age when character shaping can be done easily. The habit of enjoyment not only weakens us, it also turns us into addicts and covers us with a thick dusty layer of ignorance.

When we say, "I'm always right," we are being conservative, but when we say "I always believe in myself," we are respecting ourselves. This is a valuable trait not everyone can have. Lacking in constitution, talent, or having suffered serious failures tends to make us lose self-confidence and have a pessimistic view of all issues in life. The poet Frederick Langbridge once wrote: "Two men look out through the same bars, one sees the mud and one the stars." For our look to always be vast and immense, in addition to eliminating old prejudices, we have to overcome shallow emotions or pressuring our self to be this or that and the inability to accept ourselves and the present situation. Accept in order not to create more pressure, to understand deeply, to find ways to transform, and not to give up. Will power when not cleverly used will become a beautiful velvet curtain to cover up our true weakness and create fascinating but imaginary plays produced by the mind.

Few people expect that will power itself not only can create extraordinary things but can also help other amazing things come out. That is because one person's success becomes a great source of encouragement for another person's self-confidence to arise, heading for "the impossible" things. So for "the impossible" to become "the possible," besides our own effort to reach high, we also have the support energy of successful people before us and even the loving-kindness of the universe. Therefore when we succeed, we have the responsibility of returning those favors a humble attitude and always helping other people. In so doing, we can maintain our success. Because our whole being is non-self, the will power is also non-self. Don't turn it into a gorgeous piece of jewelry to glorify our petty self and look down on those who are still weak.

Any peak is attainable
When reaching beyond ourselves is possible
On the long road, tirelessly we keep walking
Thanks to the delightful joy of travelling

30

Hesitation

Don't worry too much about the road we have chosen or must choose because what is truly important is our attitude walking on that road.

Which choice is correct?

Life sometimes leads us to unforeseen causes and conditions causing us to face choices that can take us to a new turn in our lives. Not knowing what that turn is going to be like, we always have to be careful not to make a wrong and regrettable decision. However, there are many times when we know very well the true value of the road we must take, but we still cannot decide because we cannot overcome our own limitations. Sometimes we are greedy, wanting to "catch two fish with two hands," so we cannot bear to let go of our favorite good emotions. And maybe because of being shy and lacking self-confidence, we are afraid we might make a wrong choice or are not strong enough to cope, and have to suffer losses in the end. Of course we have to accept our wavering, see-saw position when facing a choice with both sides as our favorite. This is really a struggle that sometimes only an attitude of sacrifice can solve. If a situation requires a decision but we still hesitate and deliberate too long, the energy within us will quickly be destroyed. Then we might lose a good opportunity, or lose everything in addition to not gaining anything.

One meditation master happened to see a seriously wounded dog lying still by the roadside. Feeling sorry, he took it home for treatment and adoption. The master loved and taught the dog with great devotion. He gave it the name Tu Di (Improve Yourself) in hope that it would practice the religious way for a peaceful life. In return, the dog loved him like a parent, always hanging around him. Whenever the master went to town for Dharma teaching, it would trail along behind. Whenever he sat in meditation, it would lie with half-closed eyes beside him. One day, while he was meditating, the dog suddenly detected a familiar smell of meat being stir-fried somewhere. It was about to spring up but thought it had better not, since it had been practicing with the master for many years. So it lay down again and tried to forget the temptation. But the smell of the stir-fried meat intensified more and more. The dog stirred many times then thought it ought to go and check things out. The smell became more and more tempting. The dog could not control its old instinct, so it decided to swim across the river once to find out.

The meditation master heard the sound of the dog jumping down into the river. Guessing what was going on, he rushed to dissuade it. "Hey! Tu Di! Don't go to the other side. It's very dangerous!" The dog, startled at the sound of the master's voice, obediently turned around. But at that time it could smell the stir-fried meat very close by and its craving also heightened, so it turned its face and swam on noiselessly. The master urgently called again: "Hey, Tu Di! Come back to me, baby! This place is simple but safer!" At that time, images of the master's affection and loving care throughout the past flashed back in his mind, competing with the tempting images of the stir-fried meat it had not enjoyed for a long time. Therefore it kept swimming back and forth, unable to make up its mind. Finally it got exhausted and drowned in the middle of the river.

It was uncertain if the dog would have faced danger on the other side of the river. The meditation master only based his concern and warnings on popular knowledge of the dog's past experience of having been seriously injured. It might not have been true. Even if it were true, the dog still could have protected itself and changed the situation around in an interesting way with its intelligence and skill. We do not always understand completely our chosen road when we make a decision. It would be great if we could predict half of it correctly. We have to continue discovering the remaining part throughout our journeys.

During this journey, sometimes we see that we do not need to reach our goal quickly. The road itself can bring us many valuable experiences to prepare and reach other goals more deeply. Hence there are cases when it is not necessary to spend too much energy hesitating and trying to make up our minds. Any road is fine if we have enough faith in our true ability, or if we want to accumulate experiences and train our selves instead of competing for success and failure. Maintaining such a spirit, we will never turn ourselves into a follower of "hesitation-ism." Choosing a wrong road might not be dangerous, but constant hesitation might destroy our futures.

Those who choose love over filial piety or idealism over family must feel great anguish, regret and maybe loss. However they do not think that when they have completed their chosen path well, they have gone together with their parents. Because if they live in happiness, in love, know how to apply valuable lessons taught by their parents to build a lasting family, always try to make peace with their parents, or advise their children to remember their ancestors, then choosing love or idealism is more worthy than staying close to their parents but acting insolently or hurting them often. Even when they have to break their word with someone to choose another, they still can make up or share the pain of the person left behind if they always venerate that person's loving-kindness in a certain noble place in their heart.

Even if they spend all their life serving society, bringing peace and happiness to everyone, in their deep nature they are still actively serving their family. When their mind turns to their family, it means the accumulated energy inside them from their services is also transmitted to their loved ones. That energy can soothe and protect them from mishaps and bad luck. This image was beautifully described in the poem "*Seeing-off Song*" by the poet Tham Tam: *"Better think of my mother as a falling leaf/ Better think of my sister as a speck of dust/ Better think of my sweetheart as an intoxicating bouquet of wine."* Although the soldier thought this might be a permanent departure and asked his loved ones to consider him gone forever and not to miss him or remember him longingly, but actually from that point of time his image remained deep in their minds more than ever before. An attitude of lingering, uncertain departure will not be able to generate that kind of sacred feeling.

As a result, we should not worry too much about the road we have chosen or have to choose because what is truly important is our attitude walking on that road. Though the starting point is not very good, with time we will learn ways to accept and find "the heart" of the chosen road. No road is extremely good and no road is completely bad. The question is whether we are capable enough to use that road to serve our main goal or not. Without enough talent or skill, there are only problems and obstacles everywhere we look, and even a good chosen road would turn ordinary. Even when we fall into the situation of being "in a dilemma when to advance and retreat"—any road is full of obstacles, dangers, and can bring us bad emotions—we should still try to step forward. Maybe when we advance deeper into the interior, we will see it's quite different from the exterior, and the deeper we get, the more we discover our great potential. Therefore in order to accomplish a great goal we need to overcome the attitude of enjoying good emotions and avoiding bad ones. Jade can only be found in rocks.

Don't miss the appointment with life

It is true that no one knows all the keys to success. But if we have a thorough grasp of some basic experiences plus existing favorable conditions and especially a steady spirit to receive possible bad luck or failure, we should be bold enough to make a decision. That risk-taking is the great courage to help us succeed. That courage, of course, must be born from a foundation of experience and clear perception instead of an unrealistic dream. But it is the faith in our self—faith in the ability to cope with all failures to discover life mysteries as well as our own potential—that is the important factor helping us go forward with daring decisions. If we lack that courage, even if favorable conditions have almost fully converged at hand, we would still hesitate and continue to wait for better conditions. We should not forget that causes and conditions change constantly like flowing water, a second later is no longer a second before, for as the philosopher Heraclitus said: *"You cannot step into the same river twice."* If we keep sitting in the same place to analyze, compare, hesitate and deliberate, we will lose many valuable opportunities in life. This we will regret.

The most precious opportunity of human beings is life. Many times we have been startled seeing our youth years passing by indifferently so we keep telling ourselves to try to come back and take care of our hearts, to live more harmoniously and deeply. And many times we have missed our appointment. Unable to overcome our desire for physical comfort, enjoyment, and people's admiration, we have wasted much time and energy. We do not have a few hundred years to live, so why do we still let our lives flow in indulgence and forgetfulness? The venerable poet

Nguyen Du used to remind us: *"We see each other clearly now/ Who knows it might be a dream later on?"* Who knows whether our loved ones and we can see each other again tomorrow? If we still use the excuse of being too busy to stop and look at each other closely, open our hearts to forgive and support each other, then tomorrow everything might just be a dream. Dreams are caused by our ignorance and indecisive attitude. They are not the nature of life.

To form the habit of living deeply every moment, we should practice right away with everyday activities. Every morning when we wake up, we should not get out of bed quickly. Instead, we should sit up neatly, breathe deeply a few times to be conscious that we are still here and alive. Silently thank heaven and earth for giving us another day to live, a brand new day that we have the right to live with all our might. Yesterday maybe we were clumsy in talking, behaving or thinking that made both us and our loved ones unhappy. Luckily now we have another day to correct those mistakes. We promise ourselves to make good use of the whole day, not to let worries or afflictions harm or hurt another minute or hour anymore.

Beginning a new day with a cheerful smile on our lips will bring us much happiness and life force. We should write the word "smile" and post it on a wall, or put a flower by our bedside as a reminder for us to smile as soon as we get up to welcome life. We will remember that today we have an appointment with life as a messenger of loving-kindness. Anywhere and anytime we are conscious of being alive, we should smile; we will feel gentle in spirit and our facial muscles will also relax. The smile will help us live with ourselves in the present moment because when we smile, all worries and stress will be gone. The smile will wake up peaceful energy inside us and others; therefore it brings us closer to everyone and everything around.

Those are very practical things that we can do without having to hesitate and think hard. When we really have a grasp on life and don't let temporary emotions of like and dislike pull us down to endless irresolution, we will have enough insight, faith, and strength to advance to other great decisions. Don't forget that hesitation never shows up on the menu of those who know how to enjoy life.

Minh Niem

> *The road is not really far*
> *But there might be many shores of delusion*
> *Walking is hard because of hesitation*
> *The months and years pass by wearily*

31

Failure

> *If we realize that we are not firm enough yet, we should not be in a hurry to long for success. We should cheerfully live the "not yet successful" period of time as a welcome opportunity to develop endurance and transform our character.*

Everyone fears failure

Everyone seems to fear failure because it can cause us to lose property, energy, faith, and even hope. In general, failure always brings bad emotions, while human instinct only enjoys good emotions. How bad emotions manifest and affect people's quality of life depends on each person's view of life and their reaction to failure. If we think we will never fail because of our plentiful talent and skill or that failure is a terribly bad thing, then when we face it unexpectedly, we certainly will panic and fight back. We will have to clean up the aftermath of that failure, find ways to save face, and then worry about some unfortunate situations in the future. It is this kind of attitude that turns failure into affliction, drowning our lives.

It might also be because we are not yet used to failure, or have never failed so badly before, therefore we easily get perplexed and hold on to one person after another. Someone who just lost a job will look for another job right away; someone who accidentally ruined a great work will quickly start a new piece of work. Someone who just got jilted will speedily find another person to love. But the majority of what we try to hold on to while experiencing the emotion of failure is regrettable mistakes. The truth is we are just finding ways to soothe and hide our hurt feelings or attempting to affirm our worth. Certainly we have not yet invested our time and effort correctly and seriously for success. Tragedy always happens during such emotional explosions because that choice was not enlightened by reason.

Because of outside failures, quite a few people have tried to find their self on a spiritual path. The method of transformative practice should help them rehabilitate and recover quickly, but the wound will not heal when they hastily set big transformation goals they have to achieve soon. They mistakenly think that it is an attitude showing a determination to aim high, but actually they are just consolidating their worth. They have to do something to prove their talent or survival. In the situation of depleted energy overloaded with a new ambition, even a valid one, how can they have energy to fight on? The harder they try, the more energy they burn, and it is only natural that they would fail miserably. A snowball rolling down from a mountain top often accumulates more snow on the way, so by the time it gets to the foot of the mountain, it becomes a giant ball with a terrible power of destruction. This is the *"snowball effect."*

Only not yet successful

We should know that success must gather countless appropriate conditions, and we can't always take the lead capturing them all because they might be completely beyond our reach. Even when conditions for success lie within ourselves and seem easy to catch, but without enough experience and insight, we would not know what to add or subtract to make it happen. This is only natural. If everybody knows all the keys to success, human beings would no longer be human beings and this world would become a paradise. So when something fails, we should understand that the conditions for success are not quite right yet, maybe they are too much or not enough, but they are not exactly empty or nonsense.

The word "failure" is often misunderstood as not accomplishing anything or having nothing left. But what we have built is still there, even though sometimes it does not yet show in a practical way. Training skills, accumulated experiences and knowledge, as well as favorable factors from the outside that we have gathered will be used appropriately in succeeding successful work. Therefore when we succeed we should understand that this success is standing on the shoulder of numerous failures in the past. This is the meaning of a well-remembered saying *"Failure is the mother of success."* Lasting success is usually made from small failures initially. So from now on we should practice saying "not yet successful" instead of "failure." This way will help us from feeling depressed easily because we are conscious that opportunities have not ended, that if we lose this time we can still try another time. There never is an absolute separation between the before and the after.

Actually, failure is a very important part of life. When failing, we will withdraw ourselves. Although weighed down with very uncomfortable feelings, we have a good opportunity to look back at ourselves more deeply. At least the haughtiness, competitiveness or subjectivity inside us will decrease somewhat. Experienced people always worry when they see young people succeed too easily, especially when their successes are mainly due to good luck from the outside. They have not tasted the terrible flavor of failure or their ego has not been bruised in troubled times and then not knowing what to do. They also have not woken up and nurtured precious qualities in their heart such as loving-kindness or modesty to build mental stability. Therefore big success might develop into disaster for their own life and the people around them. We have witnessed many youngsters achieving resounding successes that die down quickly. They might reach the point when they dare not face life any more, have to seclude themselves forever, or in some cases choose a tragic ending.

Furthermore, human instinct is naturally strong. Only when facing serious failures will that energy source completely emerge. This is when human beings become stronger than ever. So do not fear failure. If we realize that we are not strong enough yet, we should not be in a hurry to long for success. We should cheerfully live the "not yet successful" period of time as a welcome opportunity to develop our endurance and transform our character. This is why those with ability and intellect often reject favorable conditions and look for harsh situations to maximize all their potential abilities. They disregard success that only brings them an ordinary sense of satisfaction to choose greater ones that triumph over the suffering shadows within them. This is authentic success.

Smile with failures

When we experience failure, the most important thing that we should do, which is also the most difficult, is to reflect on our reaction. We should try to take note of what is going on in our stream of emotions and thoughts without using our will power to suppress or reject them. We need to understand deeply the present psychological condition to evaluate accurately our inner strength. Then we can decide whether to suffer by ourselves, or to ask our loved ones for help and support instead of trying to cover up to protect our honor or to lean on others for consolation. To be able to do this, we need to practice daily the habit of always reflecting on ourselves everywhere and every time. Achieving this is already considerable progress, but if we can look back with an unprejudiced attitude, that look will reach the point where we can understand thoroughly the nature of all problems. It is possible that we might recognize our own suffering as the cause of all failures. Circumstances might have an impact but only play a secondary role.

Ambition is the suffering that often manifests the most in times of failures. Always aroused by social consciousness, we want to keep up with everyone else, although we are not sure if we need those items or if we can afford them. Ambition can cause the mind to squeeze out unfounded self-confidence. And we tend to let the desire for success take over easily instead of searching through our accumulated experiences and knowledge for ingredients that would contribute to success. If we use all of our energy just to satisfy a desire, then it is a very immature action seriously influenced by emotions. Whenever we notice that our greed is active, we should smile cheerfully to confirm that we can see it clearly and therefore it cannot fool us anymore. Maintain that observation to help it return to its selfless nature.

Accepting failure is a very important attitude that brings us closer to all living beings. It is a necessary condition in the process of taming the ego to reach perfection. When we can overcome a wounded psyche and self-consciousness about our weak egos, we have overcome more than half of our suffering from failure because the nature of failure is not necessarily suffering. Once in a while we should also ask ourselves whether we should keep holding on to exterior success, and whether it is the decisive condition for our happiness in the present. Then we can retrieve all the-scattered energies that have created the extraordinary strength within ourselves. Let us not forget that exterior failure, no matter how big, is only a part of life and cannot jeopardize the wonderful qualities we are holding in our hands.

> *Success and failure come and go*
> *The spring years continue to flow*
> *The smile on the lips is waiting,*
> *When comes the time for giving?*

32

Success

In this life there is no great or small success, only the kind that brings temporary emotions or the true happiness.

What kind of success?

When asked about success, we often think of our careers right way. This is easy to understand because income and social position have a great influence on the life of most people. Especially nowadays the global economy is in serious recession with many companies shutting down, many groups going bankrupt, and countless people being unemployed, the word "success" has become the most sensitive issue that no one dares to mention. But why don't we ask someone or ask ourselves what kind of success did we achieve? Success must be defined within a specific scope or area, not just in everything.

Suppose we are enjoying expensive and luxurious comforts or holding a social position that many dream about. We would not hesitate to acknowledge our success then. But while enjoying those things, our family happiness collapses, our loved ones depart, and our friends lose faith in us, do we still claim success? Yes, we have succeeded in a material way, but completely failed in our emotional life. Or suppose we regard love as the best thing in life and defy everything else to throw ourselves after it like a maniac. We spend countless hours, a lot of money and endless energy to catch it. We neglect our self, our job, or our important relationships around us to pamper it. We develop jealousy, narrow-mindedness or readiness to fight others to possess it. Once the object of our love belongs to us, are we really successful? Yes, we have succeeded in conquering others, but have failed with ourselves.

Which success is worth looking for?

When we go to town nowadays, we can't help feeling dazed at the sight of the large crowds in which everyone seems stressed and in a hurry as if they are running after something. If they do not know where they are going or who just scurried past, then how can they look at one another tenderly or give each other a sweet smile? They sit next to each other on the bus for hours but no one bothers to start a conversation because everyone seems very busy with plans or projects in their head. They meet daily at work, but they cannot stop to greet and wait for answers because they feel they would lose a few precious moments. Instead, they squeeze in time to read daily newspapers and go online to search for information because that would be practical and useful and an indispensable part of life. It is so extraordinary.

Many people, on the other hand, do not like others to inquire after them. They think the presence of others is not necessary and might interfere with their freedom. They do not want to tell others about their failure, or they are suspicious that others might find ways to compete or defeat them. For this reason, the business world nowadays has become a fierce battlefield in which those lacking shrewdness and ingenious tricks have to resign themselves to be vanquished. Hence human beings turn themselves into machines more and more every day and gradually lose emotional ties with each other. When they can no longer bear that kind of mechanical and superficial life, they tuck themselves within the shell of loneliness and coldness and make very wrong decisions. That kind of success really carries with it the character of destruction.

When our property is destroyed, we still have opportunities to recover it or other meaningful reasons to live, but once the sacred qualities in our hearts, such as peace, sympathy, honesty, modesty, etc., go bankrupt, we may not be able to restore them for the rest of our lives. A person without virtue is truly a miserable loser. Living without love or not being loved is no different from a hungry ghost. Therefore we should not be dazed or depressed when failing in the economic war. If we can still sit peacefully to drink cups of hot tea, to talk to friends intimately, still have patience to listen to our loved ones' difficulties, still feel touched by the miseries of life, are still eager to stand up and protect the weak and the unfortunate, then we should rejoice. To our family, society, and even this world, we have been successful in the mission of human life.

Nowadays, many youngsters are afraid to enter life after receiving their college degree. They think they must continue to get more knowledge and more certificates before they can have the self-confidence to enter the doors of success. Sociologists, meanwhile, often remind us that schools only supply us 25% of knowledge while life experience provides us 75% of the knowledge we need to accumulate. It is because of the confusion between the means of life and the goal of life that many generations of students are puzzled to the point of crisis about choosing a direction for their life after graduating from college. They dare not enter life because they fear being worsted by others, not being the prime choice of famous companies. They also fear that they will not easily win over powerful figures in society. To them, they must succeed when entering life. However, how many youngsters follow their career to find true happiness or find ways to protect the environment, help the poor, or how to maintain their people's cultural traditions, or help the community grow stronger?

Those questions are always considered far out and impractical. In their head, youngsters always think of ways to make a lot of money or show people their talent. Only then do they feel themselves valuable. Many youngsters grasp at the first opportunity to advance. Those with no real strength also try to jostle in and find ways to polish their name. They even dare to cause embarrassing scandals to attract public attention. To them, it is a big success just to get attention from many people. But, dear friends, where will that success lead you? It is true that we all need comforts in life, but if we cannot connect and take care of the wonderful values in our hearts, we will find this life insipid and empty. The happy emotion of that success will pass quickly, leaving us with a terribly lonely space that nothing can fill.

Looking at many past generations, we should carefully rethink our goal to be striven for and our present attitude toward life. We should be smart to come back and discover ourselves in order to be the master of our lives. This is the most necessary success. Learn ways to calm our thoughts. Do not let the mind think idly or worry uselessly. Try to practice controlling anger. Look for and transform part of harmful energy such as greed, selfishness, pettiness, or irresponsible ways of living. We should try to arouse potential and valuable energy that can bring us moments of relaxation and peace right in the present. We should successfully practice walking with relaxed steps, eating cozy meals with our family, or listening deeply to the difficulties of others. We should begin with those near and dear successes. Truthfully, there is no great or small success in this life, only the kind that brings temporary emotions or the true value of happiness.

Mountains are forever steady and strong
Snow can cover and fog can veil no matter how long
Have we found our own stand?
Or are we still bustling around on land?

33

Ambition

If our ambition causes us to be confused about the value of life, whether or not that ambition is fulfilled, we will not find true meaning and happiness.

From greed to ambition

Thinking that favorable conditions from outside will create lasting happiness, we always desire more than what we have. Though we know that those wishes are impractical, beyond our reach, even at a very high cost, we still want to get them by any means. This is ambition. Such ambition begins in the greedy mind, which is one of human beings' biggest afflictions. It is an affliction because it always makes us suffer, whether we can grasp it or not. When a desire is satisfied, our minds will get addicted to it and instantly increase its capacity for enjoyment, pressuring us to keep adding an appropriate amount to fill that greater capacity. And when our desires are not met, our minds will protest and resist the outcome that we are reluctantly accepting. So the greedy mind is just another aspect of the angry mind, both of which come from the ignorant mind. Not knowing what true happiness is is the most dreadful ignorance of mankind.

Throughout the ups and downs of history, human beings have eventually figured out that all the satisfactions from material possessions, power, fame and lust are only temporary. If we define this as happiness, then indeed there is no true happiness in this world. It is true that the nature of all things on Earth is impermanence—acquire then lose, succeed then fail, be together then be apart. The more we pursue this kind of happiness, the more we waste our energy because we can never own it for long. Therefore, to overcome the domination of impermanence, we should come back to our minds to discover the truth and take refuge there instead of turning outward to chase external objects. Once we have the ability to purify the energy of wanting things to go our way, all other afflictions will have no more foundation on which to exist. That state of complete absence of desire is true happiness, the kind that always exists within each of us.

In reality, our minds frequently change. It is only a phenomenon, a result of the process of looking around and leaning toward attractive external targets. However, it will stop and agreeably turn inward only after enough time to cut off its addiction to emotions prompted by external objects. Gradually it will transform, with only calmness and clarity remaining. Actually, only the energy of greedy habits is disintegrated. Like other kinds of afflictions, our greedy minds are the consequence of the erroneous workings of our psychological processes, and so long as the potential ability of those erroneous psychological processes is still there, so long is the opportunity for the greedy mind's return. We call the greedy mind "the seed of greed" to show that it is the result of what was created before, but it has not been observable or has not manifest all its power inside when it has not gathered enough supporting conditions. The greed energy of each person is different, but once it is reduced to the potential state of the seed, it is the same in everyone. This is similar to everyone's having the potential for cancer, but cancer won't develop unless there are other factors.

Even after someone has become a saint (bodhisattva), the seeds of affliction remain only as potentiality. But a saint has transformed their energy part and elevated the mind to a higher level. Once they have reached the most harmonious position between them and the universe, they will not fall back to the old level of perception any more. That means a saint's chances of returning to the ignorant mind or to the greedy mind is 0%. Anybody can become a saint.

Going beyond our reach

It is often thought that people without ambition are those without great goals or the ability to accomplish great work. It is also believed that society cannot develop if everyone lives with a complacent attitude. But what should we develop? It is correct to think that without ambition, we cannot develop our material life, but this is completely wrong in terms of building spiritual values. Looking deeply at social reality, perhaps everyone realizes that the more modern human beings become, the more bewildered they feel about the destiny of their life. They do not know where to go for peace and happiness. They vie hard with each other pursuing their ambitions by relying on their talents and skills. And they believe they have found a position very worthy of the never-ending craving of their ego. We have seen many people who are ready to let go of their conscience, to ignore close relationships and even to make enemies or kill each other only because they want to encroach on each other's claims. Cheating, lying, betrayal, jealousy, corruption, and then mental crisis, or imprisonment, are all caused by such ambition.

Another truth that everyone has to recognize is that with society getting more urbanized and modernized, human beings are getting busier and busier to the point they do not have time to take a rest. Why is this? Nobody makes us busy. Only because we want to keep up with everyone on the road to luxurious pleasures do we have to spend a lot of time planning, competing, catching, and keeping. If we have no time to nurture and begin our selves anew, how can we understand clearly and help our loved ones around us effectively. The more society develops attractive conveniences, the more human ambition is aroused and grows. Many times we have spent dozens of years working hard not to increase our level of material enjoyment, but for a reason that is not proper to mention—the desire to be recognized and admired. Nowadays people with the most power are thought to be the richest and have the most influence on society. Even when we become tired and bored with admiration, we still do not stop pursuing our ambitions. Through them, we can see our value, and chasing them is easier than returning to ourselves.

For those returning to develop a spiritual life, the greedy mind is the biggest obstacle. Though we can let go of some familiar objects of the greedy mind such as money, power, fame, and lust, it still continues to find other subtler and deeper objects to cling to. Without an object to hold on to, the mind easily gets lost and feels that life has no meaning. That first object is purity—always wanting to become a person very different from ordinary people. The next object is transformation—always wanting to improve as soon as we enter the spiritual pathway, even though the energy of afflictions from the past is still abundant. The last object is enlightenment—always wanting to become enlightened soon and be a saint (bodhisattva). This is the loftiest goal of practicing self-improvement.

Of course if we do not lay down these subtle desires, we will not have a strong motive to overcome obstacles in order to reach the ultimate goal quickly. Actually, in the transformation process, each step forward gives us a taste of happiness right away, so we do not need to rush to the end of the road. Wanting the absolute is only because we have not found true value in the relative. Therefore we just need to go on the right path, with a diligent and calm attitude like being in synchronous harmony with the universe, and then with time and favorable causes and conditions, we will reach the goal. That means attaining the goal is only the natural outcome of a correct process, not because we want it. The more we want, the more we go wrong. Practicing the path is not changing the ego self into something special, but simply to help it work accurately again.

Coming back to nourish the spiritual life is a proper attitude, but without receiving proper guidance we will easily fall into our own trap of ambition. The more we practice the path, the more we are caught and the more we struggle in affliction, and we do not understand why. There are also many people who always place their faith in externalities, so they often dream of a faraway, perfect world full of the noblest conditions, which they do not have to work hard to build. Many ambitious people almost die for some very real and achievable things in the present. Many ambitious people are driven into misery by goals that are realistic and achievable in this life. Those people with ambitious goals and dreams that are unrealistic tend to treat the other aspects of their life as useless. If our ambition causes us to be confused about the value of life, whether or not that ambition is fulfilled, we will not find true meaning and happiness. Because that value belongs to the subtle perception of the heart, ambition can only bring us satisfaction, not happiness. Ironically we have lost those precious qualities of the heart on our journey toward the goals of our ambition.

Greedy but not greedy

Actually the nature of ambition is not all bad. It can destroy us only when we are not strong or skillful enough. Like a sharp knife that is very useful but can cut our hands if we are not careful. Although not everyone with ambition gets destroyed by it, the number of people who can transform it into a useful tool for them and for life is very small. Though we see in the daily news many pictures of successful people accomplishing great work, the truth is only these people and their loved ones can understand what kind of situation they are living in. Are they still themselves, or have they "sold their soul to the devil" and become dictatorial, arrogant, suspicious, discriminating, shrewd, absent-minded, or fearful? That is too high a price to pay for the huge delusion about their talent. Therefore anyone can have ambition, but not everyone has enough ability to fulfill it.

Of course we have the right to set ambitious goals or great ideals, but the important thing is we need to evaluate accurately our real strength so as not to create wishes of a delusive nature. Once we have formally set goals, we have to gather at least five conditions in order to fulfill our ambition without it destroying us. First, try diligently to improve our skills and learn from our predecessors' experiences. Second, always carefully observe the entanglements of our greedy minds throughout the journey; when we notice it is being unduly influenced by the circumstances and is going beyond our plan and control, we should stop it right away. Third, create a balance between our normal life and our ambition, which means having the ability to live deeply in the present, although we are turning toward our targeted goal. Fourth, be clearly aware that this ambition is not the only reason for us to see our true worth, so we will not despair and suffer in case we cannot fulfill it. Fifth, always remember that we have to lean on countless favorable external conditions to help us fulfill our ambition, so we will not be proud and haughty when our goal is reached.

Having the ability to control our ambition in such a serene way means we have reached the *non-greed* level—greedy but not greedy, which we may want to distinguish by the word "aspirational."

If "greedy but not greedy" or aspirational just to enjoy a little more honor or to see our worth, then what might we aspire to achieve? There is one very worthy reason for us to develop "ambition with courage," and that is to serve everybody. Wishing and dreaming to contribute to building a society of awareness, understanding and love is a kind of ambition, which we may distinguish by "aspiration." But if society keeps losing such big-hearted and courageous people, with everyone caring only for a comfortable life or fighting for their own interests, then in what direction will society be heading and what will the future of humanity become? However, let's remember that when we walk on the road of service, we will find happiness. And the great aspiration of service needs many hands to join forces to fulfill it instead of just our own talent. Therefore, the nature of non-greed is also non-self. "Greed" that is not serving our own selfish ego is the act of a great person with a noble mind, great knowledge, and great love.

We feel ashamed watching the moon
For we have left the vast ocean too soon
Our boat knows not which ferry to enter
So busily flowing down the river

34

Knowing When Is Enough

The material world only brings us more pleasant comforts in life; it is not the most important reason for us to live.

Where is the future heading?

In the last two decades, some sociological and psychological research has shown there is no key connection between earned income and the level of personal satisfaction. People feel frustrated when they spend so much time and energy making money, but the feeling of happiness is shallow and disappears very quickly. Gradually people no longer believe in and define the sensation of material satisfaction as happiness. They have become aware that money not only cannot buy happiness, it can also destroy it.

Indeed it is so. The time we were eager to develop the industry to mass-produce high quality products to serve our increasing demand for comfort was also the time we began to lose our control of life. The time used to do our jobs leaves us very little time for our most basic human activities. We have all the comforts but we can't enjoy them fully. We are always busy with work and customers. We have no time to take care of our health, to talk to others, to learn more life experience, to prepare family meals, to listen to and understand deeply our loved ones. The worst results are never-ending ambition, and the collapse of virtue and moral qualities.

With time, we are gradually turning into robots, no longer feeling what is manifesting in our stream of emotions, in our consciousness, and the wonderful values of life going on around us. Yet we always believe we are building a very solid and bright future. How can we grasp the future if we cannot grasp the on-going present? Many a time when someone asked us if we enjoyed last autumn, we were surprised like a stranger just arriving from somewhere else: "What? Fall came already? I was too busy to notice it." Then we had no concern or regret, because paying attention to the seasons was a kind of luxurious pleasure and not businesslike. It seems anything we do nowadays is very carefully planned to see if it can bring any income or profit.

Sometimes we think that it is worth sacrificing our lives for the happiness of our children and grandchildren. But the inheritance for our youngsters is not necessarily a very big bank account. What they need most is for their loved ones to show concern, to understand and share their problems as well as their dreams in life. They need a happy family to lean on and learn from. The wealth inherited from their parents is a benefit, however they might rely on it too much, and then become too lazy to challenge themselves and easily throw themselves into hedonism. In the end, the parents made sacrifices for their children but got blamed by them instead of appreciation. The children may doubt if their parents really tried to make money for them rather than to satisfy their irresistible desire to be rich. Those youngsters will certainly get lost when they enter life, because they will not know where to go and who to trust.

Perhaps the concept of "work first, play later" is still engraved in everyone's mind. But we should ask retired people if they are really enjoying their leisure, or are they living in loneliness and forlornness? What they need now is to be understood and loved, but after many years of living with the attitude of "my way or nothing" and distrust, it's hard for their loved ones to show love and understanding. A plentiful material world might not mean anything to them anymore; they might even get sick of it and want to stay away. Their biggest longing now is to go back to their youth and live happily, cheerfully, interestingly and beautifully. The goodness and the beauty they left uncompleted is love, brotherhood, or doing something meaningful for life.

Business and non-business

Pragmatism was formed around the mid-19th century and flourished in the 20th century, especially in the United States. A mercantile form of pragmatism gives prominence to experience and practical consequences, such as having all human activities aimed at making profits. Because this demeaned form of pragmatism satisfied humanity's endless need for pleasure, it quickly received eager support from many walks of life. Business and non-business can be clearly separated on such a basis.

Whatever can produce profit is business; whatever does not produce profit or suffers losses is non-business. For example, in a meeting with friends, if we can get some useful information, or at least make some good contacts for our job, it is a worthwhile and practical meeting. On the other hand, if we spend a few hours just to hear heart-rending stories, to be reminded of stale memories of long ago, or simply to drink tea and gaze at the scenery, it is indeed a waste of time as well as impractical. Impracticality is non-business. Now, the word "practical" is used for business. An impractical person is someone without a mind for business.

Business people must always be careful to eliminate all problems regarding feelings. There is no concession or sympathy in business. Everything must follow clear principles. But who is running the business, humans or machines? A human being would need health care, rest, support, understanding, and loving-kindness. We should not quickly deem those things non-business. Without them, we cannot do business and there will be no foundation for business. But human instinct always protects the selfish ego, so human beings would rather sacrifice feelings rather than business. Doing business, we can pocket the profits ourselves, but we have to share loving-kindness. The excessive influence of business on human perception has caused so many broken relationships, internecine conflicts, and ethnic wars.

Therefore a growing business is almost synonymous with growing human suffering. People say that without business or wealth, love cannot last. But they forget that wealth means nothing without love. Why do we try to get rich if we cannot live in joy, peace, happiness and openness with everyone?

Looking for a pathway

The most confusing thing about human beings in this era is their inability to define what the means is and what the purpose of life is. The material world only brings us more pleasant comforts in life; it is not the biggest reason for us to live. We live because we are sacred living beings, a wonderful reality, so we need to develop our true nature of being that is calm, peaceful, and happy. Any of our actions should reflect this high purpose, be it loving or doing business. We cannot say that we are busy developing our means and have to wait five or ten more years before we can grasp our purpose. Now we are stuck and going haggard focusing on means, then how can we be sure we will use them to reach our purpose? With such an attitude about living, it is highly possible that we will collapse and die from focusing on those means.

Bhutan is one of the world's poorest countries, but its people always have a ready smile on their lips and feel happy with their present life. They are aware that developing a country does not necessarily mean having to sacrifice the environment or community happiness. So they set forth the GNH (Gross National Happiness) indicator to attain the purpose of life right in the present time. They do not have to go on the frivolous and dangerous road of high-grade material things. Thanks to being "unlike anyone," their life is very secure, their crime rate and divorce rates are very low, and best of all, they fully enjoy the value of life every day, so their longevity is very high.

This approach to building happiness has attracted the attention of some developed countries more and more. They have begun to listen to the deep yearnings of their people and decided to lower the GDP (Gross Domestic Product) indicator so everyone can reduce working hours and have the opportunity to return to basic activities in life. In England, about 81% of the population suggests the government should focus on helping people live in happiness rather than in wealth. They have requested a ban on commercials aimed at children to limit the tendency to worship material things. People in Japan are startled when they see that the crime rate and overtime hours have not decreased at all compared to the 1980s, even though their economy is rated number two or three in the world. Top leaders have looked at Bhutan's example of "knowing when is enough" so they have bravely proposed many projects of "less work, more play" so the GDP indicator always parallels with the GNH indicator, meaning the economy should go hand-in-hand with happiness.

Vietnam is also giving priority to economic development and is resolute on raising it to a high level. But if we are aware of the salient values of happiness, we can still avoid the failed road that other countries have taken. The country might not be wealthy, the people might have to forego material things, but we still accept it joyfully. We are determined not to live without love and happiness. Following the examples of other countries, we cannot catch two fish with two hands. So from now on we should be brave to instantly eliminate pragmatism and use all our energy to rebuild a civilized spiritual life. Only this kind of living can help us find ourselves, filter all dirt of suffering and nourish beautiful seeds of the heart. In this space, we are always conscious that all things are present in one thing; hence individualism is replaced with boundless benevolence. This is the highest happiness of humankind.

Waiting for a policy to be enacted for the public to follow takes a long time. The majority still does not believe they can be happy with few material possessions. Many also think they have to reach the high peaks of the material world before they can return to spiritual values. In reality however, even "the rich also cry" and few people want to give up high-class enjoyments. Once human greed has been expanded, it is very difficult to retract. And by that time, we will be in no mental and physical condition to feel, receive, and maintain the values of happiness. Our mind area has become dry and hardened from so-called "making a living."

Take a look back at the picture of happiness that the venerable poet Nguyen Du painted for us: *"A family shares everything together every day/ Enjoying natural sceneries and simple vegetarian meals/ Looking at the immense universe around/ The tides are in and out mornings and evenings with the clouds reflected always."* (The Tale of Kieu) Practicing a life knowing when is enough will be the only opportunity for us to ably go back and inherit the great wealth that heaven and Earth have given us. That wealth is enough to make a meaningful human life. A human life is really very short. No one knows how long we will live, so do not forsake it to run after material things. Tomorrow if we have to leave this world without having had time to truly live a worthy life, wouldn't it be a great regret?

Where were we heading yesterday?
Leaving happiness behind to stay
Still withering and pale looking
While sorrowful dreams are mourning

35

Dependence

We are never absolutely separated from the support and nurture of outside conditions, but we would not consider them excuses for our lack of responsibility in holding the helm of our life boat.

The light will go out

Life needs mutual support because all things in this world by nature cannot exist separately. At the start of something or in meeting obstacles that we are unable to cope with, the full and reasonable support of people around us is always essential. This boosts our strength and faith for us to settle down and move forward. But if the good feelings from that support repeat over and over again, it will form a habit within us that we cannot let go or have no thought of letting go. We have fallen into the situation of "emotional addiction." We always feel frustrated and insecure when good feelings are missing. This situation is *dependence*.

A blind boy went to a friend's house for a visit. Too busy talking, he did not know it was already dark outside. His friend urged him to go home and gave him a lamp. The boy laughed and asked, "Why do you give a lamp to the blind guy like me?" His friend explained: "When you hold this lamp, people will see you and get out of your way." Thinking it made sense, the boy cheerfully took hold of the lamp and left. He boldly walked straight ahead, thinking surely everyone would keep away from him. But before long, someone crashed into him and both fell down. Hurt and angry, the boy yelled. "Are you blind? Don't you see my lamp?" The other person burst out laughing heartily, "Your lamp died out already, blind boy!"

The boy could walk on the road by himself day or night with the skills he had learned. But when the lamp was handed to him, he depended entirely on it, without using his clever skills to find his way instead of combining both. He could not see the true nature of the lamp. He never knew how much oil was left or how soon the light might be blown out by the wind. Yet he depended on it absolutely. Even after a terrible fall, he was still not aware that his light went out and still blamed the other person. What a pity!

We ourselves can also find the value of happiness with our trained skills because true happiness is the peace and stability in our minds. But since life has created too many "lamps" of material and mental comforts, we have become addicted and hold on to them tightly. We spend all our time and energy to acquire them and take care of them. We get mad or hate each other because of them, too. We wander aimlessly all our lives also because of them. We let those temporary means—material and mental comforts—be our main goal in life, forgetting that the nature of those "lamps" is always controlled by circumstances. For example, we often see our income go up and down, and our honor is at times glorified and at times humiliated. Beauty and lust are attractive and boring now and then. When we lose or no longer enjoy those emotions, we will find that depending on ourselves is the safest way. Regretfully, the precious qualities in our minds have been hardened during the period that we got attached to exciting emotions derived from external objects. Although they can be revived, we have to find the correct way and this wakening process is very hard. That is the price that few people would expect. It is like when we trip over a stone and our brain secretes endorphins to relieve pain, or when we are too stressed and our brain secretes serotonin to soothe the nerves. That means our own body is very able to heal itself. Based on this structure, the medical field invented antidepressant medications such as Prozac and Paxil to help us relieve some bad emotions that our own selves could not heal right away. But the danger is that those medications will upset the biological cycles of the body, destroy nerve cells, and possibly damage our memory. What is more damaging after a period of using the medication is that the brain will make the body produce fewer natural endorphins and less serotonin or simply stop their production. When the stimulating content suddenly decreases, it will create a terribly uncomfortable feeling and force us to take even more. We will become addicted.

For that reason, drug management agencies such as the FDA in the United States have ordered a ban on these kinds of medications or they can only be used in special cases as prescribed by medical specialists. Those who abuse drugs like heroin, morphine, or cocaine with similar compositions as the two hormones above can heighten their feelings to the highest degree. After using them a few times, however, they become frenzied drug addicts and lose all basic human characteristics. Efficacious medicine can turn into toxic drugs.

Taking control of our lives

Those with a weak psychological make-up often tend to show their tendency toward dependence from childhood. We enjoy having other people help us. We think it saves us time, effort, and even brain work. Many parents love their children too much to make them work hard, even though they should only do some basic tasks that each child must experience by himself. Therefore when we grow up we often meet complications while trying to solve difficult problems. At work, we always look for ways to get the attention and support from our superiors. When meeting people, we always hope to be recognized and praised. When in love, we are often mesmerized and become assimilated to the other person. The habit of believing in the benefits of external conditions gradually gets integrated into ourselves and becomes part of our character or life style. Only when the object of our dependence is gone do we become totally devastated and suddenly wake up.

The more technology develops, the more human beings have opportunities to lean on machinery. Who does not enjoy conveniences? In the leading developed countries, machines are even used in small tasks. But the more we depend on machinery, the more we lose our inherent abilities. Many experiments show that "machinery addicted" people are usually very lazy to exercise, take notes, remember and think deeply. Therefore the number of people getting sick and absent-minded increases every year. We also trust insurance. We figure that all our activities will be safe with the care of insurance companies. We just need to pay their premiums. But the truth is that insurance companies only pay expenses for our accidents or sickness. They cannot help us get healed or share our deep personal problems. So when we need to listen patiently to others or control our anger, we have not developed skills to cope with these. We resign ourselves to fail.

Many people look for spiritual environments to take refuge after heavy losses from struggling in life. They believe that with the saints as their objects of devotion, they will not be disappointed this time as they were with human beings. But their attitude toward refuge becomes dependence when they only have great faith without any training, practice and transformation. If they try to practice the path but keep losing faith in themselves and entrusting their happiness and even their future to others, their attitude toward practice is certainly not correct. Some people are very diligent in studying and even memorizing a great number of profound religious tenets, and then they try to create for themselves a viewpoint and lifestyle very different from everyone else. But in the end they still meet countless difficulties with problems within themselves or with their loved ones around them. This is because that their attitude is only "truth begging" to paint for themselves a nice portrait, a kind of coloring of their ego with pride and apart from everybody. They certainly have not experienced anything by themselves. While religious tenets have their value as a guide or map to happiness, they are not happiness themselves.

When we are attached to the objects of our devotion and we cannot resolve our own afflictions, those objects have taken control of our lives. They might be deities and saints, our dearly loved ones, or very successful people. In the end they also cannot shoulder and solve all the difficulties and deadlocks inside us. They only play the role of an agent, not the owner, in the garden of our minds. We only need their support at those times we fail to overcome serious situations after having tried our best. If we have much experience, we will see the danger of refuge, which seriously weakens us. Therefore we would rather suffer some harm and loss of our job or wealth than depend on others. In case we are those who enjoy success and prominence yet do not want to depend on our own strength, we have to suffer the cost of the loan, the dependency. We might have power and wealth, but we would not be able to enjoy life fully because we have to keep finding ways to please more powerful people. We still do not yet have anything firm of our own.

Enough then. Stop living in exile like that. It is time we bravely emancipate ourselves from such addiction to find the value of life's true freedom. This will be a painful and difficult process. We will have to thrashing emotions with each external object of dependence being removed. But we will feel really peaceful and self-confident right afterwards because we will be on the way to regaining control of our lives. Once awakened, the luring halo of money, fame, or beauty and lust will not be strong enough to make us surrender the remaining part of our lives. Although we are never absolutely separated from the support and nurture of external conditions, especially from our loved ones, we will not consider them excuses for our lack of responsibility in holding the helm of our life's boat. Whenever we feel that we do not have enough clarity of mind or strength to continue deftly combining material and mental comforts and other external supports and our own energy, we will—at any price—let go of the external supports to come back and take control of our lives as our first priority.

Autumn will soon die
The old river will run dry
Go seek refuge for your life
In the infinity of time

36

Interdependence

Depending on one another to always be conscious of mutual respect and need is the most beautiful creation of the universe.

Cells need bodies

Never have human beings felt life to be so monotonous, dull, and irrelevant as they do now. Perhaps this is because they are gradually losing close relationships with other individuals more and more every day. With the economy developing and enjoyment increasing quickly, many people mistakenly think they can live securely and stably using their own talents and skills without needing anyone else. They limit "impractical" relationships, and dare not trust anyone because they think anybody can be their dangerous competitor. As for the young, they always want to part from their families. They believe it is an opportunity to advance on their own and to satisfy their deep longing for freedom with no more supervision, control, and scolding. Then when they are drawn into sentimental or material indulgence, the notion of a warm family or the emotional ties with their village or hamlet has no more impact on their minds. Many young people have even announced: "In my dictionary, the word 'village' doesn't exist!" "Leaving home is like leaving a prison." And since then they have been living like someone with no homeland.

The times they return to their home villages are usually when they fall into a difficult situation that they cannot cope with or solve. But that means they still believe in the loving kindness or the peaceful value of their family and loved ones. Meanwhile, other young ones do not want to publicize their failure because of pride and saving face. They would rather grin and bear it, or indulge themselves in depravity, hoping to forget everything, but certainly they would not ask their family for help. A number of other youngsters are living with their family but appear and disappear like a ghost. They also do not care about anyone, have no responsibility for anybody, and never share their problems with anyone. They have their own world. Electronic games, telephones, and the internet are places where they see themselves existing, where they feel more at ease, more self-confident, and even more "truly alive" than in life.

Only a few decades ago, people still lived very close to and in harmony with one another. Grandparents and parents always spent a lot of time shaping and teaching their offspring to become good people. They were conscious that their offspring were their continuation and also the future of society. The young generation's duty is always to love, respect, and eagerly learn the experiences of their predecessors—from practicing manners and rituals to polishing the art of interacting with other people. Their family was their first school of life. If they could live in harmony and happiness with family members, they could easily live anywhere. Because they were "rooted" in such a solid spiritual foundation, even when they had to make a living far away from home, they were always conscious that they were living for their family lineage, village, and even their homeland. When facing innumerable difficulties or temptations, they would tell themselves not to fall down; otherwise, the faith of all their loved ones would fall too. So their place of refuge was also the place of worship to help them be aware of valuing, maintaining, and trying to improve their selves.

A village was also a cradle to help the young mature. When they had problems with family and could not unburden themselves, they could run to a neighbor (who was like an uncle or an aunt to them) to pour their heart out. And they would receive heart-felt advice to go back home, concede a little, and make up with their family. Village grownups always treated the young like their own children. When they noticed one of them making a mistake, they would gladly spend time, even prepare a pot of tea or a friendly meal, to invite them over to share, and then give advice. If the advice did not work, they would take the trouble to meet the family adults directly to discuss a solution. When some families met misfortune, they would take off a whole working day to help eagerly. At times they would even stop a party as if to share our difficulties. Therefore, people in those days seldom suffered from depression, mental illness, or looked for death due to an impasse like nowadays. They would never dare leave behind a bad reputation for their family and village. They were always conscious that they were the cells while their family and village were the bodies. Cells have to rely closely on bodies or they will die.

Don't go out to sea alone

Interdependence is a compelling principle of life. Truly nothing can exist separately in this world. Thanks to having people watching out for us, we try to be careful and do our best. In the family, it is called "the family eye"; in the community, "the community eye." These eyes help us to discover the clumsiness, weakness, or difficulty that we ourselves do not see. Besides, although the criticism gives us a rather uncomfortable feeling initially, it is an opportunity for us to practice endurance and coping skills, to understand deeply our own and others' psychology. Besides, everyone has good and bad points that we can learn from. This is especially true if we get to live with experienced people because they are like a living book from which we can learn and practice. More importantly, it is thanks to living in a community that we are inspired to strive. The greatest value of an interdependent life is the opportunity it gives us to see clearly the interconnecting principle among individuals so we think less highly of our ego and develop our seed of altruism.

Those who meditate often quote, *"A tiger from the mountain will be defeated; a monk away from the Sangha will falter."* A tiger will certainly fail when it is separated from the mountain and the forest, its familiar environment. Its opponents might just be wild wolves, but due to their united strength, they can still defeat it—*"It's difficult for a ferocious tiger to fight a pack of wolves."* If a monk leaves his Sangha, a community of Buddhist practitioners protected by an abundance of diligent energy and harmony, he will easily fall into the tempting trap of life and lose his serenity in mind. This intrusion takes place gently and subtly every second and minute and is difficult to detect without the observation of the Sangha's eyes.

Certainly advice for a large number of people only has relative value because everything has exceptions. In reality there are monks with eminent awareness and self-control and nothing can change their qualities even if they live outside their community. The reason they live away from their Sangha is to expand their path of a life of service, not to seek some wild freedom for themselves. However, they always bear in mind that they are living among the Sangha, so their way of life from eating to thinking reflects the spirit of the Sangha. Hence the "independent" lifestyle is only proper when we want to strive for a higher purpose without depending on others. Even after we have built a fortune, we still remember that we have never stopped receiving loving-kindness and faith from our loved ones. Actually depending on each other to always be conscious of mutual respect and the needs of others is the most beautiful creation of in the universe.

The swans and their flock always fly in a V-formation during their migration south to avoid the cold and to look for food. With such a formation, the wing-flapping of the swan in front will help the one behind to save 70% more of its energy than when flying alone. In reality, no swan ever ventures to fly solo from north to south because the distance is sometimes several thousand miles. A remarkable thing is when the swan leader is tired, it instantly moves back to let the next one take its place. They never lead dictatorially. A more remarkable thing is when a swan suddenly gets exhausted or injured, it will be escorted by two other healthy ones and the entire flock will reduce their speed to the minimum for them to catch up. They never fail to support their own kind.

When watching a flock of swans closely attached to each other, we could be in tears. We always consider ourselves civilized but we venerate individualism to serve our petty selfishness. We do not want anyone to bother us and we also do not show concern for the suffering of others. We are even indifferent to our family members, let alone the two great words "human race." But it is actually not that great. If we do not care to love our human race, support our people, share pain and suffering with our homeland, then how are we qualified to stand steadfastly in this world? If we live just to care about ourselves then what is the meaning of life?

Therefore we should try to overcome narrow views and join hands to hoist big sails so our life boat can sail swiftly forward. Don't rely on talent or luck and don't give ourselves a position too high to be in harmony with the people around us. We do not necessarily have to become a ship captain to participate in an ocean crossing voyage to reach the shore of happiness. Each sailor just needs to know their responsibility and be ready to exchange positions when necessary. Then they can regain their positions in time to cope with sudden surges of waves from the bow. Let us walk side by side to have a chance to touch, to break down the walls of prejudice, to practice giving in and living in harmony with each other. Those are the important elements that form human beings' solid character and success. Let us live the life of understanding and loving human beings. Let us accept one another like the swans always accepting their kind. Do not create in our minds a prison of doubt, worry, and fear to deal with each other because of our excessive need for pleasure or our small, petty self. If we can still walk on the same road, still look at each other closely, still be willing to ask for help or support from each other, then we still maintain the qualities of a wonderful being. Without those qualities, we cannot be happy, because happiness only truly exists when it is shared.

Let's travel like a flock of birds
Overcoming freezing air above
Let's not sail alone on the high seas
The ocean of life always abounds with billows.

37

Weakness

Those who lack inner strength are those who suffer the most.

The habit of enjoyment

Each individual has a different physiological composition due to heredity. It is also different depending on the effects of circumstances and training. Although psychology is the deciding factor in human behavior and attitudes toward life, physiology also plays an important role in changing and forming the characteristics of human beings. Body and mind is really one tightly combined and inseparable unit. Therefore, if we have inherited the seed of strong emotions, we certainly will tend to look for good emotions and avoid bad ones from childhood on. This tendency is a natural instinct. But if we follow our instinct to satisfy our emotions without considering the consequences, we will never find the true value of happiness.

For example, even if there is nothing worth watching on TV and nothing useful on the Web pages that our eyes have been glued to, we cannot take our eyes off them. We would not know what else to do when our innermost feelings are lost and weak. We know getting up early will give us time to exercise and prepare everything well without hurrying when we get to work, but we cannot overcome the comfortable feeling of a warm bed and soft blanket. We keep reminding ourselves to consume only nutritious food to stay healthy and energetic, but we cannot turn down delicious unhealthful dishes when facing them. We are well aware that we will cause misunderstanding if we continue to be friendly with a certain person, but we cannot stay away because we cannot bear to let go of the sweet feelings we have for that person. We have realized the important value of spiritual life and are determined to practice, but we do not have enough courage to cut down on our physical pleasures and amusements.

Enjoying good feelings is similar to hating bad feelings. For example, some people do not enjoy sports, heavy manual labor or brainy work. Some people hate a disciplined lifestyle and do not like to follow too many principles at work. Some people do not appreciate straightforward suggestions or lack of respect. Our pride is easily hurt from taunts or offensive remarks. We are also aroused by sudden disruptions. When facing big difficulties, we can only cry, let alone stay calm to understand and solve the problem. We do not think we can overcome adversity, so we always plead to others for help. In other situations, we honestly want to share our opinion with some people but dare not give it for fear they would get mad and avoid us. Worse, we really want to refuse a certain request knowing we cannot handle it, but we are afraid to lose favor, so we have to put up with it.

Knowing what we should do but do not do, or knowing what we should not do but still do, this is the situation of *weakness*—unable to overcome our own selves.

When we have power in our hands, respected by many, receiving full attention when saying something, we become full of ourselves, thinking we are quite powerful. But when we are suddenly offended or slandered, we break down at once. We immediately look for allies to support us, or we take the other party to court to reclaim our honor. We think they should be rightfully punished so they would not dare meddle with us again. But we have actually failed. The law can protect our interests, but if we rely on the law to solve all our conflicts, we have inadvertently tolerated our own weakness. If we had real power, getting a few sporadic attacks would not be a problem. We could even use our talent to convert our opponents and turn war into peace.

We may be very firm when facing big adversaries, and we may never falter before violence, but nobody would expect us to be emotionally weak. Even so, we may lose all initiative when being in love. Once we hear sweet talk or moaning cries, we would be willing to accept all requests. Passion—the attitude of integrating our whole self with the emotion of love—has turned us into loyal slaves of love. Sometimes we even do crazy things like throwing away the fortune of a lifetime or severing family ties to pursue love. We think we are risking our lives for love's sake but actually we are completely drawn into the strong force of emotion. So when that love is lost, we have nothing else to live for. Two people who are madly in love and joining their lives together are no different from two weak persons trying to lean on each other.

Everyone has weak moments, actually. Those are the only times when we lose awareness and allow passion to take over, or when we are attacked suddenly by adversity and cannot fight back in time. But then our rational mind and trained energy take us back to self-control. If we let our weakness become a habit without trying to transform it, we will meet countless difficulties and even miserable failures from the ups and downs of life. Those lacking inner strength are those who suffer the most.

Inner strength

Once, two junior fellow monks and I went out to the yard to clean up fallen twigs after a big storm. Suddenly spotting a dead mouse on the road, I picked it up and put it at the base of a big tree. After a few steps, I turned around and used my hands to scoop up some sand and make a pretty grave to bury it. The two junior monks came and complimented me: "Elder brother, you're so merciful!" When they walked on, I found myself falling into a strange floating void as if something big just fell. It turned out I had just done something interesting. The act of placing the mouse at the base of the tree was sincere—it was my compassion for small animals, but the act of digging the grave to bury the mouse was insincere—it was my ego trying to prove that I was compassionate but actually it was "a thirst" for recognition. The incident happened almost 20 years ago but I still shudder every time I recall it. I never thought my ego-affliction would be so subtle and could make use of even a mouse's dead body. After that, every time I want to help somebody, I often ask myself: "What am I doing this for?" If I see that I'm being "thirsty" for good feelings, I try to stop right away.

When we think that receiving good feelings from others' recognition helps increase the value of our lives, it means we have yet to find our inner strength. But the truth is the more we expect and depend on favorable external conditions, the less we can develop our inner strength. Although we have loud and angry reactions or superficial desires, we also have a deep inner world that can only be reached in our moments of peace and calmness. Similarly, only when we dive down deep in the ocean can we see how immense and deep the ocean actually is, instead of just surges of waves coming in and going out. To find the ocean within ourselves, we should not keep identifying ourselves with our waves of emotion. This means we should practice forgetting or reducing unnecessary demands from the outside to come back and live with ourselves to understand and take control of our lives. The 13th century Vietnamese Meditation Master Tue Trung Thuong Si used to say, *"Looking within oneself is everyone's duty. One catches nothing from the outside."*

A weak psychology is closely related to a worrying and timid psychology. Maybe we are gentle, kind, and nice. We are always ready to give in to others. Even when they make mistakes or hurt us, we never get angry or retaliate. Everyone loves us and always chooses us to listen to their problems. However, they are dismayed when they work together with us. It seems we are indecisive and are always in a state of "I don't know what to do." At first, everyone thought we had a very big heart to accept everything. But eventually they discover that we are not used to coping with problems and complications. So it is safest for us to retreat to our "silent island."

Even when it is necessary to speak up to protect truth or justice, we also ignore it, avoid it, and shift the responsibility to other people. Our timid attitude has turned us into a coward. Cowardice is an important factor in creating intimidation in others. It's really a shame when we know we should do something that is within our ability, but we do not try a little more to overcome the bad feeling that is controlling our whole body. That emotion comes from an erroneous attitude about living. That erroneous attitude originates from the wrong belief that we should be ourselves and do not have to change anything. Based on this, we always look for ways to pamper or heighten our favorite feelings. If we were born with talents instead of working hard to build up our skills, our character can become weak because we can accomplish things easily without struggling. We are famous and admired by many because of it, so we forget that our true character is very weak. We have always enjoyed good feelings and now there is more opportunity to have even more good feelings. So although we are known as the most powerful person (because of our high income), we are actually the weakest (because we get hurt the easiest).

Sky-high ambition

Sometimes standing before a big memorial, especially when the energy of this memorial is combined with the great energy of admiration from the public, we suddenly feel too ordinary and ready to hide under its shadow. Weakness can lead to the attitude of dependence. Then we lose control of our lives. The weaker we are, the more we depend on others, and the more we depend on others, the weaker we become. The 12th century Vietnamese Meditation Master Quang Nghiem often advised: *"Man should have sky-high ambition/ Do not follow Buddha's footstep."* Closely imitating others, even a Buddha, only brings shame and weariness and nothing else. Spiritual transformation is an individual's own experience, which does not come from copying exactly a spiritual idol. Why do we have to do just what others do when we all have a different physical and mental composition? We can only learn about some experiences from our predecessors. We have to face and discover the rest with our own strength. Our pleasure-seeking habit has made us forget our once noble and righteous character.

The poet Che Lan Vien used to complain: *"The lots of us sleep in narrow beds/ With small dreams crushing small lives/ Happiness is contained in a beautiful dress/ While a quiet house casts a shadow over our heart."* What are our dreams? Are they to achieve honors and fame in this life? Winning the person of our dreams? Owning a luxurious and prestigious personal estate? Being respected by friends and everyone around us? What about our ideals? Living without the will power to reach lofty goals will confine our lives to a narrow space in which we will feel lost. Actually, the lofty goals are not as glorious as people might expect. Sharing our ability to serve the community or the life we are depending on is the basic responsibility of every citizen. If everyone thinks only about their own happiness, then who will take care of common goals? We would not want to blame modern science because it has brought humanity countless comforts and conveniences, yet these comforts and conveniences have inadvertently led us to strive for more and more. This has promoted wanting more material things, honor, fame, etc., instead of our ideals. It has thereby poisoned the purposes of life and drowned lofty ideals for many generations of people.

We have indeed passed the terrible wartime era, but human afflictions never end. Human beings are still busily fighting, but not in the capacity of soldiers sacrificing for their nation. We say that we love our country and are proud of our race, but have we ever asked ourselves what we have done for our country and race without including our interests? Don't think that this question is too big. Don't be mad because it touches our selfishness. Look at the truth bravely. Our country and people still stuffer from countless difficulties. If we do not shoulder them, who will? If we continue to turn away from ideals to protect "our little dream," don't ask why our lives are so small. Then we can easily go on living without any awareness of the suffering surrounding us and resign ourselves to making our loved ones suffer or to contributing to the destruction of our own homeland.

Is it really me?
Living a life so shallow, soulless and silly
Where's the hero I used to be
Just a quiet space of sad immensity

38

Repentance

*Mistakes generated by our mind must be changed by our mind itself,
not with the help of any almighty power from the outside.*

Looking back at mistakes

When we are busy pursuing objects of attraction from the outside, they will certainly distract and control our minds. Therefore the opportunity to live in awareness, holding all actions in check, will be limited, and making mistakes will be unavoidable. Of course everybody makes mistakes, unless they are saints. But that doesn't give us the right to make all kinds of mistakes without considering the consequences to ourselves or to the people around us. Overcoming our mistakes and taking responsibility for what we have done is important. Therefore, having the attitude of remorse and the desire to redeem our faults, as well as a determination to transform ourselves in order not to repeat them, is the most important thing to do for mistake-makers. This is repentance.

Usually, as soon as we realize we have just made a mistake, we quickly go to our victim to explain apologetically or to do something to make up for it. We think this is a courteous or responsible thing to do. But we do that for what purpose? It seems we are trying to compensate those persons with good feelings for the bad feelings we caused them. We hope they will not be too angry with us and think badly of us or like us less. We bring them good feelings and expect to receive good feelings, so this is just an exchange. That kind of apology is also for us and not really to heal the wound in their mind. This is why observant people do not usually accept apologies that lack sincerity or only aim at pleasing them. That kind of apology sometimes hurts them more. Therefore, according to the law of emotional balance, they really just received bad feelings from us, but now they have to give us good feelings by trying to be tolerant and cheerful, which cause them to suffer a loss.

Before trying to show repentance, we should ask ourselves if we have really recognized our mistake and why we behaved that way. We should not try to act with really touching stories with the sole purpose of restoring our good name in the other person's opinion because we will just keep spoiling our minds. The word "apology" does not mean asking the other person not to be mad at us or hate us. It must be an attitude of repentance, asking to retract our wrong words or actions and bearing all responsibility for them. Therefore we should not apologize until we can really see our mistake and be ready to accept responsibility. The worst is when we try to apologize because we are advised to do so, or we know the other persons are waiting for our apology. If we know they are really angry or hurt, then we should apologize first for their sake. But we should honestly let them know that as of now we have not yet seen our mistake. Ask them to show us what we did wrong, or promise them we will reflect on our actions carefully and tell them what we have learned as soon as possible.

If apologizing is an action aiming at treating the wound in the mind of somebody else, repenting is the attitude of coming back to treat blemishes and mistakes in our minds. Naturally which action we should do first depends on the situation, but repenting for ourselves then apologizing to others is still the most correct solution. Repentance must have two characteristics: repenting for past mistakes and resolving not to repeat them. These two elements are very important and closely related to each other. If we do not really repent, we will not be resolute in changing; if we are not resolute in changing, that repentance is only a temporary feeling to soothe the wound inside us. Changing ourselves in order not to repeat the same mistakes is much harder than showing repentance, because changing ourselves means breaking down the wall of afflictions.

Remember that transforming an affliction is different from preventing an affliction. To prevent it we just need to remind ourselves often and then use strong will power to suppress it each time it shows up. This is only a temporary solution because it will come back soon when we are diverted or our internal strength is weak. To transform an affliction, we need to have three conditions. First, we have to identify clearly which affliction prompted us to make the mistake. Second, we must have a correct and practical method to treat it. Third, we must have a strong resolution to make this transformation a priority. In addition, there is one more rather important condition in the repenting process: we should not be too anxious to transform quickly in order present our new self to the other person. This attitude will cause us to add more pressure to ourselves and inaccurately assess the level of our transformation. The other persons will certainly not blame us when they know we are trying to change ourselves, because changing ourselves is the most valuable act of apology to redeem all mistakes.

Transforming mistakes

The common psychology of most people when making mistakes is trying to find ways to salvage the situation. Though we think that we are taking responsibility for all our errors, deep in our heart we are actually hoping to reaffirm our precious ego. We want to let the other persons know that we are not that bad and that our wrong action was just a one-time mistake. Even if our action of taking responsibility can really heal the wound in their mind or help us recover our reputation in their eyes, the blemish is still intact in our minds. We should try to change the roots of the tree instead of eagerly trying to trim the canopy of the tree. If we still have not identified our affliction to really transform it, sooner or later we will repeat the same mistake with that person, or cause new mistakes with another person.

Buddhism has always affirmed *"turn around and you'll be at the shore"* (look within, meditate to be enlightened). Transformation begins when we have truly left behind the dark road to walk on the bright road. If we sustain our level of diligence throughout that journey, we will reach enlightenment. Therefore "turning around" does not mean we will get enlightenment as soon as we repent. It is just an encouragement for those turning around that they will reach the shore of enlightenment some day. In the past, we might have stupidly made big mistakes, but with a determination to change and a correct road to follow, those blemishes will be washed away and disappear. We can still come back to our whole and clean self as before. Of course the harmful energy that we created will not be wiped out easily, especially when it has left deep wounds in the mind of the other person. But with the peaceful energy generated from our sincere repentance and daily positive transformation, we can still gradually modify that harmful energy. Even if we have to suffer the consequences, meaning paying back the loan of feelings, we still have enough strength and gladly accept the consequences because they are no longer as heavy as in the beginning, especially thanks to our determination to improve.

The most awful thing is our refusal to repent. That attitude will open up many chances for us to ruin or destroy ourselves and the people around us. The young nowadays often announce emphatically: "I never feel regret about what I have done." They sound very self-confident and smart. They seem to think that feeling regret is a bad attitude for admitting a lack of maturity and showing their weakness. But actually the more we are not aware of or try to avoid our responsibility, the worse the situation gets and the weaker we become. No one wants to build a serious or lasting relationship with someone who is irresponsible. But the most important thing to notice when we make mistakes is that there might be something wrong with our psychological processes somewhere. Possibly our perception was wrong, or the seeds of affliction inside us were aroused and have been forming a bad habit or characteristic. That wound will never stop tormenting us. It will also become a big obstacle preventing good energies from developing.

Although repentance is an action to come back and readjust our minds, it should be done ceremonially. The formal practice will help us focus more easily and express correctly our attitude of repentance. We should choose a quiet space place and save plenty of time to look back at ourselves. Try to look back at our entire body and mind with a non-prejudiced attitude to understand everything deeply before finding ways to transform them. Don't get too emotional then blame or get angry at ourselves. Sometimes tormenting ourselves is a form of elevating our ego, because we do not want to admit those weaknesses are ours. But if we keep away and hate our own selves, then how can we understand deeply all the weaknesses or hidden corners of our psychology? We cannot transform them if we don't understand them yet.

We can also repent by writing a letter to ourselves. This is a simple way, yet it can bring unexpected results. First, we should sit down calmly and follow our breathing for about 15 minutes so our minds can settle down. We should also choose a quiet place and save a lot of time to write a valid letter as if we are writing to a certain loved one. We should call ourselves by the most intimate name. Ask ourselves questions about why we behaved with people that way in the recent past. Think well and sincerely write down the most correct answer. After that, we should also take note of our promise to live more deeply so we would not repeat those regrettable mistakes. This letter should be put in a place nearby so we can reread it often. We can reflect on ourselves each time we reread it. Writing such a letter will help us make a practical checklist and it will profoundly analyze our attitude toward life. That letter can also be considered our Heart Sutra.

In traditional Vietnamese culture, there is one very popular method of repenting: going to the ones we trust and respect the most to show our regret. They can be our loved ones around us, or our predecessors long gone. Whenever the emotion of regret is so strong that we cannot stand firmly, or when we need spiritual support during the time we officially turn to transformation, we should have someone to lean on and to witness. This is the attitude of rescuing our psychology from falling into a deadlock situation, not an attitude of avoiding reality. In the situation when the persons we lean on are our spiritual or blood ancestors, we can stand in front of the altar to sincerely light an incense stick, pour our heart out to them, and bow.

When bowing, we have to prostrate our whole body and especially our head down on the floor for a long while to show respect to our ancestors for their wonderful examples, and especially to the earth. The earth is also our ancestor, our kind mother who always embraces all the filthy things in this world. Let ourselves go to the heart of the earth to learn the virtues of the earth, to practice being open and adaptable with all situations and all objects without comparing or discriminating. All mistakes or sufferings originate from a big ego. So turning to somebody else is to reflect our minds, not to depend on or beg for help. Mistakes generated from our mind must be changed by our mind itself, not with the help of any almighty power from the outside. Remember that any mistake, no matter how big, is only a temporary psychological manifestation and does not represent our whole self. Do not identify ourselves with those weaknesses; otherwise we will lose self-confidence and self-esteem. However, if we are not determined to transform all those mistakes and allow them to control all our thought and actions, we will never find our true self. We will always live within the shell of our suffering. That would be the most regrettable thing in life.

Throw ourselves into the great earth
Let go of our crazy ego
Learn the virtue of adaptability
And assist all hearts and souls

39

Laziness

A lazy person is never seen in the kingdom of success.

A life left behind

Man's natural instinct is to always look for enjoyment. But the nature of enjoyment is only a temporary emotional satisfaction instead of giving us true happiness. Naturally not everyone can understand this truth and then try to tame their instinct for enjoyment, and not everyone is capable enough to control themselves. If we are victims of emotions, always drawn to unnecessary good emotions and reacting harshly to necessary bad emotions, then a weak character and a number of other habits such as dependency, boredom, hesitation, fear, and anxiety will certainly be formed within us. In addition, there is another habit of the same nature and causing big obstacles in building happiness: it is *laziness*.

Laziness is the habit of not wanting to detach ourselves from shallow, good feelings to reach deeper ones. This is like a hungry cat that wants to stay curled up on a warm blanket because it doesn't want to lose that comfortable feeling to experience the discomfort of getting up to look for food. Lazy people do little but want to enjoy much, rely on others for help, or pray for good luck instead of working hard. They always avoid heavy or tough work and look for lighter, easy work, or shift the responsibility of a hard job to others. They enjoy eating, sleeping, and entertainment. They are only interested in doing what they like. In other words, they like to do the kind of work that they have aptitude for rather than work that requires training, labor or brains. We have seen many people working eagerly, but only because they get good feelings from those jobs. For the more difficult jobs, no matter how important or how their future might be affected, they keep procrastinating and wait until the last minute to do them.

If we happen to carry around the burden of so many lazy habits, we will encounter countless problems in life. We will be very afraid to work hard, get up early or stay up late for work. When meeting co-workers not to our liking, we will not try to improve the relationship for better cooperation. We will be both the victim and the culprit of work delays and budget deficits. When choosing a life companion, we will certainly tend to find someone who will love us wholeheartedly and take care of everything for us. Marrying a lazy person is probably as bad as buying an old car. Though it consumes a lot of gasoline, it conks out after running for some distance. It has to be fixed continuously to run again, but not for much longer than previous times. Even if our spouses really want to build lasting relationships, they will suspect that we are selfish and taking advantage of them when they see our sluggish attitude and lack of effort in daily life. Numerous marriages have failed because of the lack of effort from one side. If the other side makes mistakes or falls down but this side tries their best to give support, they both can still walk together in life. However, if this side tries their best but the other side does not try to change, their marriage will fail.

Lazy people can never have a settled life or a good future. In other words, a lazy person is never seen in the kingdom of success. No matter how intelligent or talented they might be, they can never reach their goals in life if they only try half-heartedly, going forward one step and moving backward three steps.

Everybody must know the story of the tortoise racing against the hare. Nobody would think that the slow tortoise would dare challenge the naturally fast hare. But the tortoise believed strongly that its hard-working habits could compete and beat the presumption and laziness of the hare. And the tortoise did the impossible thing, setting an example for all living beings. We often say, "*Diligence makes up for intelligence.*" Indeed diligence is more important than intelligence. It is formed from training and reaches beyond ourselves, hence it is a kind of magic wand to help us overcome obstacles and build a stable life and work. Intelligence is innate, so intelligent people do not have to work or train hard to succeed or beat others, hence they often take it for granted and do not bother to study or practice more. This self-centeredness and idleness are the graves of many talents. They have "jade" inside but cannot use it.

In *The Tale of Kieu*, the venerable Nguyen Du reminded us, *"Take care of ourselves."* We should not forget that we are the ones responsible for our lives. When we are in pain or suffer, even our most beloved one cannot bear it for us. But what have we done for our life? Are we enjoying a happy life thanks to our own hard work or thanks to good luck and the support of others? While support is necessary, if we always depend on it and inadvertently ignore the ability to strive, let our learning and creativity skills rust away, our laziness will take us to roads full of difficulties ahead. How can we have enough stamina to continuously transform the negative energies in our minds if we keep procrastinating about simple activities like physical exercise and keep forgetting plans that we have made? How can we have enough ability to help our loved ones with their difficulties? If we live yet cannot reach out, cannot develop or renew, it is a worn-out, meaningless life.

Not moving half a step yet

Meditation masters often say, *"Looking back at the starting place of years ago, I see that I have not moved even half a step."* What a shame! We feel shame because we used to tell everyone about our lofty ideals, but as of now we are still empty-handed. We are ashamed of ourselves because we have seen our potential energy, yet still cannot develop it. Where have we gone and what have we done so far? Have we been pulled away from our journey of self-discovery by attractive forces around us? What we have done and are doing seems to only develop more pleasures for our ego, not reflecting the true values that we expected.

If after 10 or 20 years, we look back and realize that we have not made any step forward, it is indeed a miserable failure. Do we know the reason why? Or do we continue to put the blame on others and on the situation? Maybe we don't even know that we are just stepping in place because we mistakenly think that the attractive comforts we are grasping are the end of the journey. The main reason for our sudden shift in direction is the saturation of emotions. Suddenly we lose interest in our journey of self-discovery, especially after facing many obstacles that brought bad emotions and intense feelings. Therefore, if we want to do great work, we have to continuously try to control the development of our instincts, and know how to arouse positive energy to cope with all adversities.

Once a seed is sown in the soil, it cannot germinate and grow even with favorable conditions like sunshine, adequate moisture, fertilizer and minerals if it its development is interrupted. Just like when we rub two bamboo sticks or two pieces of flint together to make a fire, how can we get fire if we rub too weakly or keep stopping? Everything needs the factor of non-interruption to succeed. If we let laziness and sporadic inspiration interfere, they will destroy all our projects, especially the project of transforming our character. We might have great methods, great teachers' careful guidance, favorable conditions for training and practice, but if we cannot overcome laziness, we will never be able to join the ranks of the awakened people. We will always be our old self that is unable to catch up with the wonderful newness in every moment of life.

A little more

To rectify laziness, we must have a strong resolution to detach ourselves from unnecessary good emotions and practice facing necessary bad emotions. We should try to live together with our family or with stable and dynamic people so we will not always fail ourselves. Thanks to good discipline, a lively atmosphere, frequent encouraging reminders or their own examples of overcoming difficulties, we will not have any toleration of laziness. In the beginning, don't allow ourselves to be idle. We should arrange our work schedule tightly to gradually forget the intention to find amusements or endless rest. Sometimes, we should bravely take on a few important jobs and work together with a group of industrious people. Due to having the duty to fulfill and the positive work spirit of the group, we can cut down on entertainment. The best thing is to participate in various community activities and lively programs that require us to be physically and mentally active. In general, we need to begin anew our activities in a new environment so we can pull ourselves out of the attractive "labyrinth" of laziness. We can only beat it when we become part of a group's joyful and healthy activities.

Don't hope that we can let go of our long-standing laziness right away each time we make a new plan. The trick to changing the old habit of laziness soon is to "try a little more." For example, we should get up just ten minutes earlier than usual, do a difficult task five more minutes than usual before we stop, or sit down and listen to someone a little longer even though we really want to get up and do something else. Thanks to the new habit of "trying a little more," no matter how hard the mental block of laziness is, it will erode. Actually, we are just converting our old habit into a new therapy because our laziness was formed from the accumulation of "a little more." Having a little diligence replace a little laziness is a smart solution that is easy to succeed with. Just try a few minutes more and the bout of laziness will pass. On the other hand, if we resume our old habit and drop our work, we will inadvertently increase the obstruction to our energy and the door to escape it will shut tighter.

Laziness often makes us like to lie down or sleep, so whenever we feel that our will power is not strong enough to take control, we should try to go outdoors or at least do something we enjoy instead of giving up easily. Laziness is closely related to depression. Therefore we should begin doing physical exercises and readjust our diet to keep our body healthy and fit. That will help us maintain an emotional balance, to be calm and clear-minded to recognize and find efficient solutions.

In addition, we should also begin anew in our bedroom or office. Besides putting things in neat order, we should remind ourselves to return every item to its original place each time we finish using it. Upon close observation, we will see our lazy attitude manifests itself very clearly in such little acts. This technique is simple but highly effective. It helps us to be mindful of our responsibility for each of our actions. This is also a very important behavior in establishing all relationships, especially when we decide to invite a very special person to be our life companion.

Laziness is not a great affliction that can tie us to suffering, but it is a fearful obstacle, making it impossible for us to reach our dreams or even to live deeply with reality. Laziness can cause extreme bursts of emotion or sudden moments of living in total unawareness of the surrounding environment. Therefore if we try hard to overcome the old habit of laziness and move forward enthusiastically, then we have officially stepped into the kingdom of success.

Minh Niem

How startling to see the old path
We haven't yet left the labyrinth
Alas, we're thousands of miles apart
Because of each heavy footprint

40

Letting Go

The more we let go, the more we feel relieved and peaceful. It is completely different from the habit of accumulation: the more we hoard, the more we get worried and tired.

Material comforts

One day, while the Buddha was sitting in contemplation with his monks, a farmer from a far distance came running and breathlessly asked: "Dear monks, have you seen my cow herd of 12 passing by here?" The Buddha gently replied: "We've been sitting here since noon but haven't seen any cow. You might want to take a look in the other direction." The farmer was disappointed, walking away and lamenting: "Oh Heavens! My sesame crop just failed, now if my cow herd is lost too, I'll lose everything I own. How can I live?" After the farmer was gone, the Buddha looked at his students, and then said softly: "We don't have any cows to lose, right?"

The Buddha wanted to remind his students that they were living in a very favorable situation to develop their spiritual life—an environment not disturbed by success or failure, gain or loss, praise or criticism—so they should cherish it and take care of it. Not becoming spiritually successful in such a situation was a big mistake. Those monks always received support from the common people who gave food, medications, clothing and even trust and admiration. It wasn't that they could not feed themselves; they just wanted to save all their time and energy to concentrate on meditation practice to achieve far-reaching understanding and loving-kindness. Moreover, staying away from the material world to eliminate pleasures and not accruing material things, so as to be humble before others when begging for food, were very important practices. The notion of "me" and "mine" was always examined and replaced with enlightenment about the interconnected characteristic of all things in the universe and in the non-self of our original nature. Once they realized this, they could love all living beings.

Though letting go of material things is only part of the practice of a spiritual teacher, it is a very courageous action. Looking within, we see that we have the habit of holding onto material things, even common consumer goods, not to mention high-level comforts. Nowadays human beings depend a great deal on technology. How would we feel if we could not use the phone, could not watch television or could not go online for a few days? We are used to sitting in an air-conditioned car and avoiding the dust, but if for some reason we have to use the bus, would we feel uncomfortable? We have been enjoying a good livelihood, but if we suddenly lost our job and had to be careful with all our expenditures, would we feel peaceful? Certainly we would get used to living in straitened circumstances if necessary. However, dropping a good feeling to accept bad feeling takes the right attitude, strong will power and enough time to adjust.

After we have adjusted to a life of few pleasures, all of a sudden we find our space really vast. We have more time and inspiration to look deeply into all objects or problems. We feel the energy source inside us is not dispersed as it was before. Even if we have to live in those straitened circumstances reluctantly, after a period of time we will realize that life has so many more wonderful things and we can only experience those values when we dare stay away from the attractions of the material world. Actually the nature of material things is blameless, but their attractive energy has the power to arouse the inherent greed within us and claim our life force. Since ancient times, many tragedies have happened because of the power of material things. Therefore the saints and sages have always taken up the life of "three meager basic needs"—the three most basic human activities of eating, clothing, and sleeping should be kept minimal. The less we grasp and depend on external conditions, the more we nourish and maximize internal values. That is a natural principle. If we are always busy with the ordinary things, we certainly will miss the extraordinary things.

Though we do not plan to become a sage, we should practice that intellectual lifestyle to elevate the quality of our spiritual life. Maybe our boat cannot move forward because it is too heavily laden and full. To rescue it we have to boldly throw a few big cargo boxes into the ocean though they might be very valuable. Letting go becomes a useful practice only when it helps us in the struggle between the habit of pleasure-seeking and the attitude of non-attachment. It is different from letting go of something because we no longer need it. The strange thing is the more we let go, the more we feel relieved and peaceful. It is completely different from the habit of accumulation: the more we hoard, the more we get worried and tired. Besides, there are so many needy people around us, so letting go of some of our wealth is an opportunity to express human kindness.

Mental comforts

It is easy to recognize the attraction of material comforts, but seldom do we discover the addictive power of mental comforts. There are times when we would drive hundreds of miles to a friend's house just to hear them approve or praise our work. In case they disapprove or make severe criticism, we will be very unhappy and disappointed. Sometimes we look for all kinds of ways, including tricks and deceptive techniques, to get people's attention and admiration. But when someone unexpectedly fabricates a false story in the newspaper to slander us or reveal our personal life stories, we would easily have a nervous breakdown or find ways to retaliate. We think all those reactions are natural because it is the necessary self-defense instinct of human beings. However, we forget that while we are trying to reach our true value of happiness, we cannot hold on to our old instincts. Those comforts might bring us some satisfaction, but they will arouse the obstruction of afflictions inside us.

Recognition, praise, respect, and love all bring very attractive feelings. Who wouldn't like them? But if we like them, that means we do not like anything that creates bad feelings like rejection, criticism, contempt, or hatred. The nature of life, on the other hand, is always changing. Nothing and no fact stay the same for long. What we enjoy, we might become addicted to if we get it, or feel miserable if we do not.

So it is not a good idea to try to catch what we like and resist what we do not like. We will get exhausted.

We might want to help someone, for example, but we would instantly turn around because of their impolite or "I don't care" attitude. If we can let go of such pettiness, reduce the conditions for satisfying our ego in order to think only of helping, then our offer can really happen. Both the giver and the receiver will profit. Once we can let go of the greedy mind, we will step up to a higher level of consciousness. Previously, when someone offended or hurt us, it meant they owed us something (a bad emotion), and when we returned the favor (gave them a bad emotion), then it was fair according to the "law of fair exchange of emotions." However, when we let go and accept our loss, it means we agree to "give unconditionally" an emotional loan to them. Actually sooner or later the universe will draw some energy from them and transform it into a different kind of energy for us as compensation. So even though we let go honestly, sometimes we get back more.

When respected, we are not proud or think little of others because we are aware that everyone has their good points. When praised, we are humble and always conscious that our achievement is thanks to the support and help of many hands. When loved, we are conscious of our good luck so we try to limit our demands and possessiveness. Knowing how to limit ourselves before all enjoyments, even if we deserve them, is the attitude of a wise person. Besides, the practice of letting go helps us release the bad energy active in our minds so we can protect the good seeds there. We can also manage our consciousness to work in harmony with the universe, eliminating all forms of discrimination or opposition among various individuals. As a result, our survival in this life will certainly be peaceful and secure.

Letting go of material comforts is difficult but letting go of mental comforts is a hundred thousand times more difficult. However, we will receive immense, free spaciousness in our minds each time we can let go of something difficult. To be able to do it, we have to practice letting go of prejudices or petty schemes always happening in life. We follow our minds naturally without an attitude of judging or forcing it to obey us. Though we know that we have not truly let go yet, by understanding the causes and continuously observing that process, some day we will overcome it. Letting go of mental comforts is also releasing our "sacred cows." They are "cows" without clear forms, so it is easy for us to mistakenly think that we have become completely cow-less when we haven't. So we need to have trusted friends or groups to enlighten us and let us know which "cows" we are still attached to. If we have twelve cows, this means we have twelve worries; five cows, five worries; only one cow means we have one worry. Of course we would only accept this elimination technique when we have to face a choice between the habit of pleasure and letting go for peace and serenity. When we decide to practice letting go the pleasant feelings of our ego, we have actually stepped on the peaceful path of the saints, though there is still a long way to go.

> *Why bother catching and holding on to things*
> *In a hundred years, will they still be here?*
> *Let's come back and be a white cloud*
> *Gently floating leisurely in the sky*

41

Imagination

> *Circumstances usually can only hurt us, but the culprit for killing us is really our erroneous imagination.*

Living in imagination

When we by chance come across a souvenir of a loved one, all the sweet memories of yesteryear suddenly rush back to fill up our innermost heart. We can see very clearly that person's sparkling eyes and radiant smile. We can hear every gentle, tender word of comfort from the old days. We even remember the perfume scent that person used to wear. We can never forget our feeling the first time when our hands gently touched. Our minds seem to have recorded it all.

As soon as we finish talking to someone and have an interesting or memorable conversation, all the pleasant images and sounds keep coming back. These memories seem to dominate our minds. Once in a while we might giggle by ourselves, or murmur as if the conversation is not yet over. While driving on the highway, we think we are walking in a romantic environment. When the car makes a wrong turn or the car behind honks loudly, all of a sudden, we come back to ourselves. We have the impression that we are being pulled by a certain force from the outside. Actually those images in our minds were competing and overstepping reality. All that data has been stored in the unconscious, so whenever they are aroused, they reappear readily like a film put together without beginning or end. The screen for the film to reappear on is our *imagination*.

Activities of the imagination cannot be separated from *feelings*, *mental formations*, and *consciousness*. Everything happening in those areas of the mind affects our imagination. For example, upon feeling a cold wind, we might shiver and suddenly crave a steamy cup of coffee in a quiet corner shop somewhere. We must have had that kind of memory at least once in the past. Sensing the cold is the function of feeling (also called mental sensation), which quickly sends that information to consciousness for identification. When consciousness finds the most impressive data related to the cold, it will let it appear in our imagination. At that moment, if worry mixes with other mental formations, a future scene will immediately be created, sometimes vaguely, sometimes clearly. This includes a lot of old data and also a lot of brand new images. Our imagination might even come up with creative ideas so unexpected as to be shocking; it is still an ingenious re-creation being performed, either consciously or unconsciously. Therefore, no masterpiece comes solely from a sudden super-idea. Because imagination is derived from the activities of other mental factors, a change in any of the related mental factors affects imagination, causing rate change in imagination to be higher than in the other related mental factors.

Imagination plays a very important role in life. Without imagination, there would be no masterpieces or disaster prevention plans. However, imagination also makes it impossible for us to accept and live deeply in the present. It always weaves attractive dreams far away. If we see greener grass on the other side of the fence, or see a person through the lenses of prejudice, how can we see happiness in our hands to enjoy it fully? This is usually called *delusive thought*. Nowadays it seems everyone is living with delusive thoughts. Their mind is always full of images and sounds mixed together chaotically. To them, the more they can think of good ideas to bring them more income, the better. But once the imagination goes beyond a controllable level and reaches an unstoppable point, the entire conscious process will be upset and move on to more distorted forms. The forms we often see are absent-mindedness, insanity, depression, or mental disorder. We will then look at everything with completely new and strange perception. We will be in a dreamy world where we cannot recognize and locate ourselves.

These days it is easy for people to become delusional. This is caused by too big a shock when a person's spirit is weak or by a certain obsession from the past. But mostly it is from being drowned in illusions too long without anyone to wake the dreamer up. So they unintentionally assimilate reality with what they are thinking. At first the patients fall into the situation of losing self-confidence and hoping for something good and life-changing to happen. Next, they feel that what is happening around them seems to have happened somewhere else and is closely connected to their destiny. Then they try to analyze and explain it with their own vague interpretation. Over time, those thoughts are consolidated into a fixed system that nothing can change. If not treated soon, delusion will seriously influence their attitude toward life and change their personality. They may go from being good and virtuous to cruel and criminal.

The young nowadays tend to overestimate themselves and try to create far-reaching dreams representing lofty goals. In essence however, the gap between their present ability and their dreams is too big. They have never even reached goals that are close at hand, nor have they financially supported themselves to provide food, clothing and shelter. They just have an oversized ambition and imagination, which is a way for them to salvage their hope after many failures and to prove their worth to everyone. Always dreaming about something unfounded is an "imaginary illness," very close to delusion.

An overabundant imagination can sometimes put us in a situation of harming ourselves just from wanting to protect ourselves. Once there was a man rowing hurriedly against the current in a thick fog. Suddenly he saw from afar another boat rushing headlong in his direction. Alarmed, he yelled, "Hey, whose boat is that? Watch out! It's about to crash against mine!" As soon as he finished yelling the two boats collided and capsized. The early morning river water was freezing, so the man was both trembling and furious. He swam hastily to the other boat, intending to punch the other boatman out of spite. But when he turned over the boat he saw that boat had slipped out of the anchor rope and got swept down along the current. Nobody carelessly or intentionally started a fight as he had imagined.

The self-defense instinct, though very necessary, can cause erroneous actions if it is pushed too hard by outdated experiences. The habit of using accumulated experiences rather than observing existing reality is generated from excessive fear and laziness within us. We are always afraid that our favorable conditions will suffer damage and loss. We are also too lazy to observe and think deeply about the nature of objects or problems happening in the present. If we are unable to prevent the old images and sounds from coming back freely to our minds, or if we cannot concentrate on finding ways to identify impulses brought on by afflictions, we will keep having wrong perceptions and making regrettable decisions. Therefore, circumstances usually can only hurt us, but the culprit for killing us is really our erroneous imagination. Be careful with imagination!

Mere recognition

Our understanding is usually formed by accumulated knowledge and experiences. But there is one more item that few people know or can use: it is *intuition*.

Intuition is the ability to know the objects in the present moment with a crystal clear vision like seeing for the very first time. It absolutely does not include accumulated knowledge or experience to define the objects. But our instinct always leans toward enjoyment and self-defense, so we always have the habit of using old knowledge and experience to solve problems quickly and feel better that way. For example, we have two ways to eat a bowl of soup: one is to eat as we usually do, and the other is to eat as if it is the very first time. If we eat the first way, it is certainly not the way to enjoy the soup. We eat to satisfy our hunger or to finish a meal. But if we eat the second way, we will eat mindfully, undisturbed by the previous knowledge and experience about the soup to discover and enjoy it fully. This is the art of eating soup as well as the art of seizing life.

This is like many people who always want to be loved as if for the very first time; they want their beloved to look at them with a fresh look like the first time in love, even though they know a lot about each other's limitations and problems. Many people would like to be seen as they are. In reality, everyone wants to be seen afresh in the other's eyes. Because the truth is that we renew ourselves all the time—for better or maybe for worse. But the paradox is we cannot look at others or problems purely as they are. We only see everything through the shadow of the past, yet we think that we know and understand all.

Meditation is the practice to develop the ability of *mere recognition*. It is important to have a good teacher to help us form this habit from the very beginning. Each time we come to consult with the meditation master, we may have to sit all day without hearing anything interesting besides a few common and even meaningless phrases such as "Drink your tea!" and "The pine tree is there in the front yard!" Many meditation students get a headache from this strange guidance. They try their best to think of some hidden meaning behind the words of the master. But they try in vain. Finally, out of pity, the master would give them a good whacking with his cane. Then they would become awakened. Actually not any meditation student would suddenly get awakened from a cane whack. Those who do get a sudden awakening from what seems to be a common or meaningless saying are blessed with an uncomplicated mind, and understand things as they hear them, without thinking or guessing wildly.

When the meditation master says, "Drink your tea!" the students should drink-tea-like-drinking-tea. They should not drink-tea-like-not-drinking tea because their mind is busy thinking about other topics, no matter how worthy or important they may be. Drink-tea-like-drinking-tea is to recognize the fact that we are sitting and drinking tea, that the object of our contact is the tea cup. No other thought emerges in our minds. This is the most basic step of meditation practice. Just like "the pine tree in the front yard" is an obvious reality before our eyes. But the meditation students might not have seen it when they pass by every day. Or they might just glimpse at it briefly because their mind is loaded with worries and wants. The master does not want his students to keep chasing useless thoughts. He wants them to experience at once the flavor of meditation, not the theory about meditation.

Stop erroneous thinking, recognize clearly what exists around and see clearly each of our reactions to the object of contact. This is human beings' most correct attitude toward life. This attitude is also the foundation to build up wisdom. Wisdom is the ability to understand deeply the nature of all things and all matters in this world. We know clearly what to do and what not to do so we can always harmonize with the universe and achieve true happiness. In other words, to reach the depth and maybe the infinity of our consciousness, we need to limit or even isolate completely our imagination. Imagination not only makes us lose or distort reality, it also makes reality become the vista of the future or the shadow of the past. Therefore, truth must be experienced directly instead of using imagination. The more we use brain power to imagine, the more we go away from the truth and lose it.

Perhaps we do not want to become meditation students or do not need to reach the goal of wisdom. Perhaps we only want to be an ordinary person to enjoy everything life has to offer. But if we are walking on a road in spring time, yet thinking of autumn, or if we are sitting next to our beloved, yet worrying about some exciting projects, or if some people are being honest with us yet we think they are lying, what can we fully enjoy then? Happiness is already in our hands yet we still dream of faraway things, so how can we know happiness? It is true that we have a wonderful civilization nowadays thanks to great creative ideas. But upon reflection, we cannot help feeling alarmed when we know that this Earth is suffering and may be destroyed in the near future because of man's crazy dreams. Imagination based on a foundation of greed to serve the selfish need of those in power is the biggest agent to sink this existing world and lead human beings to endless harmful fantasies.

On the other hand, we can use imagination effectively if we put our imagination in a righteous framework, have the ability to observe and guide it to follow the correct path, know when to take a break, and always recognize the effect of unfavorable environments on the mental formations. If we feel that we are not strong enough to control our imagination so that it affects all our words and actions, then we should come back to practice concentration steadily, for concentration is the opposite of delusive thoughts. However if we have to go to places full of traps and obstacles before we can build solid concentration, then we should always go side by side with those who are living in awareness. They will help us by reminding us many times of who we really are, and we will get awakened to turn in the right direction.

Call me by my true name
In the midst of crazy illusion
Though uncertain how it will be
I'll still turn around for the right direction

42

Concentration

Not thinking is also a very important state that helps the mind to be more balanced and insightful.

Looking deeply at existing reality

Our mind is like a monkey, swinging from one tree branch to another, never standing still. Although the mind is for feeling, thinking, understanding, expressing emotions, or deciding, it is not like a machine that is better when busier. In contrast, when our minds are less busy, it will become more balanced and insightful. Our limitation is usually that we do not know what object to put our minds on and to what degree. The degree should be enough to solve problems as well as be appropriate to our stored energy source, since we have to use energy on other important problems. Mostly, thinking only burns away energy, causing us more stress and biasing our perception without solving anything. Therefore not thinking is also a very important state that helps the mind to be more balanced and insightful.

The philosopher Descartes once said, *"I think, therefore I am."* Many people agree with this viewpoint. They focus on their stream of thoughts to see their own presence. In other words, human beings always have to think; otherwise they are no longer a living reality. This is like many old folks who always have to find something to do to feel their existence and not feel useless or helpless in the eyes of their children or grandchildren. Actually they just have to sit quietly there, smile or always send out peaceful energy for the family to feel their presence. And that is the true presence. Similarly, when looking at a flower, we do not have to think at all to feel its wonderful presence. Sometimes it is the stream of random thoughts that pulls us out of reality. Then we have lost reality. We cannot be present with just our bodies without our minds.

Looking at a flower without thinking or being distracted by the future or the past, we will clearly see a flower blooming this morning. This is a state of full presence, or *mental concentration*. Mental concentration is the mind being still in the reality of something and recognizing clearly what is happening within us and around us. If we maintain our ability to focus on a certain object chosen in reality, with sufficient time and without distraction by other notions, we can create *concentration power*—the power of focusing. Normally, we tend to look at everything just briefly and think we already know it even though each object is constantly moving and changing Strong mental focus can send out bright energy on the object, so the more we look at it, the more we recognize its active composition or its true nature.

Life is always full of attractive phenomena that can easily make our minds run around outside all day. At the dining table or in bed, we still let our minds sink into or float on projects, plans, or sweet images of the past. With time, we gradually lose the habit of resting, or the habit of focusing on an object. On the contrary, we think that the more ideas we can come up with to bring us income, the better. It is as if humans were born just to work and make money. As a result, we overlook the dying potted plant in front of the house. We do not notice our shirt is missing a button. We are not sure how many people are currently present in our house. We do not remember what we are standing here for, or with whom we have an appointment today. How terrible! We also blame ourselves every time we realize that we are being absent-minded. But then we also defend ourselves with legitimate excuses and continue to let our minds wander around finding fun and attractive places to go to.

Meanwhile the sunshine will feel warmer if we look at it carefully. The bird chirping will sound clearer when we listen deeply. The tea fragrance will smell more delicious when we hold up the tea cup mindfully. The true presence of both our body and mind will enhance our surroundings, and we will also enjoy and profit more. Another profound truth is that when the mind is settled, being present 100% in the present moment, it can connect with peaceful energy already available in the universe. It will calm the toxic energy within us and lift up valuable qualities in the depth of our heart. In particular, mental focus helps us maintain steadily the ability to observe afflictions from the time of their birth to the moment they disappear. In other words, without mental focus, we cannot fully understand afflictions. Without understanding them, we cannot remove them.

The art of mental concentration

To practice the habit of concentration, the first condition is to be less busy. We have to give ourselves a good opportunity to come back to ourselves. We cannot order our minds to stop when we still want to catch all kinds of things. A gentle and quiet space will help us to bring our minds back and be joined with our bodies. Where the body is, the mind is too. Just like when we use a magnifying glass to catch the sunrays. They will converge in one point. Then we put a handful of dry straw underneath the magnifying glass. The converged sunrays will ignite the straw. A high degree of mental focus has the capacity to burn away part of the afflictions, making us feel lighter, calmer, and more insightful.

We should try to practice living slowly, but not too slow or it becomes unnatural. Each time we turn on a water faucet, close a door, turn on a TV, or put down a tea cup, we should observe those objects carefully. In particular, we should take careful note of what happens in our minds during the whole process. Divide each action into small parts to make the concentration experiment easier. For example, when picking up a cup of tea, we focus on three stages: picking it up, bringing it over, and drinking it. While drinking, we also focus on three stages: having just had a sip, drinking, and when the drinking is done. No matter where we are or what we do, we should apply this practice of dividing each action into small parts to observe, except for the work of a dangerous or urgent nature.

Observing our footsteps when walking in a room is also a way to develop our concentration. We just have to relax our arms alongside the body and begin to pay attention to the footsteps in three stages: lifting up the foot, moving the foot forward and putting the foot down. We can also divide each movement into three smaller parts so our focus will be even stronger: the beginning—the middle—the end of lifting the foot; the beginning—the middle—the end of stepping the foot forward; the beginning—the middle—the end of putting the foot down. Remember that we only use the mind to feel instead of looking at the footstep. This exercise, though somewhat dry, can bring us some unexpected results only after about half an hour of constant practice. The slowness will make it harder for our mind to change its target, giving it enough time to look deeply at the object and at ourselves.

Wonderful breaths

For many generations, successful mediation masters always consider the breath as the first choice for mental concentration. The breath is not only a physiological process; it is also a bridge that joins with other psychological processes. In other words, through the breath, we can know the changing states of our mind. The interesting thing is that we can feel the breath directly without the interference of any thought or experience. Don't forget that breathing is a natural process. Although we do not use will power to interfere, the breath still comes in and goes out at its own speed. Therefore, when choosing the breath as the object of focus, we must respect its naturalness. We just need to recognize and understand it, instead of forcing it to be this way or that way. In reality, we often make mistakes while breathing, wanting the breath to go our way. Perhaps we want it to be longer or shorter, softer or lighter. This is a wrong attitude that should be avoided. The difference between a natural breath and a forced breath is very delicate one that only a subtle observer can detect. Remember that we merely observe it. Do not mumble a certain phrase in our minds to remind ourselves and do not imagine anything else.

For clear observation, first we have to recognize what our breath is like. Focus on the up and down movements of the belly: breathing in, the belly goes up automatically; breathing out, the belly goes down automatically. This breathing technique is usually suitable for a small number of people because some people might get a little flustered from trying to stay with the abdominal movements. In addition, following the breath this way does not help us to feel the breath directly. Most meditation practitioners often focus on the tip of the nose, right inside the nostril or on the upper lip. This depends on each individual's nose. Breathe in a long breath deeply and take note of the air going in from the outside. Try to feel what part of the nose it touches most clearly. This is the point we need to remember to observe the breath when we let it come back naturally or in succeeding practice sessions. Then our mind tracks down the breath. Trying to control the breath will be very tiring and hard to catch because it keeps flowing.

You should practice observing the very subtle connection among the breaths, the urge to control the breath, and even the attitude of wanting to stop that control. At first we will feel a little uncomfortable. Gradually we can feel the quality of the natural breath is completely different from the controlled breath. From this, we can learn much about our attitude of frequent wanting and forcing. After observing the breath subtly like that for a short time, we will no longer want to control it. In the beginning stage, observing the breath might be boring and dull. But if we persist and breathe correctly, we will gradually find it quite varied and extremely wonderful. The truth is no two breaths are alike. They transform very subtly. With a shallow mind or that prejudice that they are all the same, we certainly will not feel or understand. Observing the breath does not just focus on its features but also its content. It is really a symphony alternating different states of panting and calming, deep and shallow, urgent and gentle.

During the practice process, sometimes we have the impression that we cannot recognize our breath. Don't worry too much! Focus on coming back to the point we have chosen, at the tip of the nose or the ups and downs of the belly. We can catch it just after a few temporary strong breaths. Remember that we should never blame ourselves during meditation practice. It is of no use. It is only the consequence of our process of living in mindlessness. Just remember to remind ourselves often. Once in a while, images, sounds, comments, worries, regrets, sadness, or bewilderment, etc., will appear in our minds. During that moment, we can temporarily focus on these new objects. In case we feel we do not have any more concentration power, we should temporarily "disregard" sudden changes around, and give priority to concentrating on the breath. But if we are ready to observe, we should only observe one psychological phenomenon at a time instead of all of them at the same time.

When those objects fade away, we should bring our minds back to the breath. It is the main focus then. The breath is our safest refuge after each trip to visit other areas, be they reactions in the body or in the mind. Don't be impatient while practicing. Don't be too anxious to solve all afflictions. Thanks to the concentration power accumulated from the breath, every time we observe such powerful changes, it will give us new experience about the nature of impermanence and the non-self of all things and all phenomena. The attitude of observing with a mind not greedy or resisting but purely with a mind of investigating and discovering will give us wonderful insights about ourselves and about life. Before, we never knew these because our minds were always full of tumult and affliction. One thing to pay attention to is that, while we are experiencing our breathing deeply, we might suddenly hear a lot of screaming or a great number of jumbled sounds. Or we might feel helpless like an uncontrollable car plunging down an abyss. Nothing is strange. Actually our minds are always tumultuous and full of conflicts and voids. We just never looked at it carefully before. Just keep on practicing, smiling and observing those strange sounds like the return of affliction. Then we will get over it.

Around us there are still so many people who live by depending on the chance of the situation, unaware of what is ravaging inside them. They look like they have no problems, but actually they are being fettered and controlled. As for us, though we have to face inner troubles, we are on the way to untangle them. Start taking good care of ourselves right now. Don't wait till affliction explodes, causing heavy damage before trying to find a solution that is too late. If we wait until we are thirsty before we dig a well, we will die of thirst. Remember, every change that leads to improvement needs work; nonetheless, the mind is complex and mysterious. Another thing to pay attention to is that it is the correct attitude toward practice that determines success, not excessive enthusiasm. Ambition in meditation practice, as in any other area, leads to pressure and making mistakes.

So, only when the mind is still can we observe steadily and carefully all constituents of our afflictions. Then we will know what to do and what not to do to transform them. And only when the power of focusing and the power of observing become well trained can the seed of wisdom begin to grow. At that time we will see clearly our status and life exactly as its true nature always is. We will suffer no longer.

> *So many years yet still drifting*
> *No safe and calm ferry for landing*
> *Come back and anchor at the old place, oh boat!*
> *To feel a peaceful and serene world coming*

43

Emotions

Emotions are momentary reactions to protect the ego's interests.

The process of emotions

When we love a certain object, we try all kinds of ways to possess it. But we get tired of it just after a short time and want to find something new, though the old object has not changed at all. This shows that we are controlled by emotions. This is similar to when someone offends us; we get angry and find ways to retaliate. At least we would say something nasty to hurt them to vent our anger. We cannot stay calm to check out the reasons and come up with a more amiable solution. This is the situation of being a slave to emotions. When we hear touching and heartrending stories from people, we cannot control our tears, get tenderhearted, and agree to all their requests. But after a few hours, we regret our impetuous decision. This action is also led by emotions.

Human activities lie within the control of a psychological system that consists of four groups (aggregates) of mental activity: feelings (sensations), perception (imagination), mental formations (intentional reactions), and consciousness (awareness). Each group is an aggregate formed and constantly affected by the other groups. For example, when drinking tea, if we can sense the hotness, the fragrance, and the taste of the tea, it is from the feelings. If we recognize this is tea and not other stuff, and we can tell what kind of tea from its fragrance, it is from perception. The notion that we like this kind of tea is mental formations. The intention of taking this tea home to treat our friends is again mental formations. On the way home, if the tea flavor still lingers in our minds, it means our mental formations as imagination are still active. When we serve the tea, if everybody says bad things about it, we will get sad and disappointed; we even tell ourselves never to do it again; this is the control of mental formations. Our cognizance or awareness throughout all of this is consciousness.

Feeling has the function of receiving what the senses accept from the outside with a positive, negative or neutral affect. Perception has the function of identifying or recognizing all the data. Consciousness has the function of being aware of all that the senses contact and storing the information in what is called mental storage, the subconscious, the unconscious or depth consciousness. Mental formations manifest love, tolerance, patience, flexibility, modesty, and even anger, discrimination, haughtiness, loneliness, despair, etc. In general, all attitudes of likes and dislikes belong to the function of mental formations.

Though each aggregate or group cannot function alone, mental formations are the direct "messengers" of the self (ego). We can also say that mental formations are the home of the self. Furthermore, all the attitudes of liking and disliking are seeds hiding deeply in subconscious storage. When these seeds are prompted by the external environment via the senses or other seeds nearby, they become a source of energy emerging on the surface of consciousness. This is the work of the mental formations. Though most mental formations embrace the characteristics of liking and disliking, only those that manifest momentary reactions without rationality and interference can be classified as emotions. In brief, we can define emotions as momentary reactions to protect the ego's interests.

The medical field defines emotions as chemical states of the brain. Any chemical state of the brain is "cleaned away" after about 15 minutes due to the constant renewal of the circulatory blood flow to the brain. The nervous system also changes constantly to send information about the happenings of the external environment or experiences already registered in the brain's storage. The nature of emotions is temporary.

Even though emotions such as jealousy or hatred might last dozens of years, their frequency always changes. Every time an emotion is expressed, it brings new knowledge and experience, making its power stronger or weaker. Furthermore, an emotion might change directions suddenly, e.g., from raging anger to passionate love if a person's ego is suddenly respected or pampered (in one form or another). It can be said that emotions are the shallow reaction part of a person's psychology. Their task is to express an attitude of content or discontent, like or dislike, or acceptance or rejection. As a result, emotions often bring us regret right afterward. Therefore, those who are regularly controlled by emotions will behave very superficially. Though they know all the right things, when a good or bad emotion explodes, they follow it like a child, instinctively, regardless of consequences.

Taking care of emotions

We cannot live without emotions because they are human sentiments. But when emotions are maximized so that they go beyond the control of reason, we lose our own self-control. We then have to accept the mistakes made while under the control of emotions and the consequences afterward.

While in love, people usually want their heart to lead the way rather than use their head to reason. This sounds very touching, as if we want to love with all our might without any careful consideration or deliberation. In actuality, we don't even know that we can't control the need to satisfy our emotions. If we used reason, it would force us to suppress that satisfaction. This is why when two persons get bored with each other, they cannot continue to live together out of kindness and affection. Even when they know that it is best to solve problems with tolerance and mutual acceptance, they still cannot do it. They are unable to overcome the need to satisfy their emotions. Instead, they think that the reason they are bored with each other is because their hearts cannot accept the other person anymore.

Of course we have to enjoy life, but the more we enjoy, the easier we get addicted to enjoyment and become weaker. Meanwhile, life does not always bring us favorable conditions. If we cannot continue to enjoy ourselves at our usual level, bad emotions will spring up and torture us. Therefore, wise people sacrifice unnecessary good emotions and accept necessary bad emotions in order to reach the loftier goal of true and lasting happiness.

Though emotions are closely related to heredity, it is the childhood environment that forms emotional strength in each person. If we are conscious of always being controlled by emotions—doing what we should not and not doing what we should—we have to be determined to rearrange our lifestyle. First, we should live with a stable person who lives with good principles and seriously follows an activity schedule. That person should be a little strict and ready to remind us every time we break a rule or promise. We can even join the armed forces or a monastery for a long period of time, to be trained in a strict and regulated environment, if we see that our lifestyle is excessively undisciplined. In the beginning stage we will meet many obstacles and troubles because we have to give up old habits to learn new habits. But once we are trained, we will feel delighted, free, and stable because we can control ourselves in all situations. In other words, we will no longer worry about being pulled or controlled by situations or other objects. Those who do not openly express emotions may not appear friendly with others, but the more we have contact and live with them, the more we trust them and feel safe. The reason is they are very patient and responsible.

If we know we are arts-oriented and often feel exhausted after unleashing emotions during a creative process, we should regularly interact with friends from different fields. Or we can try out another field completely different from our usual interest. Besides, we should try to stay away from our favorite contacts and practice socializing with people we do not normally like. Likewise, we should try to turn a deaf ear to flattery and praise and practice listening carefully to straightforward suggestions or criticism. We can also do these things to regulate the shallowest layer of emotions that we inadvertently nourish the most, which are those we feel and receive from our senses combined with our attitudes of liking and disliking.

Those are effective solutions to help us balance our emotions. When they are balanced, we will be able to observe all objects more accurately. When we can understand and can transform "stormy" emotions, our lives can have lasting peace and freedom. However, we should first find a calm and quiet place to reflect on our habitual emotions. The most ideal place is a meditation center.

At first we will learn to focus our minds on an object (concentration). This is an important basic lesson to help us develop the ability to focus steadily without the interference of other ideas. We should practice this even if it takes three months or six months to form a solid concentration habit. Without this habit, we cannot be strong enough to discover and untangle complicated and subtle psychological layers.

Actually, the main task of a meditation student is only to observe carefully all psychological phenomena with an attitude of no liking, no disliking, no prejudice, and no judgment. Just calmly observe from the time the seed of affliction is aroused and manifests itself on the surface of consciousness that it is the form of energy. Then observe the process of how that energy is continuously aroused by the external environment or other elements of the psychological process. Then observe its pushing us to talk or act, and then observe its disappearance and the cause of its disappearance. The most important thing is not to eradicate afflictions, but to clearly understand their structure. If we cannot understand afflictions, we can only suppress them and can never transform them. It is no less important to observe our attitude each time we face afflictions. A resistant attitude may conceal or expand afflictions. This skill can be practiced anytime and anywhere. Whenever the emotional energy overflows, we should stop doing our work right away, if possible, and give priority to the task of taking care of our emotion. This is like a mother who is busy cooking or sewing but as soon as she hears her baby cry, she immediately stops everything to take care of the baby first. The mother only needs to pick up the baby and comfort it a little and its cry will soften instantly. From careful observation, she will understand why her baby cries, perhaps from being thirsty for milk or from a soiled diaper, and help it in time. That subtle observation of the mother is called "right mindfulness." Right mindfulness is the antidote to all afflictions because all afflictions are isolated and melted in the strong light of right mindfulness. Therefore we can say that right mindfulness is the heart of meditation practice. We just need to develop right mindfulness steadily and the afflictions will self-destruct without any effort from us.

Afflictions originally are phenomena, so emotions are also phenomena. They were born from the erroneous operation of our psychological processes with the main cause being the erroneous perception about the ego. Remember that we cannot use reason to suppress one perception and replace it with another. What we should do is to diligently maintain the habit of observing all changes in our minds in all situations, and then we can recognize the false characteristic of those emotions. Once desires and conflicts are gone, afflictions or emotions will disappear too. Our minds will become clear and calm like a still surface of a lake without any gentle waves. When emotions are regulated and monitored within the framework of mindfulness, they will become an important and necessary material to create colors and precious flavors in because humanity is a lively reality, not inanimate wood or stone.

Far gone in an emotional coma
Unaware of our drifting whereabouts
This morning a flower comes out
Welcoming the caressing sunshine

44

Peace

Only when our mind has no more anxiety, yearning, or conflicts, and accepts and adapts to all situations can we taste peace and true happiness.

When the realm is peaceful, so is the mind

Our minds are always closely connected to the external world, since the two most basic needs of enjoyment for human beings, physical comforts and spiritual comforts, lie on the outside. So we never stop praying for favorable conditions to come to us. We only feel at peace when all our wishes can come true, or at least when we have no problems. Not long afterward, unpleasant things might rush in, or other wants and wishes might come up inside us, leaving no place for peace. When the realm is not peaceful, neither is the mind.

It is easy for us to find peace when we travel to a far and out-of-the-way countryside or to a quiet mountain area. We can temporarily put aside all worries and hurries of life. We can get nourished from the gentle and fresh scenery. We can feel life in the here and now. So our minds can really quiet down and take a break. When we find such an environment to nourish our minds, we make an effort to cherish every pleasant moment. Regrettably, our effort might not be enough. The habit of holding on to the objects that bring us familiar emotions might appear suddenly and suppress even our will power. Then all at once we might feel out of place and dazed as if we were a stranger. And if we reluctantly come to a peaceful environment, we might feel jumpy as if we were sitting on pins and needles. We even want to break the silence to feel more at ease. If we cannot talk to anyone, we might think about the past or imagine the future to kill time. Therefore, peaceful a realm can help calm the mind, but if the mind is too disturbed, no scenery can help.

Nowadays, the young often complain that life is too busy, that they have no time to relax. But when they have holidays, they find all kinds of things to do. If they do not go shopping, they go to visit friends; if they do not cook, they go online for news; if they do not watch TV, they wander the streets. They can't seem to rest. Their minds have to hold on to something or think of what they consider important, then they feel settled. They just go to sleep when they are exhausted. They only recognize the value of peace when they are sick in bed or in a terrible accident. It is true that only when our mind no longer desires or opposes any conditions, accepts reality in its absolute form, and sees the value of life in each moment, does that restful moment lead to a peaceful mind. But a peaceful mind in this case still depends on the condition of the situation and stays beyond our control. After experiencing some major accidents, many people can feel the value of life and become aware of what they should cherish, so they think they have turned a corner in life. But only a short time later, the temptations of the external world bring them back to their old consciousness. They resume their struggles and feel weary, as if they had never become aware of anything different.

Once a monk named Hui Ke wanted to practice the path with Meditation Master Bodhidharma. After many days without learning anything important from the master as expected, Hui Ke felt puzzled. Mustering all his courage, he approached the master, bowed, and pleaded for a method to quiet his mind. The meditation master said, "Give me your disquiet mind and I'll help you." Hui Ke looked carefully within himself to find his restless mind and then replied, "I looked, but I couldn't find it." The meditation master smiled and said, "I've calmed your mind already."

Our minds can suffer from restlessness, weariness, and affliction even when we want to receive good things and learn ways to elevate our heart. Of course no one can show their mind to others because it does not have a concrete shape or form. Besides, a restless mind is only a temporary psychological phenomenon; it cannot stay in the same state for long. But the meditation master suggested his student show him his disquieted mind in order to teach him a lesson: When the want is still there, the mind is not calm; when the want is gone, the mind will be calm. It is clear that the meditation master did not teach his student any method but only reminded him to come back and use the disquiet to find the quiet. The quiet that does not depend on external conditions is the true quiet. Certainly it takes more hard work to maintain that quiet mind continuously, but it is a very important starting point.

When the mind is peaceful, so is the realm

When our mind keeps a balanced state within ourselves—content with what we have, not wanting to have more or less—it means we also are balanced with all things around us. This is the important foundation for peace to be born. The wonderful thing when our minds are peaceful is that we will see all objects or all problems in a different light, which is rather accurate with what is truly happening. Because when the mind is peaceful, it is not only very clear and bright, but it can also connect with the energies emitted from the very objects and problems we are contacting. In contrast, when feeling angry or passionately in love, we are not able to see reality accurately. We seem to be in a different world.

When we see little waves on a lake's surface, we might think the lake is turbulent. Or when we Vietnamese see a mountaintop that is white, we might guess the mountain must be very old. But that is looking shallowly. We see, upon close observation, that the turbulence is only on the surface part of the lake impacted by the wind, and that underneath, the lake is calm. And we also discover that the white color on the mountain is snow, and that the mountain is actually very green. When the mind is peaceful, we will see clearly what is phenomenon or essential nature, and what is false or true. Most importantly, we have found ourselves—an honest and innocent self that has been drifting with the ups and downs of life for a long time. The peaceful mind is really our true mind, and the restless mind is only momentary delusions.

The Buddha affirmed: *"All dharmas [phenomena] are created only by the mind"*—how our minds feel is the way we feel about the world around us. Beautiful and ugly, high and low, rich and poor, and pros and cons are not the nature of reality. They are all woven by human greed-anger-ignorance. When our wants are satisfied, we think life is beautiful. And when things go against our hopes, we think life is terrible. In the meantime, all things and all beings in this world and even in the whole universe operate following natural principles: cause and effect, and causal conditions. The universe does not pamper or hate anyone. We are just too greedy. When it agrees with us, we are happy but we are never surprised and never reject it; however, when it goes against us, we feel alarmed and resist it. Therefore only when we can transform all those unnecessary energies of desires and conflicts and return to the wonderful quiet nature of our minds can we find the world around us truly peaceful, very lovely and really worth keeping.

With his profound wisdom, the Buddha used to make clear: *"When the mind is at peace, the world is at peace."* Though the world around us is still full of violence, if our heart is peaceful, it will not be affected. Furthermore, the peaceful energy inside us will link up with other peaceful energies floating everywhere in the world. When sufficient conditions are met, they will have a great effect—a peaceful world. Actually everything on the planet is very peaceful, only human beings are not and have turned things upside down. But the true nature of humanity is also always peaceful. The problem is we let the energies of greed and of conflict suppress our gentle nature. Peace is everyone's problem even though nobody can make everybody in this world peaceful. However, the peaceful energy inside each person has great interactive characteristics. It will facilitate the occurrence of peaceful conditions in everyone. Therefore every individual's peaceful energy is very essential for the family, society, the world, and even the universe.

In the song "Peaceful," the musician Quoc Bao was very subtle to note: *"A little moment of peace to soften the heart/ Peace for us to enter the night/ Peace for the flower to blossom/ Peace for the moon to rise/ Peace for the waves to caress the shore/ Unbelievable peace/ Our mind murmurs some prayers for peace."* When the mind is peaceful, even for just a little while, all angers and prejudices will disintegrate. In that little moment of peace, we can see all the wonderful reality that we normally do not: the blossoming flower, the high moon, and the endless waves caressing the shore. However, the musician affirms even more—it is due to our peaceful energy tonight that the flower blooms, the moon rises up high, and the waves caress the shore. It is true that the scenery around happens to be following its natural cycle, but this does not mean that the scenery is not related to human beings. All things and all beings are always interacting with one another. When the flower in our heart blossoms, the moon in our heart is bright and clear, the waves in our heart caress the shore, how can we not nourish those external things? And do we not ourselves expect that when our heart is at peace, compassion wakes up. This is the *Heart Sutra* of humankind.

There are two very interesting lines from the song: *"It seems from immensity another life is born for us/ It seems from togetherness we grow up and mature together."* It takes someone with painful experience who has reached a peaceful shore to write these lines. When our minds are peaceful, it is like we were born one more time—an old notion died for a new notion to be born. That is our new person. Although the new and old persons are not two separate entities, they cannot be one entity any more. The question is whether we really want and are brave enough to let the anger and hatred inside us die and allow tolerance and forgiveness to be born. Maybe they were born already but we refused to accept them. We still try to hold on to the old and withering person to satisfy our selfish and weak ego. The wonderful thing is that our new life exists thanks to the previous suffering in life. When we are aware that from togetherness we grow up, how can we blame each other? Therefore, *"Please give each other a genuine ear for listening/ To forget all problems and separations"*—not only do we forgive each other, we also cherish the moments when we can see each other, and help each other become refreshed instead of blaming or competing with each other. Only a peaceful heart can do this.

Indeed, only when our mind has no more anxiety, yearning, or conflicts, and accepts and adapts to all situations can we taste peace and true happiness. In the beginning, if we find it difficult to keep our minds calm before conflicting situations, we should temporarily find ourselves a place safe enough to calm our heart. When the heart is really peaceful, and the afflictions have been settled and transformed, we can bravely come back to be in touch with all situations and objects. Though the situations are still chaotic and our objects are still difficult, we will not find them too terrible with our new level of consciousness. We ourselves can help to change the situation. Therefore, if we know that when the mind is peaceful, the world will certainly be peaceful too, so we should try to take care of our minds instead of chasing after worldly ambitions. We should not forget that when the world is peaceful but our minds are not, we will not find our lives to be peaceful.

Minh Niem

Adjust to situation
Don't be too strong-willed
Keep the mind and not the realm
Once the mind is peaceful, the world will be too

45

Worry

> *In order to grasp life, we have to practice placing worries in an appropriate framework.*

What will the future be?

Thanks to their survival instinct, most animals have the ability to foresee circumstances that can impact their livelihood or even their lives. Swans have to migrate south with their flock before winter arrives. If left behind for some reason, a swan cannot fly thousands of miles alone to a warm area and may die from starvation in thick snow. Chameleons also change their skin color quickly to blend in with their surroundings between seasons. However, they are always afraid that sharp-eyed birds might discover their camouflage. Hence, they develop very acute observation skills; their movements are also very light and cautious.

The human race is the same. Since long ago, our ancestors worried about the future. So they learned to observe the weather, conquer wild beasts, and store seeds carefully for the following farming season. Thus worry is deeply rooted in humanity. Today we still continue to develop that effective weapon for survival. A society, no matter how civilized, can never prepare for all difficulties or sudden disasters. So anyone who can prepare thoroughly far in advance is considered smart, wise and mature. Business people always worry about losing customers, markets fluctuating or business failing. Workers keep hoping for pay raises or worry about being laid off. Students also never stop worrying about exams, afraid they will not pass entrance examinations to well-known schools. Peddlers worry when it rains. Beggars also worry when their cans are still empty at the end of the day.

However, not all worries are oriented to our survival instinct. There are targets aimed only at improving enjoyment without which we are still safe and still live well. But human perceptions are strange. Humans always think that the more comforts they have, from physical to spiritual, the safer and happier they will be, so they never stop accumulating. But the more they try to accumulate, the more they worry. Even after their aspirations have been met, they still worry. They are afraid the fruits of their labor might go bad, or they feel they are still inferior to others economically or socially. Worse still, only after a short time, they suddenly find that what they have acquired is no longer interesting. So they will enslave themselves again to get more and then worry more. Human worries are therefore endless. Perhaps they would end only with the end of their lives. All those worries come from their wrong perceptions and weak inner strength. This is a psychological illness that should be treated.

It is a vicious cycle that begins with a worry about a problem that needs to be solved once and for all within a fixed period of time. Since we have not found a solution yet, our brain keeps reminding us and we keep thinking about it. Then we worry because we have not thought of a good solution. Then we think of the problem. Then we are anxious about solving it but can't yet. And we worry again. Each time the vicious cycle is repeated, our level of bad emotions increases, and, with constant pressure, the emotional flow is blocked. If it is an important problem, our willpower will certainly apply more pressure. The stronger the pressure, the easier it is for emotions to explode. Of course if the important problem is not solved, we might incur a great loss. But we would not suffer or get a headache if we had the ability to accept it as something beyond our control—which frequently happens in this forever-changing life.

But this is easier said than done. In reality, the psychological chain reaction of fear, worry, and pressure never stops happening to protect our current interests. That psychological chain is a series of very harmful emotions. A continuous psychological deadlock will repress bad emotions to a high degree. This is a favorable opportunity for the endocrine glands to release a toxic hormone like epinephrine into the blood stream, disturbing some chemical exchange activities of the body. Medical experts have affirmed this disturbance as having a strong impact on heart problems, neurasthenia, high blood pressure, memory loss, and cancer cell development. In addition, it also makes us tired, depressed and ill-tempered, and it lowers our productive abilities.

Imagination is an important agent in bringing worries to a tense and critical level. But before imagination magnifies totally false images, it is often aroused by fear. Fear originates from the lack of confidence in our own knowledge and coping experience to solve problems and our inability to accept all situations without worrying about losing face or getting hurt.

Wonderful present moment

An old Vietnamese saying goes, *"Without far-sighted worrying, trouble will be close behind."* It is a reminder for us not to live recklessly, indulgently, unaware of the consequences of our actions; otherwise we would soon regret them. This is not to advise us to worry more. Of course if we think and plan carefully before doing something, we can get good results more easily. But reality shows that we can't always foresee accurately. Some worries are unnecessary and terribly wrong, but we seldom check them again or let some of them go. Although worries can push us to work harder and concentrate our efforts to solve problems, the immediate consequence of worries is that we cannot be fully present in the present moment to be deeply in touch with the wonderful well-being around us. When our mind is always occupied by countless confusing images and sounds, how can we notice and observe anything? The situation of losing ourselves starts here.

When we hold a glass of water up high, in the first few minutes there is no problem. But after half an hour or an hour, our arm will go numb and hurt. If we keep it up for a day, our whole body will certainly get paralyzed. Our mind is the same. If it has to put up with worries for a long time, it will become paralyzed, no longer strong and clear to recognize or solve any problem. Even when a problem to be solved is very important, if we keep sacrificing the valuable sources of energy in our mind to acquire lavish enjoyments, are we really smart?

In order to grasp life, we have to practice placing worries in an appropriate framework, but with the condition that we have enough strength and clarity of mind to observe the process of worries as it is taking place. Don't let them hold on to us everywhere and turn into a natural activity. The worry energy is very toxic. Not only does it make us frown, wither, and age faster, it also makes people around us feel paralyzed and tired. Remember that worry can also be hereditary. If we happen to inherit a large load of worries passed down from previous generations, we should try to change them once and for all so our offspring can easily step into the future.

One of the tricks to help us worry less is to accept the worst case scenario that can happen. This depends on each individual's knowledge and skill. Experienced people will give priority to keeping their mind peaceful rather than sacrificing it to have more enjoyment. Any enjoyment has only momentary value, but the mental disturbances will dominate us all our life. Actually, we just worry too much. There are many reasons to prove that life is valuable. Even if we fail sometimes, it is an important lesson for us to recheck our attitude of attachment, or to develop our endurance. When we can accept the worst loss, we have no more reason to worry, although we still save energy to solve problems in order to reduce the consequences. The attitude of not focusing too much on success or failure will help us be calm, clear-minded, and self-confident enough to find the most proper solution.

Of course we cannot always "shut our eyes" to all problems. It depends on each problem and our skills at that time. So we need to set up an appropriate process to solve problems quickly without losing too much energy. Step one, we should write down what we are worrying about. Step two, we should sit down and concentrate our mind to think of a way to solve the problem we are worrying about. In other words, avoid the situation of thinking in utter confusion all the time and everywhere. Step three, we should write down in detail the steps to solve our problem. Step four, we should focus all energy on solving the problem, if necessary. Step five, we should get rid of worries beyond our present ability to deal with them. Step six, we definitely should not bother thinking about the worries that we cannot solve. We should keep in mind that the six steps of problem solving require serenity, calmness, and no pressure on ourselves. We have to be brave to stop instantly when we feel very tense and exhausted. We can continue another time when we are calmer.

Nourish your energy to pay attention and regularly observe what is happening inside us and outside us. It is a wonderful method to help us stop thinking trivially and recover our energy. Any activity in daily life such as cooking, cleaning, talking on the phone, meeting customers, planning or making an important decision should be done mindfully and observed carefully. The most important thing is to see clearly our reaction for each activity. Stepping out in the open air for a walk to focus our mind on each step and being mindful of our breathing are effective solutions to stop worries. The energy of nature will help to refresh and calm us.

When we are too stressed, we should lie down. Lie comfortably on your back on the floor or on the bed, with two arms relaxed alongside the body, two feet turned outward, eyes closed and a gentle smile on your lips to help the facial muscles relax. After that, follow the up and down movements of the belly to be aware of the in and out breaths. About five minutes later, focus your mind on any part of the body using your direct senses, not depending on the breath anymore. If some parts of the body are sick are in pain, pay longer attention to them while sending them loving thoughts. After practicing a few times, you will feel that the ailing area is soothed and made better from the energy of the other healthy areas. While relaxing, you might fall into a deep sleep. Your body and mind at that time are supple because they are relieved from stress and worry. Just half an hour of lying in relaxation will help us regain freshness and peace.

Since long ago, we have lost the habit of taking rests. When the body is tired, the mind cannot be clear. If we keep exhausting the energies of the body and mind to serve our ambitions, we will regret it soon because of their unsalvageable collapse. Perhaps we have been so absorbed in pursuing temptations in the outside world that we completely forget that living is the main goal of life. To live is to be happy and to love one another. After so many ups and downs of life, we must know well that no loss or suffering is greater than the separation from our loved ones. What is the use of wealth or fame when we have no one around to share and appreciate it? Big worries themselves have taken us away from reality and prevented us from recognizing the wonderful values of our loved ones. What will tomorrow be like; how can we know? Come back and hold tight all the real things happening today. Living deeply today means worrying less about tomorrow.

Minh Niem

What will tomorrow be?
Who can tell or see?
In wonderful present moment
Be devoted to and cherish each other

46

Relaxation

The road leading to relaxation is by nature relaxation itself.

The means is also the end

All Vietnamese are familiar with the folk song lines *"Let's go tilling the land and planting rice seedlings together/ Now it's hard work but someday we'll be comfortably off."* The term "be comfortably off" means being content, at ease, free from stress or worry. Because we see that we are still lacking many things, all the comforts we have are not enough for us to be happy, so we always try and remind one another to "till the land" to accumulate more. We try to put up with hard work now so we can enjoy tomorrow.

But what will we enjoy tomorrow? Having a storehouse of golden rice will indeed provide us with good food and nice clothes, but will it meet all human beings' needs for happiness? Can it solve loneliness, sorrow, betrayal, or despair? Furthermore, after we have been fed and clothed, we often develop bad habits, chase after the latest trends, or dream of the different kinds of happiness farther away. Therefore a "golden rice storehouse" does not necessarily help us to be "comfortably off."

So many people have large amounts of assets but never know what "comfortable" is. They are always busy, tense, and full of fears. Sometimes we see children flying kites over the rice fields, young village women picking lotus flowers in the moonlight, or a farmer fishing in the river; these folks enjoy fully each passing moment. They are truly "comfortable," perhaps because they are always content with what they have. Though they still struggle for food and clothing, they never let work dominate their present valuable life. Their time and energy are essentially used to live really deeply, to live in harmony and to love one another.

Therefore, only when we have a great need for physical comfort do we think that "a golden rice storehouse" is the main goal of our life. On the other hand, if we have experienced the pain of separation and loss, we will see that the cozy moments by each other's side is the true reason for living. This is like the next two lines that the folk song describes: *"On the shallow field or in the deep field/ The husband ploughs, the wife transplants rice seedlings, the buffalo draws a harrow."* Having a husband, a wife, and also a buffalo like a good friend, always working hard together every day, is already a condition for happiness. To them, each passing day or each task is all happiness, and a reason to live. They do not disregard what they have in order to run after other things, especially things that they are not sure about. Perhaps they believe that the means of life are also the ends of life.

As for us, we always have many ends to pursue. When we have a new goal, we turn our back on the old goal, or treat it like a temporary means to serve the big, new goal. For example, when we need to go to point B to do something, B is our goal. At that time, only B is important. However, before arriving at B, we may have a need to relax, to practice walking after a traffic accident, or simply to walk in a lively way, then the stepping movement itself is the goal of that moving process. Walk for the sake of walking, not for arriving at someplace. We do not need to arrive because we are enjoying each of our wonderful steps. Tomorrow, maybe we might not walk again.

Isn't being able to walk a great happiness? It seems we have never seen us walking. We have never felt the deep value of someone who can still use their strong legs. We always walk quickly and hurriedly as if being chased by a ghost, as if to grasp something extremely important without which we could not live. What can be done at point B is important, but not at the expense of the entire distance of the road leading to B. The road to B is just as important as B. Both can bring us the value of happiness. Both are the means as well as the ends.

Relax now or never

People often say to each other *"Secure home, happy settlement"* meaning we have to settle down securely with good physical comforts before we can build a happy life. This viewpoint has fooled many generations of humankind, and we still believe it. But look at it again! Everyone tries their best to accumulate things hoping for a better life, but it is really strange that the more material possessions we have, the more we find them insufficient. We work hard to buy a house to our liking. But we are on the street or in the office all day. Our refrigerator is packed with food, but we eat out every day. We do not remember how many suits or pieces of clothing we own, but we hurry to different stores to buy more. Furthermore, when such things as sickness, spoiled children, family unrest, wrongdoer's harassment, etc., happen, then everything that makes up a "happy settlement" suddenly becomes meaningless.

Not relaxing in the present, we put our faith in the future. Many people think they have to wait until they retire, then they have to relax, even if they do not want to. To them, relaxation means not having to do anything. But the truth is those who miss the opportunity to live deeply in the present in the future will just sit around for days regretting the past. Without big jobs to do, they try to do miscellaneous tasks to prove they are still alive. They dread sitting around doing nothing. Only those who can accept reality in an absolute way, without hoping for anything else, can live leisurely anywhere.

Only a few decades ago, people thought that living leisurely was quite an art. Now if we say we are enjoying every second and every minute of the present, that there is nothing important we have to do, certainly everyone will look at us in surprise. We always have to say that we are very busy to show that we know how to live, that we are valuable. In the United States, people do not say that a store does well with many customers; they say the store is very busy. Even the young want to raise their level of busyness, and they are proud that they are going crazy with their work at their company. To them, if the work is not crazy, the company is not doing well. They would rather go crazy and make money to spend. They confuse emotional satisfaction and the true value of happiness and mix up the means and the ends of life. They turn all the wonderful values of life into ordinary means to serve big ambitions. Yet ambition is never enough. Therefore, we can say that we should relax now or never, because it is not a matter of time, of place, or of external elements. It depends on us and us alone.

In a number of spiritual traditions, people always direct their attention toward "freedom" or "liberation." It means that we have to find ways to overcome the control and tie of a certain person or situation. In some cases people have to leave this world before they can be free or liberated. Therefore, although they have chosen a spiritual life, they still cannot live much more leisurely, freely, and peacefully than those who are still struggling with life. Their mind is still full of worries and desires. They are still busy planning and suffering from pressure before adversities. They aim at a lofty ideal but still have not stopped to accept the present absolutely. Then how can they lead others to attain peace right here in life? Unsuccessful in the present, they draw up the future with extremely attractive vistas to tempt those who are immature and weak-hearted. Therefore those who cannot find their place in life have a strong tendency to go and look for a free or liberated world.

Upon learning of a terrible fall of the stock market, we are neither scared nor worried because we do not invest in stocks. When the economy suddenly goes into a serious recession, we can still eat and sleep well because we are not big business. When we read the news that someone commits suicide by hanging because of bankruptcy, we find ourselves really comfortable with enough salary to live on. When witnessing a couple fighting and taking each other to court, we feel happy and free because we are living a single life. When we see celebrities suffer from magazines exposing their private lives, we smile happily because we haven't been touched by the halo of fame. It is clear that when we don't run after tempting conditions in the world outside and still live peacefully, we will not be controlled and tied down. Not being tied down is being relaxed.

Relaxation only by standing outside such adverse conditions means it is still conditional. What will happen tomorrow when the favorable conditions we are holding disappear? Though we do not compete with high level enjoyments like others, we still more or less have contact with everybody, with society, and cannot avoid exchanging emotional reactions back and forth. Even if we escaped to an out-of-the-way mountain corner to avoid the control of external sights, would we feel calm and serene when the dark shadows of desires rise up inside us, or the sweet memories of the past? Relaxation from the absence of adverse conditions around is not settled yet. Those who can stay calm and unruffled when standing before success or failure, winning or losing, praise or blame are the ones who can achieve true relaxation.

Meditation Master Tran Nhan Tong of Vietnam in the 13th century used to caution everyone: *"If your house is full of treasures, stop looking for more/ Don't get attached to the scenery; that is meditation."* (From *"Cu Tran Lac Dao"*) The high peak of meditation practice is to acquire the ability of staying unmoved before all situations, whether they are favorable or unfavorable. When we can see that all the materials of peace, happiness, and relaxation lie within ourselves, then we do not ask anything else from the situation. We do not need to stay in an out-of-the-way place because we are closely related to people and to life. We have to be present to share suffering and offer joy to everyone. We have to help them find the value of relaxation right here in reality. This is really the lofty goal of human life.

Of course if we are not yet well-trained and have not yet screened or filtered all the dirt of affliction, our relaxation will be limited. Sometimes it is full and other times it is not. But we must be standing on the road of relaxation, not on any other road. That means relaxation must always be present in our every step, not at the end of the road. Truly, no road can lead to relaxation if its nature is not relaxation.

Sit still in relaxation
In touch with a floating cloud
Release the petty ego notion
To be everywhere in the here and now

47

Authoritarianism

Power in the hand of those lacking in understanding and morality is a danger for society and the whole world.

Breaking the balance

Because we think that we are much more talented and capable than others, we always scramble for priority rights to make decisions for all issues of common interests without waiting for approval or suggestions from other people. This is an authoritarian attitude. Authoritarianism is the total manifestation of ego power through the submission of others.

In their fundamental nature, all individuals are made from the collective energy source of the universe, and they are continuously influencing one another. No individual possesses a self-created self, so all individuals are equal in the nature of being, just as all the waves are born from the ocean. Though they are different in forms and looks, they are all water by nature. In truth, this wave is low so the other wave can be high; this wave is born because the other wave is gone. Though they never stop jostling each other, the nature of this wave is also the nature of that wave. In the end, all those waves are the ocean too, because there is nothing else to be called ocean other than them. Of course the ocean also includes the deep part underneath, the unborn waves. But there is neither difference nor separation between the unborn waves and the born waves. Therefore, phenomenon is also essence, and essence is phenomenon. That means no essence can be separated from phenomenon and no phenomenon can manifest without depending on essence.

The easiest way to see this is by looking at our children. Going beyond the external form and look, we will discover that our children are part of us. Both come from the same origin and have never been completely separated. Just like when we look at our body, we can see we are the continuation of our parents, grandparents, and ancestors. We have the same origin. This is also true in the relationships among us, all things and all beings. All are offspring of the great mother universe. The differences among the phenomena are the natural result of the continuous interactive processes among individuals according to the principles of cause and effect and causal conditions. But when going through the narrow and limited viewpoints of human beings, they are classified into different levels to serve the interests of the erroneous ego.

It is true that many talents and skills are the result of very hard and long training over months and years. But a talented seed was also born from the temporary union of body and mind. Before and after receiving a talent, it never stopped getting help from countless elements in the external world. In general, this self is originally and ultimately always non-self, so everything that it creates, be it talent or virtue, is also non-self. Human beings' greatest ignorance is the failure to see their own non-self nature with their perception always limited due to the differences of phenomena. Therefore we keep accumulating favorable conditions to serve the ego that we think is separate, and consider this the main task of our life. From there, showing power in front of everyone becomes a very major need of the ego.

There are authoritarians who use their power to command respect and obedience from others and do not go beyond that goal. These are authoritarians who rely on power to mobilize forces and carry out other plans with no other purpose than consolidating benefits for themselves. Besides, authoritarianism is used as a temporary effective means to generate influence or to guide those who are still weak. Fathers often think their children are not grown-up yet and must always obey their views and advice. These views came from their bitter experience and also precious experiences passed down from many ancestral generations. Group leaders also think that their members have not had opportunities to understand thoroughly all the problems, or are not yet knowledgeable enough to make good suggestions, especially since they are not responsible, so it is best that these members follow their ideas.

When we use our power to override others' viewpoints successfully, of course we have to exchange certain good feelings with them. The children understand that their father's advice comes from his good intentions for their sake. They can readily feel his love, so they can accept his scolding and forget their right to their own opinion. Likewise, group members understand that their leader's domineering behavior is for the interest of the group of which they are a part, so they accept it without demanding fair play.

However, not every authoritarian can succeed. Sometimes with claims of working on behalf of the truth or loving-kindness, they abuse their position to manifest the power of their ego, or control the interests of others. Sometimes they have good will to help others in the beginning, but half-way through, that good will is taken over and imprisoned by their greed or anger. In those cases where we use authority to guide or support others very effectively, and receive their appreciation without any reluctance, the law of emotional balance has been carried out. However, if we use power to force others to listen to us, whether publicly or disguised in a democratic format, then we have taken a big emotional loan. If the dissatisfaction or anger of the masses gets bigger, that loan gets bigger, too. It might even multiply. By one way or another, the universe will force us to settle that loan and restore the balance.

There is also the other party's direct reaction upon realizing that our authoritarianism means our disrespect for their interests or abilities. Whether they express their approval publicly or they have to accept silently, if they are deeply dissatisfied, their anger and strong opposition will build up. That energy can turn into action like non-cooperation or retaliation to rebalance the emotions. With the whole group dedicated to energetic opposition, the group will form a tsunami of resistance and overthrow that dictatorial leadership. The authoritarian system might have been built very securely and the energy of the opposition might not be strong enough yet, but with time, the balance will be established. The universe always has the responsibility to carry out the principle of cause and effect and causal conditions so that all things and all beings will not fall into chaotic situations and fighting. And if a war should happen, even just between two individuals, it is the worst way that the universe must choose to solve the problem.

Therefore, authoritarianism, for whatever purpose, destroys the emotional balance between others and us. Depending on the purpose and the severity of the intolerant attitude showed to others, we will have to accept the law of cause and effect and expect what the universe has in store for us.

Power or weakness?

In *The Tale of Kieu*, the Venerable Nguyen Du used to remind us: *"It is only rational to recognize both them and us."* The truth is everyone has their own talents, even if those talents are not appropriate to solve the problems of the present. When we think the other person is incapable and worthless, we are limiting our viewpoint about a person's totality. Nobody can live in this life full of ups and downs without some talent. That's not to mention other areas where they might be much better than us. They might be very happy with their families, loved by their friends, and trusted by everyone around. What about us? Our talent may be superior to others' in some respect, yet we have failed in our communication skills to get people to understand and gladly accept our ideas. To compare talents, we should look at our ability to control the emotions in our mind. What's the use of intimidating and defeating others when we always give up on ourselves, and still do things against our own conscience. In sum, resorting to power in order to make people listen to us is the worst solution.

Suppose there are ten people in a meeting to solve a problem. It is most ideal to get a unanimous opinion from all ten. In reality this seldom happens because everyone's viewpoints are always different. So sitting together is not just to get an opinion poll, it is also an opportunity to understand and sympathize with each other and to persuade others to drop some untimely opinions. In case one person disagrees, the majority has to select a representative to persuade that person by all means; otherwise the meeting has to be adjourned to another time. One person's discontent can ruin the harmony of the organization. When the organization loses harmony, it is difficult to get things done or to move forward. Harmony is like water and milk, which blend together.

But if one person disagrees and the group cannot come to a decision, it is also unproductive. It is also unfair if that disagreement might impact the organization's interests or survival. Therefore if we are the person whose opinion is contrary to the majority, we should yield if the problem is not too serious, if we have faith in the group's talents and sense of responsibility, and if mutual feelings have been positive. We should temporarily withdraw our opinion so the problem can be solved soon. However, when the opinion of the majority has been accepted, the majority should sincerely thank the minority for their support, and promise to try to carry out the idea effectively.

In case that person cannot be persuaded, the majority must come to a decision; otherwise the long waiting would ruin the plan. But we must sincerely apologize to that person and promise to do better in the future to reach a consensus. Another important thing is, although a few people only agree temporarily, once the consensus has been reached, no one should talk us out of it or express their discontent any more. Everything must be solved in a meeting. If we are not happy yet, we should ask for another meeting. Because once that attitude of discontent spreads out, it will unintentionally create additional opposing forces against the organization. We will bear the blame for ruining it.

The above approach will not be applicable to an organization that does not focus on building spiritual values. In reality, there are always urgent problems, so we cannot delay or keep on postponing the meeting. Another reality is those who are leaders or are responsible for the meeting do not have much time or good will to persuade each person. So most meetings follow the common practice of "the majority rules," "the minority must submit to the majority." They pay more attention to their work than "winning people's hearts."

However, submission often happens reluctantly in meetings. The truth is when people's opinions are not accepted or people are not persuaded to change in a satisfactory way, their energy of discontent is still there. If we use our leadership to intimidate them without going through negotiations, that energy of discontent will grow even stronger. Therefore, the wise attitude of those who have to play the role of a dogmatist is always finding ways to compensate emotionally and reasonably for their overstepping other people's equal rights. Deep listening and loving speech with a humble attitude are usually the most effective solution to appease emotions. If we bypass this responsibility for emotional compensation, whether intentionally or not, that association will lose balance and certainly will crack or break up in the near future.

No one wants to live with or work with a dogmatist because human beings' primary need is to have equal rights. Sometimes they might have to accept our authority because they know we are more capable and talented, we have more responsibility for a problem, or we bring them benefits. But their respect for and faith in us will decrease each time. They cannot maintain their respect for us when we do not value their opinions and abilities, from small to big tasks. We have slighted them. They think that if we are really smart, we should have the ability to make them "yield both in heart and in words" instead of using power to pressure them. The attitude of authoritarianism might be another form of weakness. Indeed, the nature of authoritarianism is to express an attitude of promoting our talent and ability; at the same time it implies an attitude of worry about others outperforming us or encroaching on our power. Hence, authoritarianism can start from weakness or will lead to weakness.

Genuine power

Authoritarianism always brings loneliness because people avoid those who do not respect them. In sentimental relationships dominance is a taboo, because the nature of sentiment is voluntary and always needs to be respected to see each other's genuine value. Even if we are parents, teachers, bosses, or supreme leaders, we still should limit expressing our power to the maximum while trying to win over people's hearts or guide them. These people might admire or deeply appreciate us but they cannot lose their fundamental right to freedom.

In Western societies, parents often create opportunities for children to develop their potential and self-control, so they usually negotiate their opinions instead of pressing them. However, there are many issues about which parents absolutely have more experience and knowledge. Unfortunately their children will only consult them and remain independent in their thinking and action. As a result, parents really suffer silently when watching their children take the wrong road without being able to stop them because the system of children rights protection is highly developed in the West and has inadvertently protected their foolishness and stupidity.

Consequently, authoritarianism is sometimes very necessary. We have to be very careful though, since it is easy to confuse the attitude of wanting to show power with the spirit of support. The borderline between egoistic and altruistic motives is sometimes as thin as a silk thread. Those with genuine power must have the ability to bring peace and happiness to other people and can embrace their suffering without considering themselves as high-minded or great. Those with genuine power do not need to use any words or gestures to draw attention, yet people still trust and follow them.

That kind of power must have come from the energy of righteousness, good character and boundless loving-kindness. All societies need such genuine powers to maintain peace and democracy. If we realize we are still abusing our power to serve our ego, we should find ways to let it go. Misusing power is not the right and safe road to build true value. Even if we cannot bring happiness and loving-kindness to others, at least we do not create any suffering or hatred in them. Power in the hand of those lacking in understanding and virtue is a danger for society and the whole world.

Unconditional loving-kindness
The power of the heart-felt consciousness
Where are you heading, little wave?
In the boundless ocean, unafraid

48

Humbleness

We can only learn humbleness when we are aware that what we have today was due to the work and support of many people.

Throwing oneself into the storm

The old Vietnamese saying "*Musk has a natural odor*" reminds us that people with real talents are like flowers with fragrance. They will automatically be discovered and admired without having to prove or affirm themselves.

The sages always work in silence and tranquility. When the work is done, they withdraw to a quiet place to preserve energy and maintain their virtuous way of life for great tasks—"Truly great men do not reveal themselves." When we receive loving energy from the public, it means we owe them a huge emotional debt. If we are really talented and virtuous, and our contributions truly bring useful values or at least joy to the public, then we can create a balance. Otherwise, the universe will gradually draw our energy to pay back the huge loan that we inadvertently borrowed. In *The Tale of Kieu*, there are two interesting lines, "*When brilliance and beauty are shown on the outside, a talented life will forever be short-lived.*" According to the Venerable Nguyen Du, if all our goodness and beauty flow out, we will not enjoy a long life or we will have a hard life. Why is that? Because we will not have anything left to nourish ourselves, nor will we bother to learn other skills. Also, when we think we are gifted, we always think little of others, and easily become a target of attack from jealous people around us.

However, nowadays people want everybody to notice them quickly. They use all kinds of sophisticated means to introduce themselves via mass media like the press, television, and the internet. They call it public relations technology. To advertise is to introduce our best to the public. We know how to maximize our strong points to attract everybody's attention. If advertisements appeal to the public, and thanks to repeat showings, we accept and believe them unconsciously. Therefore, when we discover that reality is not as perfect as what was advertised, we don't really think we have been cheated. The advertisers just haven't mentioned their bad points instead of declaring that they have no shortcomings. This is the advertisers' smart way to disguise their lack of sincerity.

In addition, the young nowadays easily become famous thanks to their shock-inducing ways. In other words, they shock and alarm everyone with their weirdness. Psychologically, the public is always interested in and curious about new things. Therefore, whether the new things are ridiculous acts, crazy expressions or vulgar images, in just a few seconds, thousands and tens of thousands of people know and talk about them. To the young, attracting the attention of such a large number of people is just great. Acting with such lack of understanding is no different from throwing themselves into the storm. However, without contributing anything useful, they dare use the energy of the public's attention and also create bad energy from disturbing everyone's consciousness. No wonder their lives are full of misfortunes and disasters.

Nobody is perfect

It is true that a gifted person is like a flower full of nectar that sooner or later will be attacked and ruined by bees and butterflies. Therefore, to nourish and use their talent for a long time, wise men in the old days advised us to always cultivate our personal character, especially *humbleness*. This virtuous energy will help us know how to limit the radiance of our talent safely and reasonably.

In Vietnamese, the term "*khiem cung*" (humbleness) is made up of two terms: "*khiem nhuong*" (humility) and "*cung kinh*" (respect). "*Khiem nhuong*" (humility) is not to give prominence to oneself in deference toward others. And "*khiem cung*" (humbleness) includes the

Understanding the Heart

attitude of respect, even if the other person is lower than us. Humility is difficult but humbleness is even more difficult. "The strong win and the weak lose" is the general tendency of today's society. We can only learn humbleness if we are aware that what we have today is thanks to the support of many people. We are also lucky to have the guidance of mature people, so we are not too satisfied about our early talent. We also get to be close and to study with the sages. We know how to look back at ourselves and clearly see our bad habits which we haven't been able to change. Sometimes as a result of an unfortunate event, we can see the deep relationship between us and other, less fortunate persons.

Many times I did not want to recognize my brother. I think I am talented, able, diligent, and have never caused any problems to my family. I even brought a good reputation to my family and my ancestors. Therefore, when witnessing some terrible things that my brother did, I declared, "From now on, you are not my brother anymore." At that moment, he looked at me for a long time. But then he understood, and silently accepted that punishment. The gap between us brothers grew more each day. I was always ashamed each time someone asked me about my brother, while he was very proud of me.

Many years later, I tried to find out why we are blood brothers yet we were so different. Until one day, by chance I overheard my sister telling a friend that most of our parents' goodness and beauty had been passed down to me. That sentence was like a thunderbolt that broke up all mistaken doubts about my status and my brother's. It turned out most of my good points include his share and most his shortcomings include my share. My brother and I are both the continuation of the same blood line. From that time, I looked at my brother with a different eye. Thanks to that, he tried to change himself very much. Then I discovered another truth. My brother has some wonderful points that I do not and he can do some things very well that I can't. I really repented and began to look back at my attitude of self-satisfaction all these years. Now both of us can talk to each other like two friends. I always tell myself to make up appropriately for him, and I know my brother is also living for me.

"*Nobody is perfect*"—indeed no one is perfect in this world. We often use the term "perfect" to refer to those who can gather so many bright lights. But all things considered, they still have dark corners. Regrettably, people always look through narrow lenses. Nobody compares a gifted scholar with a farmer. Or no one thinks that a laborer is as important as a talented leader. But the truth is the scholar cannot produce rice like the farmer, and without rice nobody can become gifted. Don't the gifted eat, too? Also it is true that the leader cannot use a broom to sweep the street every morning, because he is too busy with countless important tasks. But without street sweepers the environment will be polluted, epidemics and diseases will spread, and then will the leader be safe? Will he breathe other air instead? Therefore the scholar, farmer, leader, laborer are all equally important and respectable. Even if the scholar and leader created many useful things for life, it is only due to the favors that the universe had reserved for them. This person is ordinary so that more energy can be accumulated for that person to become extraordinary. In the end, nothing is ordinary or extraordinary. Everything is present in each other.

Few people can accept this, but it is a very deep and mysterious truth of nature. In nature, all individuals are formed from the entire universe and never stop interacting with all other individuals. There is no exception for any individual. On the contrary, the more special talents some people have, the more they owe the universe. To become a special person, they must have a special hereditary composition and grow up in a special environment. They have to depend on special favorable situations and even special needs of the community that are appropriate to their talent. All these "special" things are sent trustfully by the universe. We can say that people with outstanding talents are those entrusted by the universe to serve everybody. If they are not aware of this mission but rely on their special talent to boast, to show arrogance, or just to increase their selfish interest, the universe will certainly take it back.

Heartfelt civilization

In traditional Vietnamese culture, when sitting down to eat with the family, we have to know our seat correctly to remind ourselves who is more senior than us. Although we might have a high degree, make a lot of money, and are respected by many, when we are back home, we are still that person's junior. Whenever our parents' guests come to visit, we have to stop our work, walk over with hands together to bow our head and greet them politely. This is not just a relationship ritual but also a practice to express respect. Those seniors might have accumulated many talents and virtues. They must have lived and experienced a great deal in this life. Or they might have neglected themselves to protect the country and help build the homeland. In Buddhist tradition, there is also the greeting practice by putting two hands together in front like a lotus bud. Whether the other person is older or younger, we still put our hands together and bow our head respectfully. Besides expressing the appreciation of meeting each other, it also reminds us the other person can become a Buddha in the future, no matter whom they are or what they have done.

Not too long ago, every school in Vietnam put emphasis on the guideline *"First learn rituals, and then learn literature"*—students must give priority to improve rituals more than receiving knowledge. It means education promises to train and produce more virtuous students than knowledgeable students. Learning rituals is really practicing humbleness. Every day we should practice behaving humbly and respectfully toward our parents, teachers, neighbors, and all our friends. We should be conscious that everyone has the need for understanding and loving-kindness, and everyone can be the talented and the virtuous. Do not let differences in appearance or knowledge become dividing walls, making us proud and lack mutual respect. If we always love and respect one another like "the red crepe covers the mirror stand," then we are the future of the country and even the world.

Regrettably, together with the foreign-oriented trend of the society, schools nowadays only worry about stuffing knowledge, hoping the students will get good grades. The development of good character has been reduced to not violating school regulations; it does not include personality training so students can be well-equipped to enter life. Worse still, rituals in schools, as in some social circles, have turned into a kind of outward show lacking sincerity. Pretending to respect each other through urbane forms is the "sweetest bankruptcy" of morality.

Aware of the corruption of public morals everywhere, causing many heart-rending situations, and making people lose faith in loving-kindness and true happiness more and more every day, we all should come back and rebuild our spiritual lives. We should realize that only an understanding, clear, and peaceful mind can build a truly meaningful life. What is more meaningful when we all come together as brothers and sisters; no one will look at another with suspicion or hatred; no one will want to be glorified or to overpower anyone. There will be no more signs of deception or petty schemes. There will be no more discrimination between cultures or understandings. There will be no irresponsible or heartless people. Is this the life of the "heartfelt civilization" from our ancestors? Is this our deepest dream in the present time? We do not want to continue being "worshippers" of material goods, and inadvertently bankrupt the morality of our culture. We do not want to witness our children struggling for over half of their lifetime like us before realizing the true value of life. We just want to have relaxation in life. We just want everyone to be equal, harmonious, and loving each other.

We cannot dawdle any longer. Our ancestors are waiting for our awakening and our return. Humbleness—respecting seniors, yielding juniors—is the most ideal model for the beginning.

Like flowers blooming in the field
Lovely or plain will to non-being yield
Recognize our same essence
Return to heartfelt civilization

49

Selfishness

*Selfishness is human beings' most shallow
and mediocre attitude toward life.*

Ourselves and not ourselves

When looking at a cherry blossom, perhaps we say that it is the quintessence of the cherry tree. But when we observe more deeply, we will see that the cherry blossom is created from many other elements, like the weather, the sun, minerals, insects, and even garbage. Although these things are not cherry blossoms—at first look they do not seem to have anything to do with cherry blossoms—cherry blossoms cannot be present without these "non-cherry blossom" elements. The cherry blossom was born from the cherry tree indeed, but the cherry tree and its ancestors were also created from countless other conditions in this world. They have never been separated. In fact, there is no cherry blossom *per se*; there is only a combined form created from the non-cherry blossom elements. Actually, the term "non" should not be there, because those elements did create the combined cherry blossom form and not other kinds of blossoms.

If the cherry blossom knew the truth that the leaves, the branches, the trunk, and the roots of the cherry tree and all things outside have never stopped nourishing it, it would never dare to be proud, haughty, and selfish. The cherry blossom is only a form representing everything offered by its ancestors and even by the universe. This form only manifests for a time then changes to another form. Therefore, the cherry blossom cannot love only itself. It also has to love the leaves, the branches, the trunk, the roots, and all things around. Perhaps the cherry blossom knows this well, so it always lives life to the fullest. It cheerfully endures the bone-chilling cold so that when the warm sunshine of spring arrives, it can bloom as a fresh, lovely, and fragrant flower. The cherry blossom has lived valiantly, charmingly, and fulfilled its responsibility.

Have we ever held up our hand and wondered: whose hand is this really? Were all the talents and skills accomplished from this hand created by us or not? That question may sound simple, but we may have answered it wrongly. Look carefully at your hand again! Besides the abilities trained by ourselves, didn't it receive talented seeds passed down from ancestral generations, with the closest generation being our parents? When we cook a bowl of sour soup, we should know that our ancestors cook it together with us, too. Without their discovery and experience, how could we know how to cook sour soup? We would not even know what sour soup is. And the term "sour soup" would not exist either. Our ancestors not only exist in us through each cell but also in each of our perceptions and our ways of life. It is the truth, whether we want to recognize it or not.

We are the continuation of our blood ancestors as well as our spiritual ancestors. We are only a representative form, not a separate being. The only thing that makes us a little different from them is that we have worked with the universe to combine all those hereditary elements into a new perfect whole, to manifest a new life with a new mission. Besides, we also have to borrow more on top of what the cherry blossom had borrowed. In other words, we never stop interacting and being impacted by nature. And to become a knowledgeable person living securely today, we have depended on numerous other elements created by the human race such as the economy, politics, society, education, religion, etc. The more deeply we reflect, the more we realize that we are just like all beings, created from things that are not ourselves. Originally we are *non-self*. Therefore, every time we say "we" or look at "our" work, we must understand tacitly that it is a combined phenomenon, a joint work. That way of naming is only correct on a relative scale to help us pay attention to our sense of responsibility.

Our ancestors had many opportunities to reflect on themselves and seldom chased after external conditions, so they could easily see clearly the natural interactive principles of life. They always practiced loving others like loving themselves. It was not a matter of being noble or compassionate; it was an attitude of living that was right and appropriate with the working of the universe. To live like that is to live in understanding, peace, and happiness. Nowadays we always considered ourselves civilized, with all kinds of degrees, yet we cannot see nor accept that truth. So we keep following individualism and trying our best to accumulate interests for serving the ego that we think is ours alone. Sometimes we even encroach on others, put our grip on common property, and harm the environment and the many people around. But in the end we still do not know what happiness is.

The true self

One day King Pasenadi—of the little kingdom Kosala in India—asked Queen Malika, "Darling, whom do you love best in the world?" The queen replied, "Of course the person I love best is you, your Majesty." "I guessed you'd say that," the king smiled happily. But the queen continued, "If your Majesty permits, I'd say a little differently, but more accurately." The king was eager, "Go ahead and say it!" "Your Majesty, the person I love most is myself." The king was surprised, "What? You love yourself? I don't understand what you want to say."

The queen cautiously answered: "Allow me to ask you in reverse. Who does Your Majesty love best in the world?" The king laughed: "Who else but you, darling." The queen asked again: "But if I love another man, what would you do?" The king stammered: "Ah, I would . . . I would . . ." "You would get into a fit of thundering rage and have my head cut off, isn't that right?" the queen said, finishing his sentence. The king was flustered, "Your question was too complicated! Really complicated!" The queen went on: "Your Majesty isn't it true?" "Um, well . . . maybe you were right," the king was silent for a while then confirmed. The queen then gently explained: "Your Majesty loves me because I have brought you happiness. So when I stop bringing you happiness, you stop loving me and want to kill me right away. Therefore, you only love yourself best."

It is true that human instinct, like that of all other living beings, is always to fight for one's own interests. This is the biggest mistaken attitude for an individual who is interacting with numerous other surrounding individuals for survival. It is this mistake that leads to a serious imbalance between the huge nourishing energy sent from all things in the universe and an attitude of living for oneself only. Fairly speaking, the cherry blossom receives very few benefits from nature, but it has lived its best to offer life all its worth. As for us, although known as the most knowledgeable, we should ask ourselves how we have lived and what we have done for this life.

Don't talk about faraway things. Even with our loved ones beside us, we have seldom paid attention to their difficulties or their deep wishes and dreams. Our mind always thinks about ways to make more money, advance our position, and attract the attention and admiration of many people. It is as if everyone was responsible for loving and helping us, while we had the "privilege" of not being responsible to anyone. Actually, we have most likely tried to help a few people, but that noble gesture may never have been done without any condition. At least those people must be likable, value us, or show that they hold dear what we brought them. It is the same thing sentimentally. We might think we have loved someone with all our heart, but the truth is, we are addicted to that person's emotions and cannot get away. We think we are very high-minded when we decide to forgive someone's mistakes, but deep inside it is because we are afraid that person will not love or be friendly with us any longer, or because we want to show our generosity to everybody.

It seems we have never done something without taking along our enjoyment ego. It has become a kind of "outlook on life" in our time. The truth is selfishness is human beings' most shallow and mediocre attitude toward life—not wanting to help anybody as well as always burrowing their way through every nook and cranny to draw benefits. Perhaps that is the deep cause leading to this consequence: although human beings enjoy the most, they also suffer the most.

The purpose of morality or religion is none other than to help humans see the truth about themselves so they can re-establish their lives as righteous and in harmony with the working of the universe. That means we should always be conscious of transforming bad energies in case they develop, as well as finding ways to prevent bad energies from coming out. In other words, we must *accumulate merits*. In addition, we must have the responsibility to nourish good energies that already developed, and find ways to arouse good energies that have not had the opportunity to come out. In other words, *accumulate blessings*. Any morality or religion that cannot handle these functions leads people to worship their separate egos, incessantly creates borders to separate individuals or organizations, and causes people to neglect their precious life in the present and keep their dreams faraway. It is a kind of selfish and harmful morality or religion. Pragmatism, individualism, and theories that have a strong influence on all of society need to be re-examined. We must have the right view and clear-cut attitude to select the most righteous path that can bring the true happiness in the present.

No other path is more righteous than the path to the mind within. The mind is the origin of all suffering and happiness. We do not need to find any more faraway road. We should come back to ourselves for refuge. Within us there are plenty of conditions to set up a peaceful life with true happiness. In order to be in touch with those precious values, we have to practice letting go some unnecessary wants and conflicts. The less we make demands and get attached to the outside, the more strength we have inside. Gradually, we will be open-hearted in a natural way to share and support all people and all beings. We will have realized that all people and all other beings are also our embodiment—parts of our body. That is the true ego that each of us has the duty to find by all means. It has drifted around through all the ups and downs of life; and it used to be covered with passions and ambitions. When we have found that true self, we will have no more self-love and injuries to our pride. Our discrimination and hatred will also be destroyed.

This is the path that our ancestors walked on very successfully. We should quickly come back to continue it and try to maintain it for a bright and beautiful future for ourselves and for our children and grandchildren.

Looking at the cherry blossoms so radiant
I feel ashamed returning to my homeland
Oh, the pink petal is flying high
In a hundred years what will we find?

50

Responsibility

> *Be conscious that we are preserving our ancestors' very precious legacy, and we must have the responsibility of passing it down to our offspring.*

Bear the consequence of what we did

Never before has the word "responsibility" been mentioned repeatedly like it has been recently. In spite of daily appeals from the mass media, it does not seem to have struck people's insensitive hearts regarding what is considered public property.

People's pragmatic approach is so coarse and superficial that they not only do not want to be responsible for what they inherit, but also inconsiderately play a part in destroying it. They think that only money, power or lust is important. But suppose water or air is cut off, will they survive to chase after those things? Remember business is also non-business. Business cannot exist and remain strong when other areas are weak. Love is non-self too. Love is also created by non-love elements. That means the so-called love is nonexistent if it wants to stand separately. Yet when doing business or loving, people are ready to ignore the closely related elements around, forget all their responsibilities, and only live for their impermanent and superficial ego. No wonder they still suffer from afflictions and a hard life in the end.

The explosion of the market economy has stirred up human beings' ambitions originally tamed by the rules of conduct and morality that our forefathers had built and preserved for thousands of years. Nowadays most everyone lives in an insecure situation. It is not from the lack of food or clothing, but from the lack of understanding. They think that if they do not have plenty of comforts like others, they cannot be happy. Therefore, they quickly jump and snatch any profit as soon as they spot it, stopping at nothing. They forget that the universe is very fair. Oftentimes when we try to beat or block others, the universe might reduce our feelings or health. And when we contribute to the public, the universe will grant us unexpected gifts. The universe is not a supreme almighty. It is the combined energy of all things tangible and intangible working constantly according to the principles of cause and effect and causal conditions. When we open our heart to others or to public property, we will certainly be connected to that great potential energy source.

Therefore, our ancestors often advised, "*One can eat as much as one is virtuous.*" The universe will always feed us when we live responsibly. We will become the universe's darling child. Actually responsibility is also a benefit. It just changes from the form of labor or wealth to another form of nobler energy, but requiring non-contrived energy as the agent.

Today there are many problems crying out for everyone's responsible attention. There are many construction projects with funds being squeezed out. There are situations of schools turning into businesses. There is ruthless greed to the point of faking merchandise and foods. There is competition in the manufacture of nuclear weapons to sell to various countries and groups. There is a lot of corruption leading to a debilitated national economy, causing people's lives to be full of hardship and misery. These festering problems need to have the proper concern of the government or the United Nations to prevent or stop them from spreading. As for the environmental situation, though currently at a "dangerous" warning level, each individual can contribute to change that situation right now.

Finding upward direction

The environment is our mother, our house. If something should happen to it, we will have no place to reside and survive. We should reflect on the environment in which we are living with vigilance and understanding to see the real situation clearly.

Plastic bag problem: Plastic bags are made from PVC (Polyvinyl Chloride). When burned, they give off dioxin, which is very toxic, causes breathing problems and the coughing up of blood, reduces the immune system, and gives rise to cancers and birth defects. Using colored plastic bags to hold foods will contaminate them with metals like lead and cadmium[1]. This can damage the brain and cause lung cancer. When plastic bags are thrown down the sewers, the drainage system becomes clogged, making it possible for mosquitoes and epidemic diseases to happen. If the bags are buried in the soil, grass cannot grow, leading to soil erosion in mountainous areas.

In Wales, a southwest region of the United Kingdom, each year 480 million plastic bags are disposed. These bags take up to a thousand years to disintegrate. Wales declared the practice of cutting down the use of plastic bags, beginning in 2011. There will be a tax of 15 cents on each plastic bag used. The amount of money collected will be used for environmental protection projects. This tax has been applied in Ireland since 2002, also at 15 cents a bag, and they have collected 109 million pounds (about 153 million dollars). The number of bags used has since plummeted by 90% and garbage disposal expenses have sharply decreased. And in Saigon, every day about 5 million plastic bags are used, equivalent to 35 tons, mostly at supermarkets.

Currently Germany, France, and Holland are using bags made from potato starch or paper that can decompose after 3 months. Before now, our grandparents used lotus or banana leaves to wrap goods, and carried baskets to the market. That image, though primitive, shows a very safe and understanding way of life. It is time we need to go back and relearn the traditional life style of heartfelt civilization" and cut down on the pursuit of luxurious comforts that always make us tired and insecure. Together we should practice using only cloth bags, rattan bags, or any kind of shopping bag that is not environmentally harmful. Don't wait for the government to give warnings and fines before doing it; otherwise it will be too late to save this green planet.

Paper problem: The forests play a very important role in our survival. Thanks to wide canopies of leaves, rain water does not pour directly down onto the land, and the top soil does not get washed away with the rain or get scorched by the sun. The forests not only protect the soil but also make it more fertile. They preserve water sources so the water can slowly flow to feed the rivers during the drought season.

Therefore, areas covered with forests suffer less from droughts. The forests also have the function of reducing the sudden attacks of floods. The most important thing is that forests absorb carbon dioxide (CO_2), which is emitted from the exhaust pipes of vehicles and factories, to release oxygen (O_2) for human lungs. The forests are truly our mother lungs.

One of the big reasons for tens of thousands of forests to fall down continuously is paper production. Each ton of paper product requires 5 cubic meters of wood and 100 cubic meters of water. It is not an exaggeration to say that when the forests fall, we fall too. From now on, we should practice limiting the use of paper napkins; instead we can use a cloth napkin to wipe our mouth, and a hand towel for our hands. Even with paper cups and plates, we should only use them in unavoidable cases, instead of considering them an appropriate convenience. Going back to the old way takes some effort, but it can both treat our lazy habit and help us from becoming indirect culprits in destroying countless green forests.

Regarding the paper used in schools or offices, we should employ "best use" practices, like using both sides before discarding. Just a few decades ago, we already knew to collect used school notebooks to sell and make money for new school notebooks. In those days, a kite made from notebook paper was considered a luxury. Economic development has supplied us with plenty of everything and because of this, we have become wasteful, forgetting so many basic principles of living to stay healthy in the body and mind.

Water source problems: When the forests fall or the air is polluted, clean water sources will run dry. Currently about one-sixth of the world's population has no access to clean water, and more than 2 million people, most of them children, die of thirst or water-related diseases every year. Actually in the last 30 years, human beings' clean water needs have surpassed supply capacity. While a small number of countries are trying to set up factories to filter salt water, the majority of the remaining countries continue to spray toxic insecticides, release wastewater from the livestock-breeding industry, or use water wastefully. Environmental protection agencies in the world have predicted that in about 50 years, human beings on this planet will have to suffer chronic droughts and catch each water drop to drink if we continue to waste or pollute water sources like today.

We have probably not forgotten that we used to live through "parching thirst" periods when we had to stay up late at night to collect water from public wells for the whole family to use during the day. That tragic situation is still going on now in Africa, in some regions in Asia, and will be world-wide in the future. At that time, even if we have a great deal of money, we still won't be able to buy water, because the water will have been polluted and bid us goodbye. Even now, at a number of places, water belongs to the management of a few business groups and has become an expensive product next to electricity and gasoline. That means the poor are not allowed to use clean water. But a water source is a natural property that everyone has the right to use and no one has the right to pollute or claim their own. If we do not want that tragic situation to happen again to us and our offspring, we should be resolved to preserve water right now.

Every time we brush our teeth, remember to turn off the faucet right away. In a few minutes of mindlessness, we have wasted dozens of liters of clean water that can save a few children currently dying of thirst in the world. When washing dishes, we should use a basin. Don't run the water at full force just to wash a few dishes, even if we can afford to pay the monthly water bill. In daily activities, we waste water the most in the bathroom. From now on, we should practice limiting the use of showers. Instead, we can collect water in a bucket to bathe. This way can help us stop the water flow when it is not really necessary and know how much water we have used. This action is simple yet has an immediate effect without a public policy from the government. Our offspring will appreciate greatly our considerate way of living today when they suffer no birth defects, stunted growth, or early death, and can still see the green color on this planet.

Vehicle exhaust fumes: According to World Health Organization (WHO), every year nearly 600,000 people in Asia die from respiratory diseases related to the air. The primary culprit causing this pollution is vehicle exhaust fumes. In Beijing there are 2.6 million vehicles in traffic spouting fumes each day, and this place has been named "car city." There is one car owner for every 5 persons in Beijing. With the population of 22 million, the traffic in Beijing is not just delayed, but slowed to the point of choking too. In Hong Kong, vehicle exhaust fumes often cover the city so much that people cannot enjoy the view of the shops or the harbor for about 120 days per year. In Hanoi, each day each a person inhales into their lungs about 100mg of very toxic PM10 dust (particulate matter), 5,000mg carbon monoxide (CO), and 50mg of other fumes like nitrogen dioxide (NO_2), sulfur dioxide (SO_2) from vehicle exhaust fumes.

Every time we pick up the car key, ask ourselves a few times where we are planning to go. Go if it's necessary. If the reason is not really valid, be brave and put the key down. In addition, we should also use bicycles, cars run by non-toxic fuels like electricity, or use public transportation whenever possible. This way saves gas, does not pollute, and also restores the interaction between us and other people in the community. Waiting for the bus together is a very beautiful image. It brings us together and somewhat breaks up individualism.

Meat eating problem: The globe is getting warmer. It is estimated that in a few years, the glaciers in Iceland and the North and South poles will melt very fast, causing the ocean water level to rise. This will affect half of the world's population living along the coast, and also cause billions of tons of methane (CH_4) in the thick glaciers to break free. This is a main cause of the terrible global warming, a series of natural disasters that will happen such as drought, increasing heat, desertification, soil sinking, dead seas, wild animal extinction, and the decline of human health.

Many people in the world are alert to the *"greenhouse effect"* situation and are trying to reduce exhaust fumes from industries and transportation. But it will take a rather long time before the situation can improve, because it concerns the interests of many selfish groups or corrupt and dictatorial political regimes. Meanwhile, eating vegetarian food—all foods that are plant-based—is a solution that each individual can do right away and is highly effective in cooling down the globe. Animal husbandry contributes more than 50% of the methane waste in the atmosphere. Besides, livestock breeding for meat has increased rapidly in the recent years causing many dangerous epidemics to spread. Is it true that from the time human beings got involved with sophisticated dishes made from the lives of all kinds of animals, it was also the time when human beings lost their generous heart?

With the responsible spirit of a child, we should promise Mother Nature:

1. *Aware of the contamination to Mother Nature caused by the discarding of plastic bags which take a thousand years to disintegrate, I pledge to use only cloth bags to hold items when going shopping.*
2. *Aware that if the forests fall, I cannot breathe and will fall too, I pledge to use paper bowls, cups, or napkins in unavoidable situations only.*
3. *Aware that natural water sources are drying out and millions of people are dying of thirst in the world, I pledge to economize each handful of water even when washing or bathing.*
4. *Aware that vehicle exhaust fumes pollute the air and create acid rain that kills forests, and poisons water sources, I pledge to only drive for truly legitimate purposes and will try to use public transportation whenever possible.*
5. *Aware that livestock breeding for meat causes many life-threatening epidemics, creates wastes that increase global warming leading to natural disasters, and causes human beings to lose their noble compassion for all beings, I pledge to eat vegetarian food regularly to help soothe and preserve our mutual lives.*

Because of loving-kindness and understanding, dear Mother Nature, I would like to voluntarily sign these five pledges. I am aware that I am preserving my ancestors' valuable legacy and have the responsibility to pass it down to my offspring. I cannot allow their heart to be poor and lost in the future. If this hand continues to cause toxic energies that can destroy mutual lives, I will be guilty before you and the universe. From now on I promise to try to keep this hand really clean to lead my offspring to a better place.

Keep a careful hand
To embrace ancestral inheritance
Pass it down to descendants
Mutually find direction to ascend

[1] Cadmium (Cd) is a metal that exists in nature in the form of sulphur mixed with zinc carbonate (in zinc ores) and in the form of other metallic components to a lesser degree. Cadmium is used to make paints, industrial pigments, plastic stabilizers (PVC), NI-Cd batteries, etc.

Made in the USA
Monee, IL
20 December 2020